PRACTICAL PHILOSOPHY OF SPORT AND PHYSICAL ACTIVITY

SECOND EDITION

R. Scott Kretchmar, PhD

Penn State University

HUMAN KINETICS

Library of Congress Cataloging-in-Publication Data

Kretchmar, R. Scott (Robert Scott)
 Practical philosophy of sport and physical activity / R. Scott Kretchmar.-- 2nd ed.
   p. cm.
 Includes bibliographical references and index.
 ISBN 0-7360-0141-7 (hard cover)
 1. Sports--Philosophy. 2. Physical education and training--Philosophy. I. Title.
 GV706.K74 2005
 796'.01--dc22

                              2004013538

ISBN-10: 0-7360-0141-7
ISBN-13: 978-0-7360-0141-0

This book is a revised edition of *Practical Philosophy of Sport* published in 1994 by Human Kinetics.

Acquisitions Editor: Myles Schrag; **Developmental Editors:** D.K. Bihler and Amanda S. Ewing; **Assistant Editors:** Amanda S. Ewing, Anne Cole, and Michelle M. Rivera; **Copyeditor:** Alisha Jeddeloh; **Proofreader:** Erin Cler; **Indexer:** Betty Frizzéll; **Permission Manager:** Dalene Reeder; **Graphic Designer:** Robert Reuther; **Graphic Artist:** Dawn Sills; **Photo Manager:** Kareema McLendon; **Cover Designer:** Jack W. Davis; **Photographer (interior):** © Human Kinetics, unless otherwise noted; **Art Manager:** Kelly Hendren; **Illustrator:** Brian McElwain; **Printer:** Edwards Brothers

Printed in the United States of America   10   9   8   7   6   5   4

Human Kinetics
Web site: www.HumanKinetics.com

United States: Human Kinetics
P.O. Box 5076
Champaign, IL 61825-5076
800-747-4457
e-mail: humank@hkusa.com

Canada: Human Kinetics
475 Devonshire Road, Unit 100
Windsor, ON N8Y 2L5
800-465-7301 (in Canada only)
e-mail: info@hkcanada.com

Europe: Human Kinetics
107 Bradford Road
Stanningley
Leeds LS28 6AT, United Kingdom
+44 (0)113 255 5665
e-mail: hk@hkeurope.com

Australia: Human Kinetics
57A Price Avenue
Lower Mitcham, South Australia 5062
08 8372 0999
e-mail: info@hkaustralia.com

New Zealand: Human Kinetics
Division of Sports Distributors NZ Ltd.
P.O. Box 300 226 Albany
North Shore City, Auckland
0064 9 448 1207
e-mail: info@humankinetics.co.nz

For Janet Kretchmar,
my partner for life and my best friend

CONTENTS

PREFACE

Kinesiology professionals today work in a schizophrenic environment. On one hand, people seem almost fixated on physical prowess—on professional athletes and their remarkable feats, on the drama of the Olympic Games, and on the fate of local teams. Many individuals value physical health, good looks, youthful attitude, and long life above almost anything else. Televised sport and the income it generates have produced athletes who make more money than university presidents, world-renowned scientists, and heads of state. The leisure industry is the second largest industry in America, producing over $400 billion annually in direct spending (AAHPERD 2003).

On the other hand, physical activities are often devalued. We continue to endure stereotypes about "dumb jocks" and claims that university kinesiology programs are not intellectually challenging. Physical education is often the first subject to be cut from public schools when budgets are tightened. In a world that values productivity and work, games and play have an ambiguous status at best. And where dualistic thinking still holds sway, mind is valued over body, thinking over doing.

It is difficult to know what to make of this. Should we be flattered or disturbed? Optimistic or pessimistic? My personal conviction is that we should be optimistic, but not because sport is popular, or because people are preoccupied with how they look, or because athletes are among the best-paid performers in the world. Rather, our optimism should be rooted in something that is much more fundamental—our humanity. I hope that this book will help us come to see that to move skillfully and expressively is part of being human. I claim that this is so for all people, no matter where they live. While the form and meaning of physical activity vary under these conditions, and while the differences may be as important as the similarities, the fundamental value of movement and many of its qualities are common to the human community.

This optimism regarding movement may sound strange in a push-button, sedentary world where technology has eliminated or reduced many of the physical demands of living. Both rural and urban residents have laborsaving devices that lessen their reliance on endurance, strength, and refined motor skills. While physical skill and vigor were once requirements for human existence, they now seem to be optional.

While this is true at one level, in this book we will attempt to see why reduced activity is not really a human choice—or better said, why it is not a good choice. In order to see how movement is integrated with well-being, we need to consider alternative ways we can incorporate activity into our lives. Some ways may

In movement we find our humanity.

not work as well as others, and as movement professionals, we need to understand why this is so. Movement can be boring, painful, even alienating. Half an hour on an exercise bicycle is a torturous eternity for some people. Angry or vengeful competition can turn our opponents into hated enemies. Adolescent athletes who are pushed too hard can burn out and end up hating the very activities that once brightened their lives.

But movement can also be joyful, liberating, and a resource for friendship and community. We need to examine philosophic principles that support these positive experiences.

PURPOSE OF THE BOOK

This book is for aspiring and experienced kinesiology professionals, not for card-carrying philosophers. I do not assume a background in sport philosophy or philosophy in general. This volume should be accessible to advanced undergraduates, to experienced kinesiologists, and to any other lovers of human movement who are reasonably well-read and have an inquisitive mind.

This text may also be useful for entry-level graduate students who want an introduction to the philosophy of sport and would like to better understand philosophy's role in a field that has been associated far more with empirical science than with the humanities. Graduate students need to use this text in conjunction with other texts that provide a more in-depth treatment of various issues, such as analysis of the mind–body relationship, sport ethics, movement aesthetics, and educational philosophy.

In the acknowledgments, I mention my debt to Dallas Willard, an early mentor of mine who taught me that the value of philosophy lies in the search for practical answers, the kind that improve the lives of real people. This book has been written in that spirit. It is an attempt to see how and why skilled movement can play a central role in our search for a happy, healthy existence.

However, I am also aware that good answers are hard to come by. This volume is not an answer book or a compendium of wisdom. It is a book that raises questions that are worthy adversaries not only for kinesiologists but also for generations of philosophers. Much like science, philosophy is never finished. In both fields, we work hard to get more complete and accurate answers and then, just when we think we have it right, a new perspective presents itself and gives us pause. We return to the laboratory or the library and try to do better. This text puts us on a philosophic path, has us wrestle with potential insights, but does not lead us all the way to our destination.

COMMITMENTS AND ASSUMPTIONS

In this book I borrow from a number of philosophic traditions. I have found that answers to questions about the significance of activity do not fall under any one school of thought. For example, several existentialists pay close attention to the central role of embodiment in human development; Zen Buddhists provide insights about the power of intuitive thinking in movement; pragmatists are open to hands-on experiences and holistic understandings of personhood; anthropological philosophers help to uncover the crucial role that movement has played in our evolutionary development; and even certain idealists discuss embodiment and its significance in human culture. For instance, Plato, in spite of valuing contemplation over action, believed physical activity had an important role to play in the education of Greek citizens.

As with most philosophic works, however, this volume favors certain points of view over others. To be sure, this comes in part from personal bias. But it also comes from a commitment to find at least partial answers to philosophic questions. Those of us who are interested in applying philosophy to real-world problems are more committed to getting things at least partly right than to being comprehensive and even-handedly dispassionate. Those of us who want to put philosophy to work naturally favor positions that better explain our experiences at school, in the gymnasium, or at the clinic. We naturally gravitate toward philosophic positions that best help us solve the problems we encounter in those places.

I picture philosophy as a journey from lesser to greater clarity and insight. Because we are fighting our way through this overgrown path and have no way to get a bird's-eye view of our progress, it is difficult to say where we are at any one time. But our reflections should stimulate us to move forward even if some of the positions supported here do not exactly clear the trail. By the end of the text, we should have found some answers that will make a difference in our personal and professional lives. We should fully expect to make some progress in figuring out the nature and value of human movement.

Here are some of the commitments I have made that color the analyses in the chapters that follow:

Philosophy is a journey.

◆ *I doubt that analytical, logical analyses provide the deepest insights about movement.* While principled abstractions provide useful information about such matters as games and play, messy, lived experiences provide even better resources for insight. I appeal to uneven and varied life experiences for verification of claims while using analytic distinctions judiciously, usually only to clarify extreme positions or outline the terrain to be examined.

◆ *I am convinced that holistic understandings are more powerful than monistic or dualistic understandings.* For example, holistic medicine appears to have advantages over other forms of therapy that treat the human being simply as a collection of cells (monism) or as a composite of body plus mind (dualism). I argue for a holistic understanding of who we are as human beings, which provides important clues about how we might maximize the benefits of physical activity.

◆ *I am biased in favor of pragmatic approaches to answering movement questions.* I do not see the world as ideally fixed once and for all, even though it is fairly stable in many ways. Movement and good living seem to be intertwined in multiple ways ranging from the extrinsic use of activity for health and fitness to its intrinsic satisfactions and playful excesses. This interconnection also exists at different levels, from the chemical to the cultural, from the biological to the artistic. Movement can work toward the betterment of humankind in a variety of ways, but it can also have less salutary effects. This ambiguity is present when we try to determine what works best in our professional settings. In spite of our desire for decisive answers, this approach suggests that good professional practices are frequently built not on clear-cut, black-and-white solutions, but on solutions that are shades of gray.

◆ *I place little emphasis on the philosophy of culture.* While it is not possible to strip this book of all political, economic, and religious ideology, the text does not explicitly look at sport through the lenses provided by, for example, Marxism, capitalism, nationalism, or any particular religion. The emphasis here is on the philosophic roots of movement in human life. The text focuses on what we share as members of a common species while acknowledging that cultural, economic, and political perspectives are important.

ORGANIZATION

This text is arranged in four parts. Part I discusses the nature and tools of philosophy. Chapter 1 gives first-time philosophy students a sense of the field—what philosophers do, how philosophy complements science, and whether or not we can place any confidence in philosophic conclusions. Chapter 2 focuses on giving you the skills to think critically and clearly.

Part II turns to the nature of people. We start by looking at two of the most popular interpretations of human beings, mind–body dualism (chapter 3) and scientific materialism (chapter 4). While both positions have their strengths, I argue that they are also misleading in important ways. Thus, in chapter 5 we enter two hypothetical tournaments to see how well kinesiology can compete under the banners of dualism and materialism. We do not fare very well, so in chapter 6 we look at an alternative position called holism. Then in chapter 7 we attempt to see how holism may allow us to be more effective in the kinesiology workplace.

Part III directs us to the subject matter of kinesiology. What do we offer our students and clients? What are we about? In chapter 8 we look at movement and play. In particular, we examine the process of growing playgrounds and strategies for growing genuine players. In chapter 9 we turn to games, competition, and the significance of winning. We also examine movement as work, dance, exercise, and routine living.

Finally, in part IV we turn to professional ethics. Chapter 10 provides an introduction to ethics, including our moral responsibilities as professionals and ways we can improve our ethical behavior. Chapter 11 directs our attention to "the good life." We look at the traditional movement values of health, fun, skill, and knowledge, examining a strategy for ranking these potential contributions to good living. Then in chapter 12 we speculate on one ranking that gives priority to skill and a brand of knowledge called lived wisdom. We look at our services in terms of liberal-arts values, intrinsic goods that improve the quality of life.

We also review four profiles of the active lifestyle and draw conclusions about whether the good life is available to those who turn their backs on embodiment and choose to live their lives mostly in chairs.

FEATURES

At the start of each chapter, you will encounter a brief introduction to the topic at hand. This should stimulate your curiosity about the material to come. Accordingly, each introduction concludes with a series of provocative questions that we address somewhere in the chapter.

Next comes a brief road map of where we will be heading. This bulleted material identifies the key topics in the order in which they appear.

Philosophic exercises interrupt the text from time to time. These activities require you to think for yourself and draw some of your own conclusions. Philosophy is, after all, an active, rewarding process. It is important for all of us to practice our philosophic thinking, and these exercises provide just such an opportunity.

In most cases, it is important to complete the philosophic exercise before moving ahead. This is because you will frequently find at least partial answers to each exercise in the text that follows. While peeking at answers may save time, it does little for developing philosophic skills. More important, it takes the fun out of doing philosophy ourselves.

Where chapters are long or the material is unusually complex, brief summaries keep us on course. These summaries remind us where we have been, why we visited those places, and what we discovered.

At the end of each chapter you will find a review, a brief description of where we are headed next, and study questions. While all three elements are useful, the transition to future chapters is perhaps most important of all. The 12 chapters of the book are more places of respite on a single trail than a dozen separate trips. It is important to see the connections between where we have been and where we are going to next.

Taking philosophic trips like this is a luxury. Some individuals are pressed into work before they have a chance to think. Others are in a rush to make money, make a name for themselves, or simply get a degree and get out. Still others prefer to be told what to do. Philosophy asks you to slow down, think for yourself, and intelligently evaluate your personal and professional options.

Experience has taught many of us that we have limited opportunities to find our way on the highway of life. You might best do some planning before you pull out into the busy traffic. You will certainly have other chances to ponder and plan, but I hope you will take this opportunity to slow down and enjoy the reflective terrain in the pages ahead.

ACKNOWLEDGMENTS

I am indebted to many individuals for any ideas in this book that have merit. For all the others, I take full responsibility. In the extent to which the former is the case, I thank all of you for your good papers and books. In the extent to which the latter is true, I can only say that I should have read more carefully and listened more intently.

Many individuals who shaped my thinking are cited on the pages that follow. I read their work, was impressed by it, and shamelessly adopted it followed by an appropriate reference. Others are not included in footnotes or the bibliography, but their influence is nonetheless here. In some cases, I may have forgotten where an idea came from and improperly presented the notion as if it dropped out of the sky or, even worse, as if I were its source. In other cases, those who influenced my thinking did not write much themselves, or their publications did not fit the format and topics of this text. This too resulted in deserving names being absent from these pages.

While I was at Oberlin College, my philosophic interest was kindled by Professor Ruth Brunner. Against a background provided by the dominant pragmatic physical education philosophies of the day, she introduced me to the exciting anthropological philosophical thinking of Eleanor Metheny and the existential-tending analyses of Howard Slusher. Both were then located at the University of Southern California, so the choice of a doctoral program was not a difficult one to make. Metheny and Slusher were dynamic and inspiring—though in very different ways. As an erstwhile philosopher, I could not imagine studying at a more exciting place. A third individual at USC, Professor Dallas Willard, invited several fellow students and me into the Philosophy Department. He helped make this otherwise intimidating environment a place to learn and, most importantly, a resource for thinking that would have a practical impact on the world. I can still hear him sternly pulling us back to earth when, one day, a few advanced students reverted to some philosophic showmanship, "If philosophy does not help us live better lives," he warned, "then we have absolutely no reason to be here!"

My mentor after USC was Warren Fraleigh. I worked for him at Brockport for 13 years and loved every moment of it. He was, and still is, my surrogate father. Warren taught me a great deal of philosophy but, even more importantly, provided an example of academic courage and integrity, in short, a profile of a good person. I continue to watch and learn.

At Penn State I have been blessed with a number of fine colleagues, but most notably with Doug Anderson from the Philosophy Department. His support of my graduate students (I should say, *our* graduate students) has been most gratifying.

Over the years, we have watched a number of bright, young people grow and thrive at Penn State. Many of them are cited in the pages that follow, and all of them helped to shape the ideas that made their way into this book. Among those who wrote philosophic theses, dissertations, and articles are David Dimmick, Tim Elcombe, Luanne Fox, Alun Hardman, Doug Hochstetler, Pete Hopsicker, Rich Lally, Doug McLaughlin, Jim Nendel, Brian Richardson, Susan Saint Sing, Howard Shultz, Cesar Torres, and Kurt Zimmerman. Sigmund Loland spent a year at Penn State en route to his degree in Norway.

I am also indebted to my wife, Janet, the person to whom this volume is dedicated. She spent many evenings and weekends wondering when this volume would be completed. (I too spent many evenings and weekends wondering when this volume would be completed.) But she always understood that this book was something that had to be done, and her support during the process was invaluable. So too was the moral support provided from a distance from my children, Matt and Jen. In truth, families write books, not individuals.

◆ *Part I* ◆

THE NATURE AND METHODS OF PHILOSOPHY

In this section you will become acquainted with philosophy and its methods. It is important to start here for several reasons. First, many of you may be more comfortable with the techniques of science than those of the humanities. Second, you likely have been socialized to trust science more than philosophy. Finally, you need to understand where and how philosophy fits in—what it does and how it can join science in providing more complete answers to our questions.

The following two chapters provide an introduction to philosophy that starts from the ground up. In chapter 1, you begin by testing your philosophic readiness and learning to identify basic philosophic questions. In chapter 2, you will use the methods of philosophy on two complex ethical questions—the moral acceptability of running up the score on an overmatched opponent, and the ethics of using performance-enhancing substances in order to improve competitive capabilities.

1

Philosophy and Kinesiology

© SportsChrome

A clever management slogan underlines the confidence we place in scientific inquiry: "In God we trust. Everyone else—data!"

We live in an age dominated by data and the powerful tools of science. Most college kinesiology programs have a full menu of science courses—chemistry, biology, physiology, biomechanics, motor learning, motor control, fitness assessment, exercise prescription, and more. Even sociology and psychology of sport are empirical sciences that rely heavily on controlled studies, actual measurements, and statistically significant findings.

On the other hand, kinesiology curricula in the arts and humanities—in the history, literature, poetry, music, art, and philosophy of physical activity—is much smaller, if it exists at all. In addition, advanced skill classes that provide firsthand experience in the joy of movement are few and far between. Many believe that liberal arts and subjective experiences in physical activity provide more enrichment than essential knowledge, particularly in preparing for the workplace.

Without a doubt, that point of view has some force. Imagine that you are a kinesiologist and need to help an accident victim, a physical educator who teaches a yoga class, or a cardiac rehabilitation specialist who must facilitate someone's recovery from bypass surgery. If you had time to study either exercise physiology and biomechanics or history and philosophy of physical activity, but not both, which would you select? Most people would immediately choose the science courses. And this is quite possibly the right choice—well-trained professionals need the information that science courses provide.

Nevertheless, we are seldom faced with such all-or-nothing choices, and the purpose of this text is not to pit science against philosophy. As mentioned in the preface, pragmatic thinking avoids unhelpful either–or dichotomies. The spirit of this book is friendly to the arts, humanities, *and* sciences of physical activity. Science does not tell the whole story of movement, and neither does philosophy. Each one plays a part in complete professional preparation. In order to see what philosophy does and how it can make a contribution, we need to ask the following questions:

◆ Do philosophic issues deserve our attention? If so, which ones are most important, particularly for the workplace?

◆ Do philosophic methods work?

CHAPTER OBJECTIVES

In this chapter, you will

◆ *become acquainted with philosophy,*

◆ *assess your readiness to think philosophically, and*

◆ *examine the distinctiveness of philosophy and its relationship to empirical science.*

◆ How can we be sure that the methods work when most philosophy seems to amount to little more than opinion?

◆ Do philosophic answers really make a difference in our day-to-day lives? Can philosophic insight help us teach a student or heal an injured athlete more efficiently and quickly?

THE NATURE OF PHILOSOPHY

Philosophy literally means "the love of wisdom." Notice that it does not mean the love of facts. Philosophy requires us to go beyond facts. It relies on judgment, discernment, and a kind of reflective vision that extracts something interesting or useful, often from nothing more than everyday experience.

Wisdom, or as Plato called it, right opinion, can affect every choice we make and everything we do. Consequently, philosophy is a broad, fundamental discipline—one that could be called, as in fact it once was, the mother of the sciences. But philosophy is also mystifying because it does not literally measure anything and thus has no need for microscopes, hand dynamometers, or test tubes. For some, this makes philosophy difficult to describe and to perform. For many more, it makes philosophy difficult to trust.

Determining Your Philosophic Readiness

Perhaps you have been practicing philosophy your whole life, putting stock in philosophic reasoning without fully realizing it. Or perhaps you have been dodging philosophic questions and leaving them for others. In this book you will be asked both to trust philosophy and to think philosophically. Are you ready?

Philosophic Exercise

At this moment, you are at a certain level of readiness to find philosophic questions and deal with them. This might be called your Philosophic Readiness Quotient, or PRQ. You can get a rough measure of your own PRQ by completing the Philosophic Readiness Inventory. Choose the number that best corresponds to your degree of agreement or disagreement with each statement, and record your answers on a separate sheet of paper. You should complete the inventory before reading further because the discussion that follows may bias you toward certain choices, making it difficult to obtain a meaningful score.

Philosophic Readiness Inventory

			Rating Scale			
Strongly Agree						Strongly Disagree
1	2	3	4	5	6	7

Set 1

1. I frequently wonder about the meaning of life, about why I am here.
2. Whether or not I am a member of a religious organization, I regard myself as a spiritual person.
3. Compared to others, I think of myself as more introspective and reflective.
4. I often find myself pondering questions of ethics, of what is right and wrong.
5. I think of my life more as an adventure story than a routine journey.

Set 2

1. I am confident that philosophy is not just a matter of talking in circles.
2. While there may be more than one defensible position on the value of exercise, not all positions are equally valid.
3. I believe that some logical arguments, like the one that follows, are enlightening and persuasive: Because I have a moral obligation to tell all my clients who are uninformed the truth about their condition, and because Jane is a client of mine who is uninformed, it follows that I have a moral obligation to inform Jane truthfully of her condition.
4. Not everything in life is relative. We can confidently make judgments about what is more or less important—for example, that love is among the top human values.
5. It is possible to distinguish good sportsmanship from poor sportsmanship across cultures in the modern world. For instance, I can see that attempting to deceive officials into making a favorable call is questionable behavior no matter where it occurs.

Set 3

1. Insights about morally right and wrong professional practice should affect my behavior on the job.
2. Philosophic conclusions about ethics and the so-called good life should affect what we teach our children.
3. Some ideas and principles are so important that they are worth fighting for, even at great risk to oneself.
4. It may be as important to put philosophic insights into practice as it is to make use of scientific findings.
5. Spiritual or materialistic value commitments should make a difference in how people actually live their lives.

Add up the responses from each set, then add the subtotals for your total PRQ. Compare your three subscores and your grand total with the norms on page 21.

Interpreting Your PRQ

The Philosophic Readiness Inventory measures three readiness factors: philosophic curiosity, confidence, and commitment. These factors correspond to three of the questions we asked about philosophy at the start of the chapter:

◆ Do philosophic questions deserve our attention? (curiosity)

◆ Do philosophy methods work? (confidence)

◆ Do philosophic answers matter? (commitment)

Your score from set 1 indicates your interest in philosophic questions, or the degree to which you wonder, question, and play with ideas. It may tell you something about your capacity to be amazed, intrigued, even perplexed by your life and the world around you.

Set 2 measures your confidence in the tools of philosophy. You could have a high score on curiosity (subscore 1) yet be skeptical about the way philosophic thinking works. Or you might not be very interested in philosophic issues, even though you think the methods are reliable. Thus subscores 1 and 2 have a degree of independence from one another.

Set 3 measures your belief in the importance of philosophic answers, either as ends in themselves (it is good to know principles of ethics, period) or as means to other ends (principles of ethics can help a person be a better kinesiologist). If you had a low score for set 2, it is likely that your score for set 3 is low as well. If you do not believe that philosophic methods work, it would be strange for you to believe that philosophic answers are useful. However, the converse is not true. You might trust philosophic methods, have a high score for set 2, still have a low score for set 3, and not see how philosophic answers apply to life. Thus subscores 2 and 3 have degrees of reliance on one another.

If this short exercise gave you some insight into your attitudes toward philosophy, you now have a sense for how ready you are to move ahead. If your scores were low, you begin with a healthy degree of skepticism or doubt, an attitude long esteemed in philosophic circles. In effect, your scores say, "Show me how this stuff works before I invest too much time or energy on it." In some ways, this is an advantage because you will undoubtedly hold philosophy to the test.

If your scores were relatively high, you are undoubtedly interested in moving ahead. You have probably already had rewarding personal experiences with philosophy. Like an athlete who comes to a team with some skills and positive attitudes already formed, you begin with an advantage. You should, for instance, be more creative in returning tough philosophic passing shots that come your way. Those who need to spend time on basic skills will be more mechanical in their thinking and less able to deal successfully with such volleys.

Is play good for both adults and children?

What Makes Philosophy Unique?

Some people believe that philosophic questions are easy to spot. See if you can identify which of the following are genuinely philosophic:

1. Is play good for both adults and children?

2. How does a therapist get a sedentary person to adopt a physically active lifestyle?

3. Should allied health or medical professionals always tell their clients the truth? If not, what are the exceptions?

If you answered that all three questions are philosophic, you are right. If you think that all three need not be philosophic, you are right again. Virtually any question offers some possibilities for philosophic analysis, but the opposite is also true—virtually any question presents opportunities for measurement and other nonphilosophic treatments.

The issue is not so much finding questions that are purely philosophical, but locating the philosophic perspective as opposed to scientific perspectives. For the previous three questions, answers may come from chemists, physiologists, sociologists, and many others. But scholars in these various areas adopt a different standpoint than the one taken by philosophers. They look for answers in other places and employ other tools.

Philosophic Exercise

A research team that includes a chemist, physiologist, sociologist, psychologist, and philosopher addressed the three questions according to their own disciplines. Table 1.1 shows their responses. Can you see differences between the perspectives? If your answer is yes, try a few more:

a. Where would you start? With philosophy? Chemistry? Somewhere else? And, if it matters, where would you go second, third, and last? Give at least one reason in defense of your ranking.

b. Which discipline provides the most useful answers for your professional purposes? Rank them from most important to least important and again, give a rationale for your choices.

Answer questions a and b for the first question in table 1.1, then check your reasoning against my own, which begins after the table. Repeat this procedure with the third question. (The second question will be used later in this chapter.)

TABLE 1.1 Questions From Different Perspectives

Question	Chemistry	Physiology	Sociology	Psychology	Philosophy
1. Is play good for both adults and children?	Can we find a change in brain chemistry for players as opposed to nonplayers? If so, does this change have different functions for children and adults?	How does play affect physiological development? How does the play of children affect, for example, the circulatory system? The nervous system?	How do different cultures view the play of children and adults? Do certain societies discourage adult play? If so, why?	Do children who have good play experiences grow up with more self-confidence? Does play have any similar effect on adults?	What is play? Does it come in different gradations, such as deep play or shallow play? Are children more likely to experience deep play or shallow play? Which are adults more likely to experience?
2. How does a teacher or therapist get a sedentary person to adopt a physically active lifestyle?	Are there chemical profiles that predict inactivity or lack of energy? Are there genetic or chemical markers that support or discourage activity? What is an endorphin? How powerful is it?	What physiological barriers lie in the transition to an active lifestyle? How fast and durably can they be affected? Where should one start? Where do endorphins come in?	How can the social barriers to activity be overcome? Can society develop policies that encourage activity, such as incentives for walking, biking, or playing outdoors?	How does one motivate a person to move? What incentives might help? What barriers must be overcome? How powerful is the so-called endorphin high?	What is the experience of an endorphin high? Is it memorable? If not, what else will make activity meaningful?

(continued)

TABLE 1.1 (continued)

Question	Chemistry	Physiology	Sociology	Psychology	Philosophy
3. Should allied health or medical professionals always tell their clients the truth? If not, what are the exceptions?	What are the biochemical facts of a disease or injury? What are the probabilities of recovery? What are the results of chemical analysis of risk factors?	What are the physiological facts of the disease or injury? What are the probabilities of recovery? What are the results of physiological analysis of risk factors?	What are the common practices in this culture? If a person is seriously ill or injured, does a medical person communicate this, or a family member, or a spiritual leader?	What is the psychological impact of the truth on health and recovery? Is the individual strong enough to deal with this information?	How would the medical professionals want to be treated if they were in this situation? If there are circumstances for withholding the truth, what principles should inform such judgments?

If you made judgments about where to start and where to find more and less valuable answers, you have demonstrated that the five approaches to knowledge are different. You should have noticed that they use very different tools and look for explanations in different places. If you have taken courses in each of these areas, you are well aware from personal experience that chemists are not philosophers, and sociologists aren't physiologists.

Is there a correct answer to question *a,* or a place to start looking for answers? I'm not sure that there is. Notice that the sequence of disciplines in table 1.1 moves left to right, from the building blocks of chemistry to the lived human experiences of philosophy, from smaller elements to larger, more complex combinations of elements.

Focusing on the first question, about the value of play for adults and children, we could argue for starting most anywhere. The more scientifically oriented might want to begin with chemistry. Chemicals are physical and measurable. They affect all plant and animal actions, including human play. Further, everyone relies on answers from chemistry. A physiologist, for instance, cannot completely understand physiological responses to play without also understanding the chemistry of play. No play occurs apart from chemicals (causation from the part to the whole), and no play takes place without consequences at the chemical level (causation from the whole to the part). Because chemicals are involved at both levels, it would not be a bad decision to start with fundamental explanations—the chemistry of play.

But some of you may argue that because the topic of interest is human play, we need to begin with lived experience and thus with philosophy. Philosophic analysis can do some descriptive ground clearing. For instance, it might explain how and why being off work and at play can be two very different experiences. Individuals can be away from the job and still be thoroughly bored. We need a description of play that explains how this phenomenon involves more than merely being away from work or other duties.

Chemists might want to wait for this description if it will help them find the right subjects and thus avoid committing serious mistakes. What if they drew blood from a group of individuals who were off work but were also bored? Would the results say much about the chemistry of those who play? And as a health practitioner, would you want to use these results in arguing for the value of play therapy?

Question *b* asked you which answers are most useful in the workplace. Again, I am not sure that there is a conclusive response. A physiologist studying play using animal models such as mice runs the many risks that go with making generalizations from animals to humans and from the laboratory to the natural world. The insights of a sociologist on play in the context of friendships, culture, and history would complement the physiologist's work in important ways, because children and adults experience play in some context or other. A physiologist, for instance, might not notice the issue of guilt in adult play, but in certain contexts, such as work-oriented cultures, guilt is important in understanding the leisure behavior of adults in contrast to children. Physiological answers without sociocultural insights are often one-sided and incomplete; likewise, sociological answers alone will not suffice.

As noted earlier, questions of the best place to start and the most valuable answers assume that there are differences between disciplines. We are ready to make some generalizations about these differences, which will help us see more clearly what philosophy can add to our knowledge of human movement.

The Measurement Turn

Chemists, physiologists, sociologists, psychologists, anthropologists, biologists, and other scientists take what might be called the measurement turn. They try to measure things that they can see, hear, feel, taste, or smell. They analyze atomic structures, cardiovascular responses, observed behavior, and so on. They take these measurements with tools ranging from mass spectrometers to validated surveys. But regardless of the tools, when asked to justify a conclusion or finding, they refer to the products of measurement—data.

Philosophers do not usually rely on data, though most would admit they are very much dependent on sensory experiences and real-life events. Nearly all would acknowledge that they think with an intelligence that is profoundly limited because it is embodied, it is the product of evolution, and it is embedded in a particular language, history, and culture. In contrast to the scientist's tendency to gather data, philosophers are not interested in measuring anything empirically.

Philosophic study includes intangibles—descriptions of human experiences like hope, trust, and love; analyses of relationships between things like games and play; and speculations on the value of human enterprises such as cooperating in contrast to competing. If asked to join a research team on question 1 (see table 1.1 on pages 9-10), philosophers would be content to leave the gathering of chemical, physiological, and sociopsychological data to the others. They would spend their time instead examining play on the basis of lived experience, logical distinctions, and speculations about its value. Although, such judgments rest on nothing palpable and are not supported by statistically significant findings. Philosophers rely on intelligent recognition, discernment, plausibility, and logic.

THE CASE FOR PHILOSOPHY

Interdisciplinary research teams, like the one symbolized in table 1.1, are now fairly common because we can find more comprehensive, accurate, and powerful answers by approaching problems from many directions at once. Even some professional preparation programs are now grounded in the science and wisdom of many fields. Professionals prepared in this way seem to be more effective than their peers. They cure people faster, prevent disease more effectively, improve athletic performance more consistently, and change lives for the better more regularly (Weil 1997; Coles 1989; Jackson and Csikszentmihalyi 1999).

But how can philosophy, a discipline that dispenses no pills and knows little of gene transplants, increase our effectiveness? Let's use question 2—how to get a chronically inactive person to adopt an active lifestyle—to see how intangibles make tangible differences. We'll look at five arguments that support this point.

The Common-Sense Argument

Common sense suggests that because we are trying to change human behavior, we need someone on the research team who understands how people think, what people know, and how people come to understand these things. The sociologist's data, for instance, might indicate that many people do not understand why movement is important. The active lifestyle is not meaningful for these individuals, and this is one reason for their unwillingness to adopt an active lifestyle.

But how do things become meaningful for human beings? A philosopher who can clearly articulate differences between intrinsic and extrinsic meanings, personal and impersonal significance, and simple and complex meanings could be invaluable in helping the team determine where to go in search of answers to this question. Once again, common sense suggests that for human problems, someone who knows about human thinking from a subjective standpoint could be helpful.

The Missing-Information Argument

Let's suppose that the conversation turns to the so-called endorphin high, a subjective state that active individuals often experience. Might we enhance behavioral

From the kitchen of: _____

Common Sense

1. *Begin with a generous amount of firsthand experience.*
2. *Add in skills of careful observation.*
3. *Mix together and set aside for several years.*
4. *Retrieve the mixture by means of a good memory.*
5. *Place in a slow oven of careful thinking for as long as necessary for useful conclusions to rise to the surface.*
6. *Remove from the oven and enjoy.*

Serves 1 for a lifetime. Quantity is usually sufficient to feed all others who are nearby.

Firsthand contact with the world + careful observation + a good memory + clear thinking = good judgments.

change, the physiologist suggests, if we could get more people to experience this euphoric state? The chemist agrees and proceeds to obtain data on what an endorphin is and how its chemical makeup can produce pleasurable states of mind. The physiologist provides information on exercise thresholds that generate the release of endorphins. The sociologist discusses the kinds of social support that promote exercise. And finally, the psychologist produces data on self-efficacy, barriers to exercise, and their respective roles in promoting and inhibiting activity. So what's missing?

One thing that's missing is a description of what it is like actually to live an endorphin high. But even more important is information on how this experience fits into human life. The good life is not composed of one continuous endorphin high. People want more. They seek challenges; they thirst for meaning; they thrive on love and community; they try to make the world a better place (MacIntyre 1984; Keen and Valley-Fox 1989; Bellah et al. 1985, 1991; Midgley 1994; Singer 1995). By pointing out the limits of an endorphin-based motivational strategy, a philosopher can provide a value context for a more accurate portrayal of human interest. Endorphins affect and are affected by persons, not machines.

We need all the information, including experience.

The Argument Against Reductionism

Reductionists believe that any phenomenon can be understood in terms of its smaller parts. According to reductionism, changing from a sedentary to a more active lifestyle can and should be reduced to simpler elements, to root causes. Where do the secrets for changing behavior lie? Not in lived experience, because experience is a product of psychological mechanisms and enculturation. Then do they reside at these two locations? Not entirely, because enculturated thinking is determined by evolution, anatomy, and physiology. Are these three factors the final root causes? Not quite, because each of them depends on chemistry and physics. So, the reductionist might say that the secrets to changing a sedentary person into an active one lie in brain chemistry and particle physics.

This tidy conclusion, however, presents a problem. While reductionist models work well for certain mechanical operations, they have not been very effective in explaining complex, real-world behavior (Gleick 1987; Midgley 1994; Ridley 2003). Because of this, it appears that the answers to modified behavior do not lie simply in particle physics or brain chemistry. To be sure, part of the answer lies there because human beings are chemically tethered organisms. But to get a more complete answer to behavioral change, we have to resist the urge merely to reduce lived experience to biochemistry, the elements of which can never be experienced.

This claim is based on the fact that neither you nor I have ever met an endorphin and we never will, apart from a textbook or test tube. What we experience after a good workout is a delightful calm, a slight buzzing or tingling sensation, a sense of well-being. As human beings we react to that feeling, not the chemicals that may cause those subjective states. We seek calm, not the company of

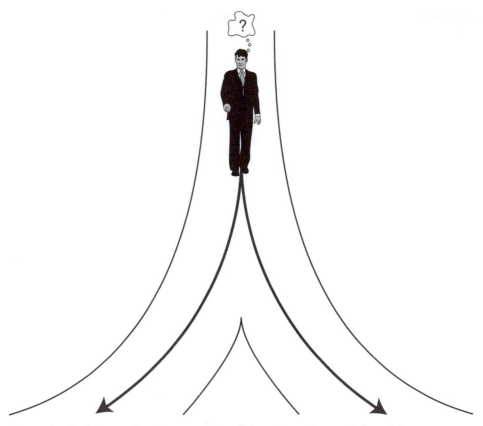

We need to look in two directions . . . toward the parts and toward the whole.

endorphins. Philosophers focus on what it is like to live an endorphin high. Thus philosophers can provide a counterbalance to those who look for all the answers in antecedent causes.

The Argument Against Linear Causation

Reductionism is closely related to principles of linear causation. When scientists reduce complex human behavior to mechanical structures, they begin to expect the regularity associated with machines. Linearity takes its cues from physics, specifically the Newtonian principles of mechanics. Linearity suggests that doubling a cause (say, the length of a lever between the fulcrum and point of force) results in a predictable increase in the effect (the ability to move objects). With each change in the length of the lever, the new effect could be plotted along what would become a straight line; thus the term *linear causation*.

The problem is that the linear model does not help us understand many things in the world. It is insufficient for forecasting the weather and it is surely insufficient for explaining human behavior. Small causes, it turns out, can have

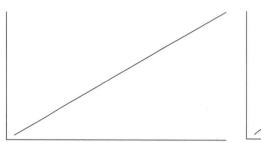

Human behavior does not go like this . . .   **it goes like this.**

unexpectedly big effects, and vice versa. This results in chaos, where we can observe general patterns but cannot predict individual events with any certainty (Gleick 1987).

If weather patterns are chaotic, human behavioral patterns are at least as complex. Consequently, promoting change from a sedentary to an active lifestyle cannot be based on any linear model alone. Interventions to increase an individual's activity must be calculated from complex interactions among history, gender, age, aspirations, genetic makeup, skills, past experiences, chemistry, and other variables. In real life, more of something that once helped, like exercising with a friend, is not always better. A philosopher will serve as a counterbalance for attempts to produce interventions on a simplistic linear model.

The Argument Against Single-Direction Causation

If we see the shortcomings of linear causation, we should also see that causation goes both ways, not just in one direction. This is important for philosophy for the following reason: If ideas are simply the result of a chain of electrical, chemical, physiological, and cultural events, then ideas become merely the dependent offspring of that chain. We would not need to take ideas seriously. But if ideas also work the other way, affecting enculturation, brain structures, and electrochemical actions, then intangibles and tangibles are on an equal playing field (Ridley 2003).

In such a world, an active lifestyle is influenced by the mechanisms and realities described by the other members of the research team, but the reverse is also true. Active living with all of its subjective highs and lows influences everything from social arrangements to the architecture of the brain. The effects of thinking are real in an empirical sense and thus need to be taken seriously.

Conclusions

Table 1.1 suggests that philosophy complements our understanding. Philosophy provides a unique perspective that is not concerned with empirical measurements. It also provides unique information such as descriptions of lived experience, logical distinctions, and speculations about what is good. Philosophic input is

Cells ➤ Ideas

Human behavior does not work like this . . .

Cells ➤ Ideas
⬅

it works like this.

important if we want to honor common sense; avoid missing important information; and temper thinking that is reductionistic, looks for linear causation, and is based on causal relationships that run only in one direction.

Some of these ideas may be perplexing, but throughout the book examples from activity settings will put them more fully into context. You will learn how to become a professional who values ideas and human experience and uses them along with information from the sciences. As a holistic professional in a science-oriented field, consider a simple proposition: Ideas are real. Human experience matters and must be studied on its own terms. We can investigate even intangibles like values and make reasoned judgments about them.

Philosophic Exercise

One of the strongest cases for the importance of philosophy rests on the relationship between behavior and values. It is said that values drive our behavior; we choose what we find worthwhile, interesting, or good. To see if this is true in your own life, write down three things that you hope to accomplish in your life. Then, identify the values that seem to be present in these goals.

Many individuals find values like love, pleasure, knowledge, progress, security, friendship, and excitement behind their choices. What did you find? Can you agree with the claim that values drive behavior, including your own? If you can, you have found yet another argument that supports philosophy.

PHILOSOPHIC QUESTIONS

The experiences or ideas that philosophy studies fall into several categories. We can use question 3 from table 1.1 to see how far our philosophic work goes. The question is this: Should allied health or medical professionals always tell their clients the truth?

Questions About the Nature of Things

This is an area of philosophy called metaphysics. It is concerned with what things and actions are and how they are similar or dissimilar to one another. It is descriptive. It lays out the characteristics of physical things like chairs, nonphysical things like hope, speculative things like heaven, and all actions, such as running and believing. Following are some metaphysical questions:

◆ What is a health or medical professional?

◆ What is the difference between a person in a profession and in a trade?

◆ What is a client or patient?

◆ What relationship exists between the professional and client?

◆ Is the relationship one of equality or inequality? If it is one of inequality, where does the inequality lie?

◆ What counts as telling the truth? Is truth something that has degrees? Or is it an all-or-nothing sort of reality?

Questions About the Value of Things

This area of philosophy is usually called axiology. It attempts to uncover reasons for calling certain objects, actions, or states of affairs "good." Rather than being concerned with what *is,* it focuses on what *should be.* Rather than looking at the characteristics of certain actions, it asks how people should act. It looks at specific values such as excellence, truth, and broad values such as what makes the good life. Following are some axiological questions:

◆ To what extent is a professional's integrity at stake when deciding what to tell a client? Should that be an overriding issue?

◆ Would the client be better off knowing or not knowing? What exactly do we mean by better off? Happier? More peaceful? More knowledgeable?

◆ How can a professional's decision to tell or not tell affect the life of your client in the best way possible?

Questions About Good Behavior

This area is called ethics. It is closely related to axiology. While it is concerned with what is good in life, it focuses on how individuals affect each other for better or worse. It looks at how individuals should treat one another and how they should treat themselves. Following are some ethical questions:

◆ When is a professional permitted to be paternalistic—when it's for the client's own good? When dealing with young children? When working with the uninformed?

◆ Should professionals tell the truth as a part of their basic moral obligation to clients?

◆ Are there any extenuating circumstances that would permit or even require that the truth not be told? If so, what are they?

Ethics looks at how individuals should treat one another and how they should treat themselves.

Questions About What People Know

This branch of philosophy is called epistemology. It concerns the theory of knowledge—what human beings know, how they know it, and with what assurance they hold different beliefs. It looks at the specifics of understanding, such as the knowledge that may be present in the reflexes of young children, as well as larger problems, such as doubts about the ability of human beings to know anything at all. Following are some epistemological questions:

◆ Can you know with any assurance that you are right about any of the previous questions—about what a professional is, what counts as the truth, whether or not telling the truth is a moral obligation?

◆ How would you substantiate your claims?

◆ If you intuit that in a specific case telling the truth is not the best policy, is that intuition a form of knowing?

◆ Should professionals trust intuitive insights?

Questions About What Is Beautiful

This is the area of aesthetics. Like axiology, it is concerned with what is good. But aesthetics focuses on matters of sensual, artistic good—what is beautiful or pleasing to the eyes, ears, palate, fingertips, or overall human experience.

Consider, for example, the following aesthetic questions. Remember that both the professional and client are living stories based on certain themes, roles, and expectations.

◆ How will a decision about telling the truth affect the coherence of those stories?

◆ For the professional, will telling the truth be courageous?

◆ For the client, will the new knowledge provide tranquility?

Philosophic Exercise

To make certain that you have a sense for the range and philosophic character of the five question categories (metaphysics, axiology, ethics, epistemology, and aesthetics), write a two- or three-sentence answer to one question under each category of questions. Answer them in any order you see fit. Do not label them as metaphysical or epistemological answers, but again make sure you have one of each. Then share them with classmates or a colleague. Can they pick out the five types of questions and put the traditional labels on them?

REVIEW

Philosophy is the art and science of wondering about reality, posing questions related to that wonder, and pursuing answers to those questions in a reflective manner. Philosophic questions are everywhere and are virtually impossible to avoid. Almost any question can be turned in philosophic and nonphilosophic directions. Philosophers attempt to answer questions logically, speculatively, and descriptively. This reflective methodology provides distinctive information about the lived experience of human existence. Its presence in an interdisciplinary research project is important due to common sense, missing information, and the limits of reductionism, linear causation, and single-direction causality.

Philosophers ask several types of questions that address the nature of things, value, good behavior, knowledge, and beauty. The tendency to ask and pursue philosophic questions is related to philosophic curiosity, confidence, and commitment to the usefulness of philosophic insight.

LOOKING AHEAD

Now that you have a basic understanding of philosophy and the role it can play in answering practical questions, it is time to practice the skill itself. In chapter 2 you will have an opportunity to test your reasoning skills on two philosophic problems. You will learn how philosophers think and practice philosophical thinking yourself.

CHECKING YOUR UNDERSTANDING

1. *Can you describe your own readiness to think philosophically in terms of curiosity, confidence in philosophic methods, and belief in the usefulness of philosophic answers? Can you explain why the three measures are more or less independent of one another? Can you also explain why a low score on confidence should result in a low score on utility? Based on your own personal experiences and background, can you explain why your scores on the Philosophic Readiness Inventory are high, middle, or low?*

2. *Take a general question such as, "What is the value of sport?" and describe how a philosopher, psychologist, sociologist, physiologist, and chemist might go about answering it. What is the difference between the way philosophers and scholars in other fields would answer?*

3. *How could you change the mind of someone who sees philosophy as a waste of time? Can you identify five concrete arguments for the importance of philosophy?*

4. *Describe the range of philosophic questions. Take a topic like modern dance and formulate at least one question about it from each of the five areas of philosophy.*

Norms for Philosophic Readiness Inventory

Category	Low	Middle	High
Set 1 Philosophic Curiosity	16-35	12-15	5-11
Set 2 Philosophic Confidence	17-35	13-16	5-12
Set 3 Philosophic Usefulness	17-35	12-16	5-11
Total PRQ	50-105	37-47	15-34

2

Pursuing Philosophic Answers

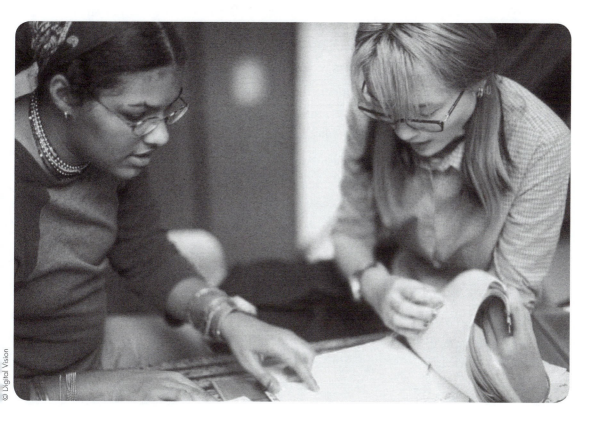

Now that we've learned to identify and ask philosophic questions, it's time to take the next step—searching for answers. This is the most challenging part of the philosophic endeavor because many people doubt that the tools of philosophy work. While they might acknowledge the importance of philosophy and even agree that its answers could and should affect the way we live, they avoid philosophy because in their view it doesn't get them anywhere. Philosophic evidence is an oxymoron because all arguments are subjective. For this reason many people believe that philosophic conclusions are simply personal opinions.

In everyday life, however, most of us behave as if philosophic positions are more powerful than this skepticism would suggest. For example, when we encounter parents who say that sport should be fun and competition should not be too serious, and then observe these same parents placing tremendous pressure on their kids to win, excel, and perhaps even get college scholarships, we can conclude that their stated beliefs and behaviors are inconsistent. We can provide concrete reasons to defend our view. If these parents were to challenge our conclusion, we could show them exactly where the ideas of play and childhood conflict with the ideas of serious competition and a heavy load of extrinsic values.

When we take such pains to defend our views, we show our true philosophic colors. Philosophic conclusions are not simply opinions, even if we cannot strictly prove them true or false, because our behavior shows that they carry persuasive weight. In light of this tendency to give at least some credence to philosophic processes, we can ask the following questions:

◆ What techniques do experienced philosophers use?

◆ Do all philosophers use the same methods?

◆ Are there any foolproof methods? Or do all philosophic techniques have strengths and weaknesses?

◆ Do you currently possess the skills necessary to work through a philosophic problem?

CHAPTER OBJECTIVES

In this chapter, you will

◆ *learn the steps of philosophic procedure;*

◆ *use inductive, deductive, and intuitive thinking to wrestle with two philosophy problems; and*

◆ *review the strengths and weaknesses of philosophic methods.*

INITIATING A PHILOSOPHIC ANALYSIS

No one has ever agreed upon a single set of procedures for doing philosophy. The road map in this chapter is but one formulation of a multitude of possible approaches. However, most philosophers recommend the following steps.

1. Develop a thesis. Much philosophy begins with a hunch. It is important to formalize this idea and write it down to help you see what you are really thinking about. This step provides a focus for gathering information and arguments. If there is no thesis, then there is probably no focus, and any reflection on the problem is likely to meander without coming to any forceful conclusion.

The thesis in philosophy is analogous to the hypothesis in science. Just as hypotheses do not need to be correct to be useful, it is not crucial that your philosophic hunches turn out to be accurate. Their utility lies primarily in their capacity to help you focus on a problem and search for relevant arguments. Moreover, once an investigation begins, you can modify your hypothesis and change the direction of your study.

2. Clarify the problem. A thesis gives only the bare bones of the philosophic problem. Many issues are usually too large or ambiguous and stand in need of clarification. Philosophers have to declare what assumptions they are making, what they are looking at, what they are choosing to ignore, what definitions they will use, and so on. This step turns a general focus (step 1) into a clear, workable problem that has a chance of being solved.

3. Search for arguments. Finding a thesis and clarifying the problem merely sets the stage for the more interesting work of philosophy—finding persuasive arguments. No simple formula tells us where to find these arguments, but most philosophers use a combination of inductive, deductive, and intuitive–descriptive thinking to make their case. We will examine how these tools work, though you have probably already used them informally and developed a degree of argumentative skill in using each one.

Inductive Reasoning

Inductive reasoning is based on the human intellectual ability to move from the specific to the general, from concrete examples to abstract understandings (see figure 2.1). If we were analyzing oranges, we might line up four or five types of oranges and identify general characteristics that describe all of them in spite of their individual differences. We might say something about their shape, color, and structure, qualities that distinguish them from other objects like potatoes, books, and baseballs.

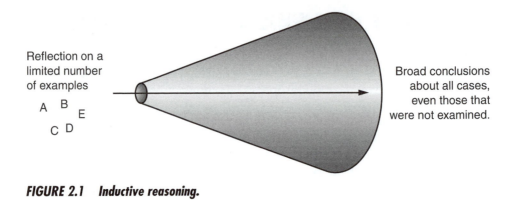

Reflection on a limited number of examples

A B
  E
  C D

Broad conclusions about all cases, even those that were not examined.

FIGURE 2.1 **Inductive reasoning.**

Philosophic Exercise

Your task in this exercise is to describe the core characteristics of sport, the central features found in almost all examples of this unique domain of human behavior.

1. Write down five exemplars of sport, such as a collegiate soccer game or a singles tennis match. For each of the five examples, ask yourself the following questions:
    ◆ What do these activities have in common?
    ◆ What general characteristics distinguish these activities from other human endeavors such as dancing, studying for a final exam, or exercising? For instance, some have argued that sport involves a test of physical skill. Is physical skill a feature that is common to all five of your examples? If so, this helps distinguish sport endeavors from intellectual tests like final exams, which do not rely on motor capabilities.
2. List three to six characteristics of sport that capture at least some of its distinctiveness. Did you have the necessary skills to look at a few particular examples and induce or generalize broad features of the phenomenon? Does your description distinguish sport from the activities listed in step 1, namely dancing, studying for a final exam, and exercising?

Intuitive Reasoning

Intuitive reasoning is based on the human intellectual ability to see something directly and describe it faithfully. For this kind of thinking, we do not have to gather multiple examples of our object of interest; one will do. We reflect on it, add features to it, subtract features from it, and observe how it changes (see figure 2.2). If a certain addition or subtraction does not change the exemplar very much, we might conclude that the modifications are not central to the character of the item. On the other hand, if a change transforms the object, we might claim that the variation was crucial to the integrity of the exemplar.

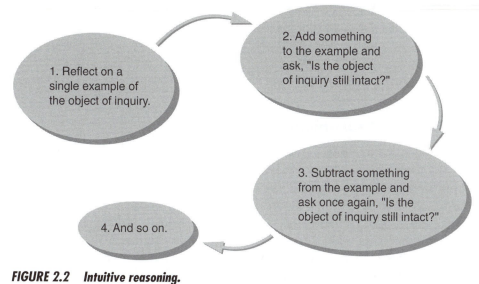

FIGURE 2.2 *Intuitive reasoning.*

Philosophic Exercise

Your task in this exercise is to describe the relationship between following the rules of the game and satisfying the demands of good sportsmanship. Are people who follow the rules necessarily good sports? Are athletes who intentionally break rules necessarily bad sports? Start by imagining a single exemplar, such as the behavior of the catcher as she receives the pitches in a game of softball. Picture a few tosses coming in, the catcher receiving them, the umpire making the call, and the catcher throwing the ball back to the pitcher. Not much of interest here. But now vary the scene to better allow you to intuit information about sportsmanship.

Imagine the catcher framing a pitch, holding the glove and her body in a way that creates the illusion of a strike. Imagine the catcher pulling a pitch to try to get a strike called, quickly moving the glove from outside to inside the strike zone a fraction of a second after the ball hits the mitt. Imagine the catcher holding a pitch, remaining motionless after catching a pitch in an attempt to pressure the umpire into calling that pitch a strike whether or not delivery was actually in the strike zone. Now for the crucial part: What do you see as you visualize these variations? The catcher broke no game rules in any of the three cases, but do you still see good sportsmanship?

You can also try the opposite and picture the catcher breaking a rule. Say that the catcher has some sandpaper hidden in her glove. Before returning the ball to the pitcher, this individual roughs up the ball to give the pitcher an advantage. What do you intuit about good sportsmanship—has it disappeared or is it still there? Now picture the catcher pushing a batter out of the way just before a pitch arrives, because the catcher knows that the pitcher plans to throw at the hitter's head. Again, the catcher has broken a game rule because catchers are not allowed to interfere with batters. But the catcher may have saved the batter from serious injury. What has happened to good sportsmanship? Is it still there or not?

How good are you at intuitive reasoning? It takes skill to come up with variations that produce interesting and useful differences, and it takes skill to observe changes in your object of interest—in this case, good sportsmanship. It also takes skill to faithfully record what you see. What did you learn about the relationship between following game rules and good sportsmanship? Write down two or three conclusions.

Deductive Reasoning

Deductive reasoning is based on the human intellectual ability to move from the general to the specific, from several broad premises to a few concrete conclusions. In this kind of reasoning you begin with facts (propositions whose truth has been demonstrated) or hypotheses (propositions whose truth is still in question) and attempt to see what follows. Derivations from facts often take this form: "*Because* this is the case, then such-and-such must be true." The formulation from hypotheses often goes like this: "*If* this is the case, or *supposing* that this is the case, then such-and-such must be true" (see figure 2.3).

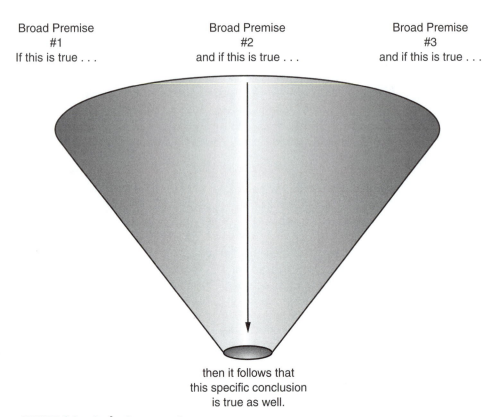

Broad Premise #1
If this is true . . .

Broad Premise #2
and if this is true . . .

Broad Premise #3
and if this is true . . .

then it follows that
this specific conclusion
is true as well.

FIGURE 2.3 Deductive reasoning.

Philosophic Exercise

Your task in this exercise is to determine if playacting in games like professional soccer is consistent with the purpose of the activity. When a player exaggerates contact from an opponent by dramatically falling to the ground, holding his leg, and writhing around as if in extreme pain, is he still pursuing soccer objectives? Does this strategy for winning soccer games make sense? Is it self-defeating?

We can start by formulating some broad premises that will lead us to one or more specific conclusions. Remember that premises can be hypotheses or facts. In this case, we will frame them as suppositions rather than facts.

Premise 1: Suppose that the purpose of contest in soccer is to see who displays superior skills during any given game.

Premise 2: Suppose too that these skills feature playing the ball, defending space, passing, and so on—all the strategic and physical skills outlined in the rules of soccer, as interpreted and commonly applied by the soccer community.

Premise 3: Suppose further that playacting is, in part, a physical skill that can influence the outcome of soccer matches. It can be practiced, and like other skills, it can be done well or poorly.

Premise 4: Suppose, in addition, that playacting can serve as a substitute for the featured skills. For instance, a team that is highly skilled at faking injuries could occasionally win games even though it exhibited poorer dribbling, passing, and shooting skills during that game.

Premise 5: Finally, suppose that playacting is difficult to detect. Referees cannot see inside the head of the injured player to determine if he is really hurt or not, making it difficult to rid the game of such tactics.

Now that these hypothetical premises are in place, what can you conclude about playacting in soccer? You may be able to make some descriptive statements about why it exists and why it has not been eliminated. You may also be able to make some value judgments about its contributions to or detractions from soccer. If you are uncomfortable with any of your descriptions or value judgments, it could be that you are also uncomfortable with one or more of the premises. As you will see later in this chapter, this is one of the weaknesses of deductive reasoning—your conclusions are only as good as your premises allow them to be.

APPLYING PHILOSOPHIC REASONING TO COMPLEX ISSUES

The exercises in the previous sections have prepared you to wrestle with a full-blown philosophic controversy. You will apply all three methods to a single issue and weigh the evidence you have gathered. The following case studies produce strong arguments both for and against any single conclusion, so you will have to judge where the strongest reasoning lies.

In the appendix, you will find two provocative articles, one by Dixon on the ethics of running up the score on a weaker opponent, the other by Gardner on the morality of taking performance-enhancing substances in order to improve performance. Read them to become familiar with the problems and to see if you agree with the authors' arguments. After completing the articles, consult the following case studies.

In the two essays, I have provided editorial inserts that indicate where each author formulates a thesis, clarifies the problem, and searches for arguments. The case studies discuss these editorial inserts.

In addition, I have provided a brief bibliography for each essay. The bibliographies will allow you to research what other philosophers have said about these two sport problems. These readings could be useful for a class debate, a paper, or simply to satisfy your own philosophic curiosity.

Case Study 1: The Ethics of Running Up the Score

Case study 1 focuses on the ethics of running up the score in a lopsided contest. Dixon argues that, under most circumstances, there is nothing inherently unsporting about continuing to try one's hardest when leading by a very wide margin. This advice contradicts the traditional tenets of sportsmanship that urge competitors not to embarrass overmatched opponents. Who is right?

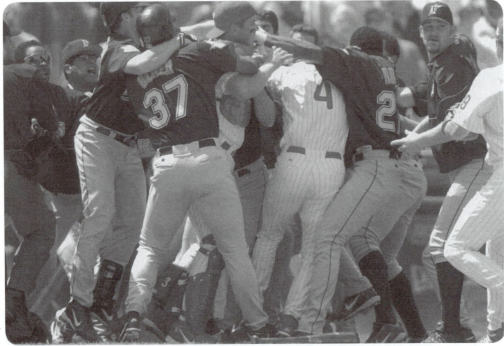

Is running up the score morally defensible?

Analysis of the Problem

Read the description of Dixon's essay in the five numbered paragraphs. Then return to the essay to see if you can find these points. Ask yourself if the following interpretations are faithful to Dixon's text. Finally, respond to the questions in the short exercise at the end of each paragraph.

1. Dixon formulates a thesis (before and including section I). He claims that there is nothing unsporting about maximizing the margin of superiority in a game after securing victory in a one-sided contest. He is saying that it is morally acceptable to run up the score. This is a general hypothesis.

Short exercise: Is this issue interesting? Is it worth examining? Do we find examples of this dilemma at different levels of sport? Do lopsided victories occur frequently? Are you clear about how athletes should behave when beating opponents badly?

2. Dixon clarifies his problem (section II). Dixon already has the problem, but he has not yet pinpointed the precise claim he wants to defend. The problem of whether or not "pouring it on" is proper behavior is too large and unwieldy. Thus he begins with some caveats about what he is *not* claiming and some descriptions of the smaller subject he *will* be examining. In order to effectively evaluate his argument, you need to understand these clarifications, particularly his admission that in some situations running up the score is not morally defensible, such as in certain noncompetitive or recreation settings and where there is any intent to harm or humiliate.

Short exercise: By the end of Dixon's definitions and caveats, do you think he has sufficiently clarified his claim? Has he cleared away the underbrush enough so that both you and he are looking at the same issue?

3. Dixon searches for arguments (section IIIA). Dixon claims that in competitive sport, where there is a mutual interest in the accurate determination of superiority, continued effort in lopsided games is permissible, perhaps even morally required. We could structure this argument deductively:

◆ Premise 1: If athletes play for accurate and complete knowledge of superiority, and

◆ Premise 2: If victory by itself does not provide that knowledge, and

◆ Premise 3: If continued play that affects the magnitude of victory helps to supply that desired information, then

◆ Conclusion: Continuing to compete even after victory has been secured helps athletes get what they play for.

Short exercise: Do you like this deductive argument? If not, where is the problem? Is it in the premises? For example, is knowledge of superiority the primary value at stake in competitive sport? Is it true that victory alone has limited ability to provide this knowledge? When a football team is far ahead, do they learn more about their ability by continuing to complete long passes and otherwise dominate an overmatched opponent?

Are additional premises needed? If so, what is missing? For instance, does premise 3 need further modification? Under what conditions might running up the score provide important information on superiority? Under what conditions might this be redundant?

Is the move from the premises to the conclusion valid? For example, is premise 1 solid? Don't athletes play for different reasons? If so, continued effort in a lopsided contest may not make complete sense.

4. Dixon provides a second argument (section IIIB). He claims that even in playful situations, continued effort in lopsided contests is morally acceptable. We could phrase this argument in intuitive–descriptive terms:

◆ Play does not require generosity, easing up, or in any way not taking winning seriously. Play is more compatible with all-out performance, innovation, and freedom than it is with pandering to those who are losing.

◆ It is simply more fun for both sides if the game goes on at full speed, particularly when it is understood that losers in blowouts have no reason to feel strongly humiliated as long as they continued to play hard, did not cheat, and so on.

◆ While lopsided games are not as good as even ones, when they take place players gain nothing by killing the clock, grinding out meaningless plays, or otherwise performing well below their capabilities. Boredom descends on both players and fans when such strategies are employed. In other words, when we vary the exemplar of a lopsided contest to include all-out performance, we intuit more play.

This descriptive analysis draws a relationship between play and a spirit of generosity (Dixon says they are not necessarily connected in competitive sport) and between playing hard and enjoyment (Dixon says they are positively related; he argues that the cure for lopsided contests is worse than the disease because easing up promotes boredom). Do you buy this descriptive account? Is there some sound logic here? How do you define play? When an opponent rubs it in, does this tend to extinguish play or not? Is there any antidote for lopsided contests that would salvage the spirit of play?

5. Dixon provides a final argument (section IIIC) that avoiding running up the score is not required by high-minded virtues of sportsmanship—that is, by any deep, genuine concern for the welfare of the opponent. We could structure this argument inductively:

◆ Sample A: A person who played hard to the end but lost by a huge margin.

◆ Sample B: A person who refused to cheat or intimidate officials in spite of the fact that she was behind by a large margin.

◆ Sample C: A person who did not bemoan his fate, ask for favors, or seek sympathy in spite of losing a game by an unusually large number of points.

Dixon asks himself: What is common in these three cases?

His answer: The athletes all lost by lopsided scores.

Dixon asks himself: Were the three athletes strongly humiliated?

His answer: No. They simply lost a game. While they may have been disappointed as athletes, they were not humiliated as persons. Strong humiliation is related to character defect, and none of the three compromised his or her integrity. In fact, observers can see some honor here. All three played courageously and honestly to the very end.

Dixon then draws some inductive generalizations from these three examples that are pertinent to his final argument:

◆ Lopsided defeats alone produce little harm even though they may be distasteful.

◆ When dominating weaker opponents, virtuous athletes need not let up.

Short exercise: Do you agree with these abstractions from the three examples? What if Dixon had given himself more difficult samples, such as a case where an athlete was shown to be utterly incompetent? Would he still be able to conclude that there was no significant harm?

Summary

Through deduction, description, and inductive thinking, Dixon has tried to clarify a muddy ethical problem. He provides arguments in favor of certain sporting behavior that has often been regarded as improper. While his arguments in support of running up the score are not conclusive, they have some persuasive power.

Short exercise: If you think that Dixon's arguments are not particularly weighty, you have an obligation to show where his reasoning is faulty and provide stronger evidence. Can you collect any counterarguments that show that Dixon is wrong, or at least that the case for running up the score is not as clear as he thinks it is? The brief bibliography that follows includes articles by individuals who believe that Dixon was mistaken as well as responses by Dixon that clarify and defend his original position.

Dixon, N. 1992. On sportsmanship and "running up the score." *Journal of the Philosophy of Sport* 19:1-13.

Hardman, A., L. Fox, D. McLaughlin, and K. Zimmerman. 1996. On sportsmanship and running up the score: Issues of incompetence and humiliation. *Journal of the Philosophy of Sport* 23:58-69.

Dixon, N. 1998. Why losing by a wide margin is not in itself a disgrace: Response to Hardman, Fox, McLaughlin, and Zimmerman. *Journal of the Philosophy of Sport* 25:61-70.

Feezell, R. 1999. Sportsmanship and blowouts: Baseball and beyond. *Journal of the Philosophy of Sport* 26:68-78.

Dixon, N. 2000. The inevitability of disappointment: Reply to Feezell. *Journal of the Philosophy of Sport* 27:93-99.

Case Study 2: The Ethics of Taking Performance-Enhancing Drugs

The second case study covers a major problem in sport—the use of performance-enhancing substances. While most sport organizations ban any number of drugs and other aids, many athletes and scholars question whether such bans are justified. And, of course, many athletes around the world, from baseball players to weightlifters, ignore these prohibitions and attempt to avoid detection when they are tested for drugs.

Some argue that adult athletes who understand the risks of such supplements as anabolic steroids should be allowed to use them. Others claim that there is something morally wrong with using drugs to improve performance and the pursuit of championships or medals. Who is right?

Analysis of the problem

Read my description of Gardner's essay in the following five paragraphs. Then return to the appendix to see if you can find the points in the original article. Ask yourself if my interpretations are faithful to Gardner's text. Finally, respond to the questions in the short exercises.

1. Gardner formulates a thesis (beginning of article). He claims that there have been no compelling arguments for banning performance-enhancing drugs, at least not on the grounds that they provide an unfair advantage. He needs arguments that support his position that rules against drug usage are arbitrary, inconsistent, or otherwise unjustified.

© Empics

Where do you draw the line on performance aids?

Short exercise: Is this an interesting issue? In the world of sport, is drug-enhanced performance still an ethical problem? Are you clear about issues of fair play and performance enhancement? Where do you draw the line on performance aids? Are the following enhancers acceptable or not? How would you defend your decisions?

- High-tech equipment
- Nutritional supplements
- Help from a sport psychologist
- Prayer for divine intervention
- Steroid injections to restore performance
- Wheat germ
- Aspirin
- Natural aids like the infusion of your own blood (blood doping)

2. Gardner clarifies his problem (introduction and section titled "What Is an Unfair Advantage?"). Gardner has a large and unwieldy issue to deal with. Because the ethics of drug usage in sport are so complex, he must take considerable pains to reduce the problem to a manageable size and to clarify exactly what he will be claiming. In order to clearly evaluate his argument about unfair advantages and drugs, you need to understand his stipulations about the following:

- What counts as a performance-enhancing drug?
- What if certain drugs do not really enhance performance? What are you to assume in this regard?
- What about arguments besides unfair advantage (e.g., harm, coercion, unnaturalness)? Are you to consider these or not?
- Is it not true that unfair advantages are commonplace in sport and are tolerated without moral condemnation? If so, the issue cannot be one of unfair advantage per se, rather *how* the advantage was gained. True?
- If unfair advantages are gained in ways that are morally unacceptable, would you not expect rules to prohibit such means, and would that not justify such rules?

At the end of this section, Gardner believes he has cleared away the brush and is ready to meet the arguments head-on. For instance, you should no longer be distracted by the argument that taking anabolic steroids provides an unfair advantage simply because it involves breaking a rule that others follow. Although Gardner would agree that this is unfair, he would remind you that the larger question is justifying that rule. Why is the rule there in the first place? Is taking drugs a morally objectionable means for gaining an advantage? That is the key question.

Short exercise: Are you clear on what the argument is about? Do you know all you need to know about the drugs, the kind of competition, the age of the performers, and so on? If not, write down any additional facts or assumptions that need to be on the philosophic table before the argument begins.

3. Gardner searches for arguments (section titled "An Advantage Over Other Athletes"). Gardner argues that a variety of complaints about drug usage as improper or somehow unsporting are not persuasive. He shows this by using an inductive train of thought in reference to the claim that drugs provide an unfair advantage because they are not equally accessible to all competitors. For example, in some countries so-called designer drugs are not available, or for some individuals in developing countries, costs for certain drugs may be prohibitive. The inductive argument might look like this:

Sample A: A golfer who has wealthy parents and the best coaching that money can buy.

Sample B: A bobsledder who lives in a country with strong scientific and technological support for the sport.

Sample C: A skier who performs exceptionally well in part because he was born in Norway.

Gardner asks: What is common to all of these cases?

His answer: They all involve unfair advantage because these athletes have unequal access to performance-favoring conditions.

Gardner then asks: Are these advantages morally acceptable?

His answer: Yes. They are ethical, even if they are not ideal. Athletes with such advantages are allowed to compete. No one discounts their victories, and

Do skiers born in Scandinavia enjoy an unfair advantage?

no one holds them morally blameworthy for benefiting from the advantages. Our collective moral judgment has been, "This is part of sport."

From these particulars and others, Gardner can abstract his broader claim about unequal access to drugs such as anabolic steroids. If unequal access to any number of performance-enhancing factors were commonplace and morally unobjectionable, why would we single out unequal access to anabolic steroids as an unethical way to show superiority?

Short exercise: Do you agree with Gardner that the unequal access argument is inconclusive? As far as access goes, are there any relevant differences between being born in Norway and being able to afford steroids? Does the freedom to choose affect the moral status of behavior? One is not free to choose where one will be born, but choice does exist regarding the use of steroids.

4. Gardner provides a further argument (section titled "An Advantage Over Other Athletes"). We can frame the case he makes here in intuitive–descriptive terms. Some who favor the banning of drugs argue that athletes do not earn the advantages they gain from anabolic steroids. Gains from popping pills require no training, sacrifice, or effort. Sport should reward those who work harder, not those who have better pharmacists.

Gardner's descriptive counteranalysis goes something like this: While sport has much to do with measuring merit, effort is not the only way to show merit. In fact, diverse sports require different levels of effort. Training for baseball is not the same as training for football or distance running. Likewise, athletes in the same sport, depending on their dispositions and genetic endowments, may find success with considerably less effort than their peers. But we do not discount their accomplishments just because they did not have to work as hard as someone else.

Short exercise: Gardner wants you to agree with his intuitive–descriptive conclusions. When he subtracted high levels of effort from his exemplar by imagining success from a naturally gifted athlete, he still saw or intuited athletic merit. Do you? Effort, or at least high levels of it, Gardner concludes, is not a requirement for athletic merit. Do you agree that banning performance-enhancing drugs because they reduce effort is not a conclusive argument? How important is consistency?

5. Gardner provides a final argument (section titled "An Advantage Over the Sport"). Gardner considers claims that the use of drugs compromises the integrity of sport—it provides solutions to sport problems that end up ruining the activity. We can frame one of his arguments in deductive terms.

Premise 1: All new technologies or methods that ruin the game by making the sport test too easy should be prohibited.

Premise 2: The use of square-grooved golf clubs makes the golfing sport test too easy.

Premise 3: The increased strength stimulated by steroid use does not threaten sport tests by making them too easy.

Conclusions: The use of square-grooved golf clubs should be prohibited; the use of steroids should not be prohibited.

Once again, Gardner believes he has provided a persuasive argument.

Short exercise: If you disagree, you need to identify weaknesses in his premises, look for missing premises, or argue that his conclusion is not warranted. Is premise 1 controversial? Do sport-governing boards outlaw technologies that might undermine their sport? Under premise 3, is it true that steroids do not ruin sport tests by making them too easy? Could they have that effect, at least in some sports? Which sports could be harmed if athletes became too strong?

Summary

Through inductive, intuitive, and deductive arguments, Gardner believes he has provided evidence to support his contention that the unfair-advantage argument for prohibiting drugs in sport is inconclusive. He argues that we are inconsistent when we claim that steroids provide an unfair advantage or when we accept any number of comparable conditions that are unfair.

Short exercise: If you think that Gardner's arguments are weak, or that evidence on the opposing side is stronger, you have an obligation to show the superiority of your view. Remember, Gardner has limited his discussion to only one facet of the issue. Even if Gardner is right about unfair advantages, drug usage could be justifiably banned for other reasons such as harm to oneself or the coercion of others to take dangerous drugs. If you are interested in more information on this topic, refer to the following bibliography.

Brown, M. 1980. Drugs, ethics, and sport. *Journal of the Philosophy of Sport 7*: 15-23.

Simon, R. 1985. Good competition and drug-enhanced performance. *Journal of the Philosophy of Sport* 11:6-13.

Gardner, R. 1989. On performance-enhancing substances and the unfair advantage argument. *Journal of the Philosophy of Sport* 16:59-73.

Schneider, A. 1993-94. Why Olympic athletes should avoid the use and seek the elimination of performance-enhancing substances and practices from the Olympic Games. *Journal of the Philosophy of Sport* 20-21:64-81.

Burke, M., and T. Roberts. 1997. Drugs in sport: An issue of morality or sentimentality? *Journal of the Philosophy of Sport* 24:99-113.

Kretchmar, S. 1999. The ethics of performance-enhancing substances in sport. *Bulletin: International Council of Sport Science and Physical Education* 27:19-21.

Holowchak, A. 2002. Ergogenic aids and the limits of human performance in sport: Ethical issues and aesthetic considerations. *Journal of the Philosophy of Sport* 29:75-86.

CONCLUSIONS ABOUT PHILOSOPHIC REASONING

As we discussed in chapter 1, in this age of science and hard data many individuals have little confidence in philosophic methods. Because philosophy does not literally measure anything, it is thought not to produce any reliable results. However, as important as good data are, this is surely an extreme position.

First, scientific thinking and data gathering are difficult, skill-based procedures. Often we forget that the current truths of science turn out to be errors for the next generation of scholars. How many times, for instance, have recommendations on diet and exercise changed over the past 100 years? A certain food is deemed dangerous, then another study finds it acceptable, then further research suggests that it should be consumed only in moderation.

As late as the 1990s, physiologists in our field recommended relatively high amounts of exercise. Their data supported the old cliché of no pain, no gain. Then new data came along, showing that lesser amounts of exercise have nearly the same health benefits as more strenuous amounts, and health recommendations changed dramatically.

All this shows that the search for truth is difficult even when it involves a controlled study and draws conclusions from so-called hard data. Consequently, we should not single out philosophy for not being able to prove things once and for all. Philosophic truths are often revised when new arguments, perspectives, and thinking come along, but scientific truths are often revised as well.

We also learned that philosophic methods are designed to persuade, not to prove. Philosophers often have to base conclusions on the weight of the evidence. They have to make rational judgment calls. Rarely do philosophers find slam-dunk arguments that leave no room for doubt. But this is no reason to abandon philosophic thinking. All of us want to make personal and professional judgments using the best information available. We do not hold back on recommending dietary or exercise interventions to clients just because some study 10 years from now may show our practices to be faulty.

Likewise in philosophy, we may not be able to prove that running up the score is morally indefensible or that taking steroids is unethical, but we must still act. Our professional recommendations and personal decisions must be based on the best thinking we can produce today. Then we must read some more, reflect some more, and remain open to the possibility that we do not have it quite right, just as scientists diligently try to replicate findings, experiment with new paradigms, and seek different data to see if old truths hold up.

Both scientific and philosophic thinking take a great deal of patience and skill. Either procedure can be done well or poorly. Scientific data can be accurate or flawed, and conclusions drawn from them can be accurate, misleading, or flat-out wrong. Philosophical ideas, values, and logic can also be clear or ambiguous, consistent or inconsistent, persuasive or weak.

In this chapter we focused on three kinds of thinking that philosophers use in various combinations. This showed that philosophic thinking is not mysterious or otherwise unspecifiable. Philosophers do not have license to think in any way they choose. When we hear philosophic arguments that move us, it is usually because the methodology was sound.

The brief exercises in the two case studies zeroed in on places where philosophic thinking goes well or poorly. Following are some ideas that provide further evidence that philosophic procedures are skill-based and have varying degrees of success. This section will also help you identify places where you need additional practice.

Pitfalls of Inductive Reasoning

Inductive reasoning is not a foolproof methodology. Sloppy procedures, or what some call leaky thinking, can scuttle the most promising line of inductive thought. Here are some common problems.

◆ Mixed samples. In the exercise on page 26, you were given the metaphysical task of describing the nature of sport. After creating a list of five sport examples, you induced broad statements about what was common to each example and, at the same time, distinguished sport from other human endeavors. The validity and utility of your thinking were based on the examples. With good examples, you had a good chance to pull off the analysis. With bad or mixed examples, you might have drawn some misleading conclusions.

I suggested intercollegiate soccer and singles tennis because they are noncontroversial examples of sport. I left out activities such as chess or cheerleading in order to avoid the problems caused by a mixed sample. If we want to know about the nature of apples, we need genuine varieties of apples from which to generalize, not a combination of apples and oranges. If we want to know what the nature of sport is, we need genuine sports from which to generalize, not a combination of sport, dance, exercise, or other movement activities.

◆ Incomplete samples. In order to generalize effectively, we need a reasonably complete sample. If we use only two examples of sport—say, football and baseball—we might conclude that sport requires tests involving objects called balls. But if the list includes swimming and gymnastics, it is clear that ball-related tests are not distinguishing features of sport. The longer and more representative set of examples prevents us from making this mistake.

◆ Faulty abstraction. When we are looking at examples of sport, nothing automatically tells us the insightful characteristics we are searching for. We have to find the elements; we have to abstract them. When we make a good generalization, we need to be able to recognize it as such; conversely, we need to get rid of those that do not work.

For instance, if we look at our five examples of sport and see people in each one, we could abstract the principle that sport requires people. While this may be true, it is not very helpful because it does not distinguish sport from thousands of other activities in which people engage. This generalization is too broad to be of much use. If, however, we recognize that all examples include a test of some sort that is solved through physical skills, we might be on to something more significant. Many activities are not tests, and many activities that are tests do not require motor coordination or strength. Physically demanding tests get us closer to the distinctive domain of activity called sport. It is a more useful description.

Pitfalls of Intuitive Reasoning

Intuitive reasoning also demands exacting skills. When these skills are lacking, the engine of intuitive thinking may jump its tracks. Here are some examples of how this can happen.

◆ Bias. On page 27 we thought about catching in softball and varied it. When we varied catching to look at framing, pulling, and holding a pitch in order to get a favorable call from the umpire, we tried to see if sportsmanship was lost even though no rules were broken. This is where biases may play a role.

If you had been taught by a coach who presented these three techniques as strategy, and if you admired this coach, you might have no problem identifying these acts as fully compatible with good sportsmanship. But are you seeing the situation objectively? Have your previous experiences colored your insights? Intuitive sight is never immune from bias.

◆ Weak variations. As we look at the example of a softball catcher performing her duties, nothing tells us where to go next. Nothing tells us to vary our reflections this or that way. Consequently, we may come up with variations that produce little fruit. For example, we might picture the catcher playing a day game, and then vary the scene to see her playing a night game. That particular variation does not help us see much about rule-following and sportsmanship. The variation needs to go somewhere else. Perhaps we need some experience with baseball or softball to know where these interesting moral places are. My own selection of framing, pulling, and holding pitches comes from my familiarity with baseball as a coach, player, and fan. Weak variations are more likely to come from those who do not know the subject at hand. This provides one argument for the claim that good sport philosophy depends at least in part on firsthand knowledge of sport.

Can we still intuit good sportsmanship when picturing a catcher framing, pulling, or holding a pitch?

Pitfalls of Deductive Reasoning

Deductive reasoning is also not exempt from procedural problems. Here are some common difficulties.

◆ Faulty premises. On page 29 you looked at five premises about playacting in soccer. Even though these were presented as suppositions and not facts, it could be that one or more of these hypothetical statements are not believable. If the premises are faulty, the conclusions are likely to be faulty too.

Premise 1, for example, stipulates that the primary purpose of soccer is to learn who displays superior skill during a game. Some might not accept that supposition. They could argue that the primary purpose is to win, whether by superior skill, luck, umpiring error, or intimidation. Of course, if we do not accept that superior skill is the primary purpose of soccer, then the deductive argument falls apart. We will not see playacting as an inconsistent behavior, because with the rejection of premise 1, soccer is not necessarily about game skills. Successful playacting is consistent with winning in at least one sense of the term.

◆ Incorrect deductions. When we look at the five premises on page 29, no obvious deductive conclusion jumps out from the page. The philosopher has to find it, and it is possible to make a mistake here. Valid conclusions must follow logically from the premises.

Premises 1, 2, and 3 allow us to say the following: Although playacting is a physical skill used in soccer, it does *not* necessarily follow that it is a physical skill that the game condones. We would need another premise to nail down that finding. Another example comes from premise 5, which stipulates officials' difficulty in detecting playacting. From that premise we are not allowed to say that playacting is permitted in soccer only because it cannot be detected. While this might be an implication of premise 5, it does not guarantee this conclusion. In short, you must be sure that deductive conclusions do not outrun their premises.

REVIEW

Philosophic reflection requires patience and discipline. Like much scientific work, philosophic insights are provisional—they are the best answers we have at the time. And as in science, old philosophical truths are replaced by better conclusions. Unlike some science, however, the spirit of philosophy is to enlighten and to persuade, not to prove. Philosophy has merit even without assurances of proof or absolute certainty.

Most philosophers take three steps to address a problem:

1. Formulating a thesis
2. Clarifying the problem
3. Searching for arguments

The search for answers often involves inductive, intuitive, and deductive reasoning. Each method has its strengths and weaknesses.

LOOKING AHEAD

In the next chapter we stop talking about philosophy and begin working on it. Our first step is to examine the nature of people as potential movers. Everything that we discover in a humanistic philosophy of physical activity depends on getting *us* right. This is because philosophic prescriptions depend on our vision of human beings and their true interests and needs. We begin with a popular interpretation of people called mind–body dualism.

CHECKING YOUR UNDERSTANDING

1. *Describe the steps that most philosophers take and why each one is important. Why is it important to formulate a thesis and clarify the problem before beginning the search for arguments and answers?*

2. *Identify the basic methods at your disposal in the search for answers. Describe how each one works.*

3. *Take the problem of running up the score or of taking anabolic steroids to enhance performance and identify one inductive, deductive, and intuitive argument for the author's conclusion.*

4. *Explain why philosophy's inability to prove its conclusions is not necessarily a fatal flaw. Compare philosophic findings with those of scientific inquiry.*

5. *Describe one weakness of each of the three philosophic methods presented in this chapter.*

◆ *Part II* ◆

HUMAN BEINGS AND PHYSICAL ACTIVITY

This section addresses fundamental questions for activity professions: Who are our students and clients? What does it mean to be human, and how can we most effectively serve these individuals?

In chapters 3 and 4 we will look at dualistic and materialistic answers to the question about what it means to be human. After discussing serious concerns about the adequacy of these two approaches, in chapter 5 we'll watch kinesiology compete poorly in dualistic and materialistic tournaments. In chapter 6 you will learn about holism, a position that enjoys some of the advantages of both dualism and materialism. And in chapter 7 you will see how holism can help you become a more effective practitioner.

3

Mind–Body Dualism

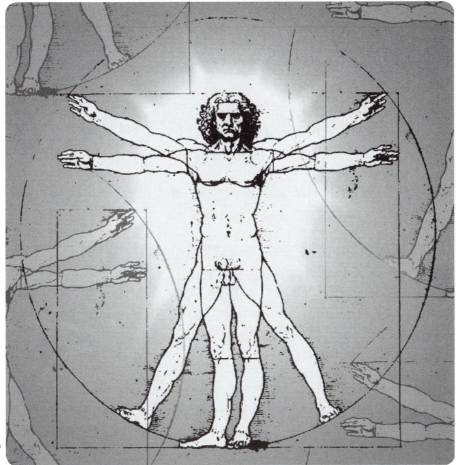

© Digital Vision

Philosophers, psychologists, biologists, and others who study human nature have yet to agree on what a person is. And practitioners—educators, physical therapists, coaches, trainers, and medical personnel—have yet to agree on how to help the people who come to them.

These theoretical and practical dilemmas are connected. Theoretical questions about what it means to be a person are not simply ivory-tower concerns; the answers make a difference in the workplace. When practitioners have different ideas of what a human being is, they hold different assumptions about how human beings might react to various interventions. If a person is a machine, for example, then mechanical treatments should work. If a person is a mind, or has some sort of spiritual dimension, then more cognitive interventions might be called for. It is unfortunate that kinesiologists have not spent more time on the question of human nature because it is the foundation of everything we do. If we embrace a faulty image of our students, athletes, and clients, our work with them will not go well.

Much of kinesiology's theory and practice is based on three positions on human nature—dualism, materialism, and holism. All three make sense. All three have been put into practice and have produced good results. One could even argue that some of our most effective teachers, coaches, and trainers have combined all three positions in their practice. Nevertheless, it is important to understand the claims of these positions about what human beings are and how they can most efficiently be maintained, fixed, and improved. We will start with mind–body dualism, asking the following questions:

◆ Is it not true that people have both minds and bodies?

◆ Are minds more valuable than bodies?

◆ Do our minds direct our bodies?

◆ When we teach, coach, or advise our students and clients, should we direct our instruction to their minds?

◆ Does it not stand to reason that information is the key to behavioral change?

CHAPTER OBJECTIVES

In this chapter, you will

◆ *learn the basic characteristics of mind–body dualism,*

◆ *see five different forms of dualism, and*

◆ *identify theoretical and practical problems with dualism.*

INTRODUCTION TO DUALISM

Dualists are impressed by the radically different characteristics of thought and matter (Descartes 1641/1960). Physical stuff is extended in space and has a variety of qualities like shape, color, weight, and molecular structure. Mental stuff is entirely different. Delight in skiing down a slope, for instance, has no shape, color, weight, or molecular structure. Yet the concrete joy that the skier experiences is unmistakable and is just as real as the accompanying electrical activity in the skier's cranium. The dualist does not want to dismiss subjectivity just because its "material" is intangible.

This approach leaves us with two separate parts, a mechanical body connected somehow to an immaterial mind. It also makes kinesiology a divided field with two research agendas and two kinds of interventions. To understand movement in the classroom and to improve performance on the field, we have to deal with two distinct realities—physics, circulatory systems, and oxygen delivery on the one hand, and ideas, motives, and fears on the other.

This is a reasonably attractive idea. Kinesiologists who practice dualism take the subjective seriously. For this reason alone, dualism may have significant

Whom are we teaching? A machine? A mind?

advantages over other philosophies such as scientific materialism that largely ignore perception and experience. As a whole, we *are* affected by our perspectives and our feelings. One of my favorite graduate professors, Dallas Willard, was fond of saying, "An idea is just as real as a tree." Dualism takes this important statement to heart.

Nevertheless, dualism also carries unfortunate baggage that causes both theoretical and practical problems. In order to understand how these difficulties affect kinesiology, we need to first look at the various ways that dualism shows up in the profession.

FIVE KINDS OF DUALISM

Substance, value, behavior, language, and knowledge dualisms are different facets of the same vision of human life. Even so, they affect kinesiology in different ways. As you read the following descriptions you may be able to discern the effects that each form can have on kinesiology. Table 3.1 summarizes these effects, which we'll discuss in more detail later in the chapter.

Substance Dualism

Substance dualism lies near the heart of dualistic thinking and practice. It rests on Descartes' insight that physical matter and thinking are radically different from one another. The body is extended in space and so it is much like baseball bats and rocks. The body can be measured, dissected, and treated like any other

TABLE 3.1 Five Kinds of Dualism

Name	Assertion	Effects on kinesiology	Result
1. Substance dualism	A human being is composed of two things, mind and body	Tendency to believe that we educate or otherwise tend to the body, not the whole person	Deification of the mind
2. Value dualism	Mind and mental activities are superior to the body and physical activities	Tendency to think that mainstream education is intellectual education; efforts to make ourselves appear scholarly or otherwise intellectual	Deification of intellectual education
3. Behavior dualism	All physical doing must be preceded by thinking	Tendency to compartmentalize thinking, to believe that thinking takes place apart from action	Deification of thinking over doing
4. Language dualism	Verbal symbols are radically different from and superior to other kinds of symbols	Tendency to overlook activity as a significant form of meaningful expression and communication	Deification of verbal language
5. Knowledge dualism	Knowing that (understanding) is superior to knowing how (the capacity to do)	Tendency to associate intelligence with only one form of knowing and to devalue action, particularly when it is physical	Deification of understanding over intuitive insight

object. The body, like all physical objects, must obey the laws of physics. The body is a kinetic machine whose actions can be described in terms of levers, forces, and material properties.

The substance dualist also acknowledges thinking, the subjective side of life. Thoughts are radically unlike matter. Ideas, as already noted, have no physical properties such as shape and size. They do not obey the laws of physics, but seem to be governed by rules of logic, coherence, and other tenets of clear thinking.

Finally, substance dualists note that mind and body interact. The body affects thoughts, and thoughts affect the body. While this connection between a physical entity and a nonphysical entity is difficult to explain, dualists nevertheless know from personal experience and scientific experimentation that the body and mind affect each other.

Value Dualism

Value dualism is grounded in substance dualism. The human being is still composed of mind and body, but here the emphasis is on the relative value of the two halves. Plato placed mind above body, preferring thought, ideals, and perfection over emotion and mediocrity. At best, physical training provides some balance in life and is valuable in education as a complement to more intellectual acquisitions. At worst, our carnal nature is the source of perceptual error, animal desire, emotional disturbance, and ultimately pain and death (Plato 1951).

Behavior Dualism

Behavior dualism is a type of value dualism because it highlights the dependence of the body-machine on the mind-operator (Ryle 1949). Behavior dualism suggests that all actions are composed of two parts, thinking followed by doing. The body cannot act on its own because it is only a machine, so it must await commands from the mind. Behavior dualism views mind and body in an asymmetrical relationship where the body depends on the mind.

Language Dualism

Language dualism, like behavior dualism, is a type of value dualism. This school of thought focuses on symbolism, or letting one thing stand for another. According to some, the ability to make and use symbols is a hallmark of being human, distinguishing us

Like oil and water, both mind and body are important. But how do we get them to mix?

from lower forms of animal life (Cassirer 1944). This theory takes a dualistic turn when intellectual symbolic processes are distinguished from, and valued over, nonintellectual symbolizations. Language in prose, poetry, and other spoken and written forms, as well as mathematical symbols in physics and other sciences, are commonly thought of as intellectual in nature. Standing, as they do, at the heart of many IQ, SAT, GRE, and other intelligence and academic achievement tests, they are thought to show the workings of the human mind at its best.

Symbol systems that do not rely primarily on words or numbers—for instance, those in music, painting, and sport—are often associated with so-called nonintellectual endeavors, and they enjoy lesser academic status.

Knowledge Dualism

Knowledge dualism holds that "knowing" occurs in two ways and at two different levels (Scheffler 1965; Polanyi 1966). First, there is "knowing that," or propositional knowing, which is genuine understanding. Propositional knowing allows us to explain what we know—for instance, why some sport techniques work better than others, or how and why circulation improves with exercise interventions. A second, inferior kind of knowing is "know how," or procedural knowledge. People with this kind of knowledge can do things, such as kick a football or play a piano, but they cannot explain how. According to knowledge dualism, people with this kind of knowledge do not really understand what they are doing. This compromises the value of their accomplishments.

Philosophic Exercise

Rank the five forms of dualism from the one that is most visible to the one that is least visible in your current or future kinesiology profession. For example, in teaching or coaching, behavior dualism might be most relevant. Coaches often say, "Think before you move." In the allied medical fields, substance dualism may be most obvious. The "machine," after all, needs to be fixed.

Next, provide at least one reason for your top and bottom rankings. You can then use the following discussion to see if your intuitions match my own about the utility of the five most popular dualisms.

ASSETS AND LIABILITIES

Dualism gives us a prism through which to see our clients as well as our students, athletes, and ourselves. This prism is helpful when we direct it toward certain objects and turn it in a certain way, but it also produces distortions when misused. Most scholars believe that the distortions are so significant that we need to abandon dualism. Nevertheless, because dualism holds some partial truths and durable attractions, we will discuss the assets and liabilities of each form.

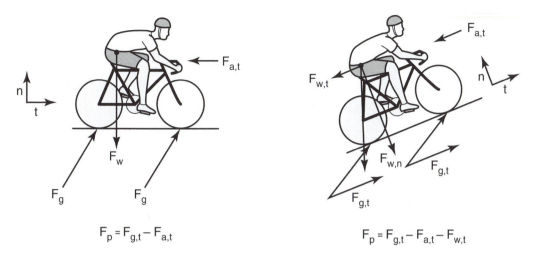

$$F_p = F_{g,t} - F_{a,t}$$ $$F_p = F_{g,t} - F_{a,t} - F_{w,t}$$

We cannot understand the movements of physical beings if we view them as the mere work of machines.

Reprinted, by permission, from R.M. Enoka, 2002, *Neuromechanics of Human Movement,* 3rd ed. (Champaign, IL: Human Kinetics), 270-271.

Substance Dualism

For substance dualism thoughts have no physical properties and bodies are like machines. The rise of modern science was stimulated in part by Descartes, who helped us examine the human body as just another physical object. Treating the body as a machine has resulted in better health, better movement performance, and far better understanding of how everything from genes to physiology influences us. Likewise, by preserving the significance of the mind, dualism allows us to talk about motives, inspiration, goals, and attitudes as real and powerful forces for improving the lives of our clients.

Theoretical Problems

◆ Dualists have never explained how mind and body affect one another. How can something immaterial move something material, and vice versa?

◆ If the mind is entirely immaterial, where is it? How can something that has no physical properties be anywhere at all?

◆ Do we ever have pure mind and pure body? These seem to be unreal abstractions, because our thoughts are always embodied and our body is always minded.

Practical Problems

◆ If mind and body are separable, how much attention should we give to each one? Do they each deserve equal amounts? Perhaps one deserves 70% and the other deserves 30%. Or as is often the case in public education, we might devote 90% of our attention to intellectual education and a mere 10% to art, music, and physical education. As kinesiologists, once we divide the person into parts we run the risk of becoming a mere "body shop," and we are relegated to maintenance and other auxiliary functions.

◆ What would it be like to teach the mind but not the body? How can we teach the body but not the mind? Could kinesiologists ever devise a therapy aimed purely at the physical? Would we want to do so, even if we could?

Philosophic Exercise

The way we speak and act perpetuates substance dualism. See if you can correct some of the following dualistic statements, and then speculate on how a dualist would respond differently in the case study.

◆ "A mind is a terrible thing to waste" (popular educational advertisement)

◆ "The Body Shoppe" (sign outside a fitness establishment)

◆ "Education of the physical" versus "Education through the physical" (slogans of two different philosophies of physical education in the mid-1900s)

Case Study

A recent graduate in kinesiology was taught to devote equal time to the three components of the human being—the affective (emotions), the psychomotor (skills), and the biological (movements). When devising lesson plans, she develops different sets of activities and assesses the three components separately. At the end of each unit she can confidently claim that she has taught the whole person.

Value Dualism

Value dualism is attractive for a number of reasons. Plato (1951) was right that our sense perceptions could be mistaken, that our passions could lead us astray, and that our mortal bodies would decay. In a way, the body is the source of our fragility and many of our difficulties in living from day to day. Conversely, our thoughts and purposes can inspire us to achieve excellence, perhaps even approach perfection.

We can reflect on ideals as Plato claimed we could. We can observe an imperfect jump shot, for example, and imagine how it might be improved or even perfected. John Wooden, the legendary basketball coach from UCLA who won nine national championships at that institution, was an idealist with a vision. He refused to allow himself or his players to cave into base desires, let alone to be satisfied with mediocrity. He is an inspiring example of mind over matter, of what it is like to find a transcendent purpose in the seemingly inconsequential activity of playing a game.

Theoretical Problems

◆ It is not clear that the mind is the source of our salvation and the body the source of our ills. Our sense perceptions are usually reliable, so we can trust the body. On the other hand, we can have evil thoughts of greed, envy, excessive retribution, and so on. Thus, there are times when we should not trust our mind to guide our actions.

◆ It is not clear that we can reflect on perfection, or even that there is such a thing. Would we be able to agree on the perfect jump shot or perfect health just because we all reflected on exactly the same thing? Perhaps we do not need a world of reified perfection, but only one of improvement toward excellence.

◆ Why would we want to cast doubt on the value of the aesthetic and sensual? Are these things not part of the good life simply because they are not products of reflection? Do we not want to relish climbing a mountain, swimming through water, or hitting a golf ball on the sweet spot of the clubface?

Practical Problems

◆ Should kinesiologists distrust the sensual experiences inherent in movement? Should we warn our clients about the dangerous allure of the sensual, or should we celebrate it as part of the charm of our domain? Value dualism suggests we should be cautious about the sensual and we should emphasize more durable outcomes, such as excellence in performance (Weiss 1969; Simon 2004) and character development (McCloy 1940; Clifford and Feezell 1997).

◆ How are we to deal with performances that fall short of perfection? What are we to do with people who come to us with far less than ideal capabilities? It is one thing for John Wooden to guide a group of highly motivated and skilled individuals toward perfection, but what about average athletes, students, and clients? Value dualism may be somewhat cold and impersonal when it presents us with the ideal objectives of kinesiology.

◆ Should we agree that intellectual education is more valuable than physical education? Should we add more intellectual content to our field just to make it more legitimate? Should we require undergraduate kinesiology students to take mostly theory courses with little or no performance?

We should celebrate the sensual.

Philosophic Exercise

Because we perpetuate value dualism by how we speak and act, try to eliminate this brand of dualism from the following three statements and the case study.

◆ "The spirit is strong, but the flesh is weak" (common religious claim)

◆ "I think, therefore I am" (Descartes' famous description of our fundamental nature)

◆ "Mind over matter" (recommendation for success)

Case Study

A soccer player has sustained a career-threatening spinal injury. He has two options for surgery. The first involves high health risks and offers only moderate chances for success, but if successful, it might allow the individual to play soccer again. The second option requires the fusion of two vertebrae, promises a much higher chance for success, and allows for a reasonably normal life, albeit without soccer. Both the surgeon and physical therapist recommend the second option, asking, "Why would you risk your well-being for soccer?"

Behavior Dualism

Behavior dualism is a logical outcome of dividing the person into two parts. Bodies cannot act alone; they need guidance. In physical education classes, teachers explain a movement before the students try it themselves. In clinical settings, practitioners describe the values of an active lifestyle as a precursor to behavioral change. Behavior dualism shows the significance of understanding and motivation in the movement domain. This means we must teach the mind before we can get results from the body.

Theoretical Problems

◆ Behavior dualism may rest on a false distinction—if thinking is just another form of doing, then it too is a skill that can be done well or poorly. What we are left with is not pure insight directing physical activity, but one fallible skill preceding another. Also, if thinking is a form of doing, what informs it? Previous thinking? If so, we then fall into an infinite regress where each thought is a form of doing that requires previous thinking, *ad infinitum*.

◆ The claim that thinking precedes doing is not always born out of experience. When athletes get into "the zone," ideas and actions merge into one, and behavior flows effortlessly. We also know that too much or the wrong kind of thinking can hinder performance, leading to the paralysis by analysis phenomenon.

◆ Reflective thinking may not be particularly helpful before or during performance. It could be that another kind of thinking, intuitive insight, works better. Intuitive insight might be part and parcel of skill, not something that directs later motor activity.

When athletes are in the zone, they do not reflect first and act second.

Practical Problems

◆ If reflective thinking works as well as dualists claim, we should devote considerably more practice time to theory, biomechanics, and other verbalizations about performance. However, most veteran trainers and coaches have learned through experience that too much talk is counterproductive. Patients, athletes, and students need to gain experience in the movement setting itself if they are to heal, improve, and learn.

◆ Behavior dualism suggests that all good performances are the product of previous thought. A record-breaking performance is actually a great proposition in sneakers. But what if athletes cannot exactly say why they broke the record—what new strategy they tried, what biomechanical principle they used, or what physiological law they employed? What if athletes consistently perform well and still cannot get in touch with the theory that supposedly is responsible for that excellence? Was it just extraordinary luck? Such athletes *know* how to perform in marvelous ways, but such knowing does not seem to be simply the product of previous abstract thinking.

◆ Should our profession emphasize knowing the theory of moving well or developing the skills to move well? For dualism, theory takes the preeminent role. Because we have precious little time with our students and clients, efficiency might suggest that we focus on theory—once they understand the theory, they can work it out on their own. But any program that produces knowledgeable individuals, who still do not move, has failed. Many people understand and appreciate why they should exercise, but they still do not exercise. Because of this, rationalistic behavior dualism does not seem to work very well (Dishman 1994).

Philosophic Exercise

As with the first two forms of dualism, behavior dualism shows up in our speech and actions. Attempt to eliminate behavior dualism from the following three statements and the case study.

◆ "Think before you move" (recommendation from a physical-education instructor)

◆ "Theory always precedes practice" (statement from a kinesiology research manual)

◆ "Can't the coach tell him how to hit a curve ball? What's the matter with this guy?" (frustrated parent watching her son strike out for the third time in a Little League game)

Case Study

A fitness instructor has just met an overweight teenager. Her concerned parents have told the instructor that it is impossible to get this 15-year-old away from computer games and the television. The instructor decides that the teen needs a little motivational information. He gives her handouts on longevity, obesity, diet, and the principles of caloric intake and expenditure. He also provides a list of physical activities that she could pursue in her free time. "There you have it," he concludes. "Do you understand now why you must exercise and change your eating habits?" She nods, and the fitness instructor leaves the session confident that the knowledge he provided will have its intended effect.

Language Dualism

Language dualism highlights the significance of verbal and mathematical symbols. Creating a word or number to stand in for something else is an impressive intellectual feat, one that is hard to find in lower levels of animal life. Words and numbers are also efficient methods for recording information and for communicating. People who are gifted in their ability to use language or numbers have considerable power. While symbols also come in the form of music, art, and gestures, language trumps them because of its efficiency.

Theoretical Problems

◆ It may be true that *all* forms of symbolization advanced as humans developed so-called higher powers of intelligence. Rough drawings on cave walls evolved into the art of Rembrandt, basic competitive activity turned into complex games, and Neanderthal gestures evolved into dance. Perhaps the hallmark of human intelligence is our ability to use symbols in general, not just those symbols that involve words and numbers.

◆ Sometimes when we have an idea, words fail us. In such cases, we may need to expresses ourselves by drawing, dancing, or gesturing. If sophisticated thinking tends to produce ineffable concepts, then nonverbal symbol systems may actually have an advantage. Polanyi (1958, 1966, and with Prosch in 1975), for instance, argues that art represents creative human thinking at its best. In

© Jumpfoto

Movement is an alternative way to "talk."

other words, art conveys insight at this most challenging intellectual level where words and numbers cannot do the job.

Practical Problems

◆ If numbers and words are the most valuable symbols, then we should spend most of our time developing these particular capabilities. This would reduce the importance of nonverbal exploration, discovery, expression, invention, and creation. In other words the liberal arts side of our educational and human contributions would fall into question. We would probably be pushed more toward movement utility for health and fitness.

◆ Movement is so important to so many people. Dancers, hikers, and many other movers tend to be passionate about movement. Take away their movement and they get surly or worse. But if movement is not a powerful symbolic system, how can we account for this passion? Movement can become very personal, expressing who we are and what we value all without a word or mathematical formula. Why should kinesiologists support language dualism and thus endorse the expansion of the English and math curriculum at the expense of physical education?

◆ Does language dualism imply that we have not done our job if we have not encouraged our students and clients to convert movement experiences to words? Perhaps we should shorten activity time and increase reflective time. We are left with the interesting question of whether or not real education occurs when it does not involve the conversion to words or numbers.

Philosophic Exercise

Language dualism also makes itself known in language and action. Attempt to eliminate this dualism from the following statements and the case study.

◆ "If you haven't written it down, you don't know it" (recommendation about learning)

◆ "The pen is mightier than the sword" (Edward Lytton, 19th-century English novelist)

◆ "If you don't talk to me, I won't know if anything's wrong" (frustrated parent to her child)

Case Study

Facing significant budget cuts, a school board meets to discuss the fate of physical education, interscholastic sport, and the performing arts. One member of the board summarizes the majority viewpoint saying, "We know that our students are scoring below the mean on language arts and math, and we know how crucial those skills are for the students' future. On the other hand, sports, music, theater, and the like are more recreational activities than basic academic skills. If we are going to cut anything, it should be these nonessentials."

Knowledge Dualism

Knowledge dualism emphasizes understanding how and why things work. It is one thing to become a good high jumper simply by trial and error. It is another for the jumper to explain the mechanisms he uses to achieve success. The knowledge produced by science and the humanities gives us a perspective on our world that allows us to manipulate, modify, and choose intelligently. Kinesiology is a field in which we strive through multiple disciplines to better understand, predict, and improve human movement.

Theoretical Problems

◆ It could be that there are multiple ways of knowing. Is it possible to understand something without being able to explain it? If so, propositional or declarative knowledge may be overrated.

◆ We may gain understanding through inductive and deductive reasoning, experienced-based speculation, and subjective interpretations. If this is the case, then propositional knowledge is not entirely objective.

◆ Emphasizing propositional understanding to the exclusion of the know-how that produces such knowledge leaves individuals uneducated in important ways. To appreciate a truth is not the same thing as having the capacity to produce it. Thus, procedural knowledge is also important.

Practical Problems

◆ If understanding is the true goal of education, do we have to de-emphasize skill? For instance, if knowledge dualism is right, we might conclude that it is more important for our clients to understand tennis than to be able to play it well.

◆ Should we use understanding as the highest end of physical education, a powerful means, or both? Is Teaching Games for Understanding (TGFU), for instance, on the right track when it highlights the efficacy of understanding in physical education?

◆ Is it possible to bypass understanding when developing skillful players? Is it more efficient to do so?

What are the limits of theory and understanding?

Philosophic Exercise

Attempt to eliminate language dualism from the following statements and the case study.

◆ "She's just a technician" (reference to an accomplished physical therapist without an advanced degree)

◆ "Athletes are doers, not thinkers" (claim about many athletes' lack of understanding about movement)

◆ "There is only one way to understand the mechanisms that determine good cardiovascular health: Do good research" (claim from a physiology textbook)

Case Study

Two baseball coaches are facing one another in a key game. One has coached the game for over 40 years. The other is a second-year coach who has the latest information on baseball, from the biomechanics of hitting to the complicated statistics on hundreds of different strategies. In spite of his superior training, the younger coach realizes that the older mentor still has an advantage—he has an uncanny ability to make exactly the right coaching move at exactly the right time. The second-year coach is sure that he understands the game better than the older coach, so why is he still at a disadvantage?

REVIEW

Mind–body dualism is an attractive perspective on the nature of human beings because it acknowledges both material reality and subjective existence. Dualism comes in at least five forms. Each form, while attractive, has theoretical and practical weaknesses. These problems suggest that we need to speak differently about people and their behavior, and we need to act differently wherever practices grounded in dualism are the norm. Because substance dualism separates people from their bodies, because the four varieties of value dualism favor mind over body, and because dualistic methodologies may not work well in our professional settings, we need to look for other interpretations of what it means to be a human being.

LOOKING AHEAD

In the next chapter, we will examine another set of conclusions on what a person is. This approach, called materialism, solves all the problems of a two-part person by suggesting that human beings are only one kind of matter. But this solution also has certain implications for kinesiology, some that are helpful and some that introduce new difficulties.

CHECKING YOUR UNDERSTANDING

1. *Define mind–body dualism. Describe each of its five forms.*

2. *For each of the five dualisms, provide one reason for its popularity. Why did its practitioners think they had the right idea?*

3. *Describe one theoretical and one practical problem of each of the five dualisms.*

4. *Provide practical tips on how kinesiologists should talk and act if we are to minimize the negative effects of these five dualisms. For example, can we avoid using the terms "mind" and "body"? And, can we develop methods that are not aimed at separate mental and physical elements?*

4

Scientific Materialism

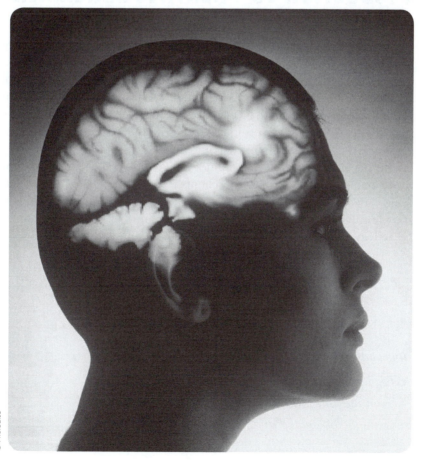

© Photodisc

The most useful alternative to dualism in the field of kinesiology has been scientific materialism. It suggests that there is only one substance in the world, not two. Anything that exists must be physical, including the mind and other intangibles.

In one stroke, scientific materialism eliminates dualistic problems with the relationship between the mental and the physical. On the other hand, materialism raises new concerns about the private, unobservable, subjective part of human existence. One of the strengths of dualism turns out to be one of the weaknesses of materialism. For under this latter school of thought, only physical stuff exists . . . period! This raises important questions.

◆ Does materialism provide a modern, scientific vision of humanity?

◆ How does materialism deal with daily experience, the subjective side of life?

◆ Does materialism provide concrete, effective methodologies for the workplace?

INTRODUCTION TO SCIENTIFIC MATERIALISM

Scientific materialism is grounded in the belief that everything in the world can be explained by principles of math and physics. The roots of this idea reach as far back as ancient India (Raju 1985). During the Enlightenment, scientific materialism was a reaction against spiritualism and any suggestion that causation occurs outside of physical systems (Midgley 1994). It soon became part of the scientific canon to believe that only atoms and space exist and nothing else, including anything spiritual. Even ideas, motives, and hopes are written off as inconsequential "appearances" that accompany various brain states.

These beliefs suggest that we should not look to subjective experience to find out how to motivate our students and clients to have an active lifestyle. Rather, we should have them perform activities that produce certain brain states characteristic of individuals who are habitually active and happy. These brain states and the activity that gave rise to them might then stimulate future activity and

CHAPTER OBJECTIVES

In this chapter, you will

◆ *become acquainted with scientific materialism,*

◆ *examine four kinds of materialism in kinesiology, and*

◆ *evaluate theoretical and practical problems with materialism.*

The world according to materialism = atoms + void.

comparable brain states. In this way, kinesiologists bypass consciousness and still produce active human beings who have agreeable lives.

Some forms of scientific materialism exceed the boundaries of good science (Midgley 1994; Wallace 2000). Scientific materialism is an extreme position that is based as much on unexamined bias and belief as it is on demonstrable fact. Consequently, you don't have to be a scientific materialist in order to be a good scientist. In fact, to be a good scientist in kinesiology, you probably would not want to be a scientific materialist.

Good science is broader than materialism and is based on certain principles:

◆ It requires rigorous scrutiny of the subject matter and controlled experimentation rather than casual observation.

◆ It requires appropriate analysis that is typically quantitative.

◆ It often relies on some form of reductionism and a search for underlying mechanisms.

◆ It usually results in predictions or other generalizations that can be retested for validity.

◆ It is grounded in a healthy skepticism toward common understandings and other received beliefs.

All of these principles have helped to produce a tremendous amount of knowledge in physiology, biomechanics, sports medicine and cardiac rehabilitation, teaching, and athletics. These principles have also improved qualitative research in psychology, sociology, and even philosophy of physical activity, helping researchers eliminate bias, opinion, and other sources of inaccuracy.

If scientific materialism is also based on these principles, how can it be extreme? And in what ways is this unwarranted extension of scientific thinking damaging to kinesiology?

FOUR KINDS OF SCIENTIFIC MATERIALISM

We will examine four ways in which scientific materialism shows up in our field. Much like the five faces of dualism that we discussed in chapter 3, these four elements are an interrelated cluster of beliefs that inform scientific inquiry and daily practice. We will discuss them separately only for the purpose of clarity.

Measurement Materialism

Measurement materialism deifies observation, data gathering, and analysis. It operates under the belief that we can secure and analyze information in ways

© Photodisc

The goals of measurement materialism are gathering undistorted data and factual conclusions.

that avoid contamination from bias, interpretation, or any other source of error that the scientist might introduce. It hopes to accurately portray the world without prejudice or any other distortion.

An ideal framework for discovery would be one where data are mechanically gathered by some fail-safe measurement device. They are then automatically and faithfully transmitted or converted to some digital form that can be statistically treated, where the statistical methods used are perfectly matched to the discovery desired and the outcome is entirely immune to incorrect interpretations.

The subjective domain of experience and consciousness is taboo for at least two reasons (Wallace 2000). First, experience is entirely private. An observer can only surmise what the subject is thinking at any moment in time. The observer cannot ever have the other person's experience. Second, subjective reports are notoriously unreliable. Personal perspective and bias often cloud our vision, preventing us from seeing the way things are. Subjective reports do not provide reality, only personal perceptions of reality.

Monistic Materialism

Monistic materialism is a redundant name. Materialists are monists because they believe that there is only one substance in the universe, not two as dualists believe. Monists view the world as a giant, complex machine. All causation is physical—one lever moving another lever, one atom striking another atom, one brain state leading to another brain state.

While monists will admit that it is often difficult to measure the physical factors that cause later events, they attribute this to two conditions. First, the technology may not exist currently to measure everything. Genes, for instance, were hard at work in causal chains of events long before technology was able to identify, measure, and begin to unravel their secrets. Future technology, it is hoped, will eventually put us in touch with everything that needs to be measured. Second, reality is remarkably complex. Consequently, current failures to predict future events accurately can be attributed to the complexity of causal mechanisms. If and when that complexity is sorted out, perfect predictability will be assured.

In the meantime, monists argue that they are on the right track by assuming that there is nothing out there but atoms and space. They do not believe they should turn their backs on scientific progress by reverting to some sort of spiritualism where intangible, unpredictable causes are thought to influence the future.

Reductive Materialism

Reductive materialism follows from materialistic monism. It claims that the larger can always be explained by the smaller. Complex wholes are the product of their parts. Consequently, if kinesiologists understand the parts, they will also understand the whole.

Scientists who adhere to this ideology assume that fruitful inquiry lies in one direction only, from the macro toward the micro. They look only for underlying mechanisms. Overarching mechanisms either do not exist or are unimportant because their existence and operation can be explained by their underlying causes. Causal action always lies in the direction of the underlying mechanism, all the way down to the subatomic level.

At the heart of the debate between dualism and monism lies the reduction of consciousness to brain states. Anxiety about facing a longtime opponent in tennis can be explained entirely in terms of electrical and chemical mechanisms in the athlete's brain. Anxiety cannot yet be fully explained, but someday it will be, when the right technology exists. Reductionism debunks our subjective indulgences, pretensions, and fantasies (Lewis 1947).

Physicalism

Physicalism is another type of scientific materialism that informs both theoretical inquiry and practice. According to physicalism, we live in a mindless, meaningless

universe. We are simply the product of a grand evolutionary accident. There is no way to make any sense of it, and no telos, or ultimate end, will redeem anything we do. Because the world consists of nothing more than atoms bouncing off one another, goals make no sense except as inconsequential by-products of our evolution.

From a physicalist perspective, ethics are nothing more than the complex workings of our selfish genes (Dawkins 1989). Reflecting, wondering, and loving are nothing more than the operations of our computer-like brains (Dennett 1991). Play and work are artificial categories that describe mechanistic needs to elevate or decrease arousal (Ellis 1973). A good golf swing is nothing more than the right side of the brain taking over at precisely the right time (Wiren and Coop 1978). The fun experienced in a gym class is nothing more than a brain state influenced by dopamine (Blakemore 2004). Culture, ethics, and ideals are nothing more than fancy window dressing for the biology that lies underneath.

Merely a site to elevate arousal levels, or more than that?

© Photodisc

ASSETS AND LIABILITIES

Like dualism, scientific materialism provides a prism through which to understand human movement. As we have seen, it has been an attractive, no-nonsense alternative across the centuries. It has its own theoretical and practical strengths and weaknesses.

In the following sections we'll discuss the appeal of the four kinds of scientific materialism and then detail their theoretical and practical problems. The end of each section has exercises that give you an opportunity to correct excesses in materialism.

Measurement Materialism

Measurement materialism is attractive because it focuses on much of what is good about science. Scientific procedures attempt to remove bias and error, and scientists are appropriately skeptical about what is real. Measurement materialists attempt to accurately assess real things and rationally interpret the data to discover concrete, indisputable facts.

Personal bias—particularly parochial, self-serving, and unexamined beliefs—should not ground a discipline like ours. Neither should we try to measure things that do not exist or that we cannot access. The subjective domain is difficult to access, and there *is* a sense that our ideas are strictly private. Objectivity is also welcome when we look at some of kinesiology's inaccurate claims from the past that gained life through a combination of robust biases and inadequate data. Within the last half century we made several incorrect claims:

◆ Women cannot successfully compete in endurance events and it is dangerous for them to try.

◆ The elderly cannot add muscle regardless of diet and weight training.

◆ High-intensity exercise is required to produce significant cardiovascular health benefits.

◆ Athletics automatically promotes the development of good character traits like teamwork, fair play, and dedication.

A little more objectivity and dispassionate testing might have shortened the life span of some of these claims. Even today we need some healthy skepticism about what is real and what is imaginary so that we might discover sooner rather than later which of our current sacred cows deserve to be gored.

Theoretical Problems

◆ Measurement materialists underestimate how difficult it is to achieve pure objectivity. The scientific process is riddled with subjective judgments, including decisions about what to study, which hypotheses hold the most promise, how best to gather data, and most important, what the data mean. Subjective judgments play a central role in scientific procedures.

◆ Measurement materialists do not acknowledge the legitimate debate over what is real and what is not. Can anyone say with assurance that a rock is more real than an experience of love? Many quantum physicists are not sure that matter is really the ultimate stuff of the universe (Greene 2004). And some proponents of chaos theory argue that causation does not work solely on Newtonian, or mechanical, principles of physics. It may not be wise for kinesiologists to put all of their eggs in the same basket of physical matter.

◆ Finally, kinesiologists who live the colorful world of exercise, dance, and sport hardly want to dismiss our powerful inner feelings as mere fantasies. Ideas affect our future projects. In this sense, ideas are both objective and real. For example, say that I am planning to run as soon as I finish working for the day. Those subjective, nonphysical plans will get me out on the jogging trail. It would be strange for me to say that I was deceived by my ideas, that it is actually my brain state that gets me running. I fully understand that brain states accompany and, in some complicated way, are responsible for my daily experiences. However, it is the wonderful experiences of running that I encounter, not brain loops and electrical impulses. Materialism takes what seems to be obvious in kinesiology and stands it on its head. It identifies the lived experience of moving as unreal, while identifying brain states and other underlying mechanisms—things that we never experience in daily life—as real.

Which work better, tips about brain states or swing sensations?

© Photodisc

Practical Problems

◆ Measurement materialism places teachers in a difficult situation when it comes to a student's subjective report of liking or disliking an activity. Because the report could be biased or could even be a lie, the teacher might want to dismiss it, telling the student, "I'm sorry. I only deal with concrete reality. What you're feeling is of no interest to me and of no importance in this class." On the heels of such insensitivity, the teacher's rapport and effectiveness with the student would undoubtedly plummet.

◆ Measurement materialism also places skill teachers in a bind. They are torn between providing subjective cues that seem to work, and objective information about body states that have little or no bearing on performance. A materialist who is well versed in brain waves and their correlation with good golf swings might be torn about giving the following kinds of input to the learner.

> Approach 1: "You're using the left side of your brain too much. Try harder to get those neurons on the right side firing more regularly! Concentrate, right side, come on!"
>
> Approach 2: "At the start of the downswing, make it feel like gravity is pulling your hands down to the ball."

Philosophic Exercise

Materialism, much like mind–body dualism, has become part of how we talk, think, and act in kinesiology. See if you can modify the following statements to remove elements of excessive measurement materialism.

- ◆ "Data!" (creed of some scientific canons)
- ◆ "Science is objective and produces hard data; philosophy is subjective and produces soft data" (common distinction made between the physical sciences and the humanities)
- ◆ "The athlete is simply a complex machine" (tenet of some scientific materialists)

Case Study

A cardiac-rehabilitation specialist is working with a postoperative cardiac patient recovering from triple-bypass surgery. The patient reports tremendous stress at the prospect of even the most basic exercise such as walking. He resists the specialist's efforts to get him out of his chair and back to his normal life.

The cardiac-rehabilitation specialist has been taught that the roots of the problem are at the chemical, biological, or physiological level. She wants to employ scientifically sound procedures in getting this individual to move again, so she turns to textbooks for an explanation of her patient's slow recovery.

Monistic Materialism

Monistic materialism is attractive because it is logical. It is an extension of a mechanistic vision of the world and its inhabitants. It would rid the world of superstition, spirits, or a god that fills in the gaps of scientific ignorance. The belief that physical things affect other physical things has a simple, honest, courageous ring to it. While we might like the comfort that hopes and dreams offer, monists claim that we are better off realizing that the keys to improving life lie in understanding material reality, not idealistic intangibles. If kinesiologists want to improve health, performance, and body composition, they should examine genes and other biological mechanisms, not subjective attitudes. Removing superstition from science, after all, accounts for much of the success of empirical study. In order to continue making progress, monists argue that we should deal with only one substance, physical matter.

Theoretical Problems

◆ Attempts to predict human behavior on the basis of material conditions alone have not been very successful. Monistic materialists have difficulty explaining actions, reactions, and behaviors in terms of matter and physical mechanisms only.

◆ This lack of success, as mentioned earlier, has resulted in two unsatisfactory defenses. One claims that when technology improves, we will be able to measure matter more effectively and thus improve predictions. The second defense claims that the incredible complexity of the world is what frustrates accurate prediction. When we eventually unravel the complexity, we will find more complete answers. While both explanations may have an element of truth to them, it is also possible that the materialistic model is inadequate. No matter how far technology advances, and no matter how much machine-like complexity we unravel, we still will not understand human behavior. Something will still be missing, perhaps something intangible.

◆ Monistic materialists have never demonstrated that consciousness or other intangibles cannot influence causality. No studies or mathematical formulas have demonstrated that we can only explain behavior in terms of particles acting on particles. Ultimately this is a dogmatic claim, a tenet of monistic faith (Midgley 1994; Wallace 2000; Clark 2003).

We do not have the luxury of working with isolated portions of the anatomy in a controlled environment.

Practical Problems

◆ Monistic materialism works better in some situations than others. It does very well with mechanistic calculations in biomechanics, and for some physiological research, prediction accuracy is quite good. But these are controlled studies, conducted in carefully constructed environments, with only isolated portions of the anatomy. The problem for kinesiologists is that in a controlled environment we do not have the luxury of dealing with an abstract circulatory system or an anonymous ankle. We must deal with people in complex social and environmental circumstances, people who have unique values and individual stories.

◆ Monistic materialism does not account for the success of many practitioners in kinesiology, practitioners who somehow use more information than that provided by physiological and chemical tests. Some of the most successful exercise specialists do not attribute their achievement to the superior attention they pay to numbers. On the contrary, they have a unique ability to reach the *person*. They appear to be dealing with the world of human consciousness, beliefs, and values. While materialism provides part of the story (numbers do matter), data may not tell the whole story.

Philosophic Exercise

See if you can modify the following statements and case study to reduce excessive monism.

◆ "Given enough scientific information, I will be able to predict with nearly 100% accuracy which of my clients will persist with their exercise programs and which ones will quit" (claim of some practitioners)

◆ "There simply has to be some physiological or biomechanical explanation" (statement by a frustrated coach whose Olympic athlete continues to underperform)

◆ "Cells are the building blocks of life" (biological statement about the direction of causation)

Case Study

An athletic trainer has a client with a serious injury to the medial collateral ligament. It does not require surgery, just rest and rehabilitation. The trainer might use several different strategies to treat the problem, and he weighs the factors that bear upon his decision—likelihood, speed, and degree of recovery; cost; anatomy of the problem; physiology of the injury; and latest research findings on such injuries. The trainer tells this athlete that statistically he fits a certain therapeutic profile and will use a specific five-week sequence of rehabilitative interventions.

Reductive Materialism

Reductive materialism is attractive because we do find out how things work by moving from the larger to the smaller (Ridley 2003). The genome project, for example, has astounding implications for everything from how and why we contract certain diseases to how and why people have different dispositions. Genes are powerful, microscopic engines with built-in blueprints, so we cannot entirely dismiss the ethical claim that we are our "selfish genes." Our genes affect whether or not we share court time with another tennis player or hog the court ourselves, whether or not we spend another 15 minutes with one of our particularly needy clients or head home to dinner and relaxation.

Theoretical Problems

◆ Some reductionist models assume one-way causation, from the smaller to the larger. Chemicals have causative effects on genes, genes on biology, biology on physiology, physiology on psychology, and so on. One reason for looking for underlying mechanisms is to find the real causes of a chain of events. The problem with this picture is that causation may actually work in two directions—from the smaller to the larger *and* from the larger to the smaller (Wallace 2000). This is called circular, mediated, or reciprocal causation and is a fairly standard model for understanding complex interactions among potential causes. Any belief in strictly one-way, micro-to-macro causation may be misplaced.

◆ Fixating on the micro also limits inquiry to a narrow group of scholars and research methods, namely, math and physics. If human motor performance is caused by particles, then mathematicians and physicists are likely to find the important answers to questions about human existence. But this runs counter to our intuition and cannot explain success at other levels of scientific inquiry. Biological laws like homeostasis affect smaller elements like genes and chemicals. Psychological reactions such as fear affect biological laws, genetic expression, and chemicals in the body. Strong reductionism would turn kinesiology into a field that focuses on math, physics, and chemistry, while dismissing other useful disciplines that provide a larger picture of human existence.

Practical Problems

◆ Sometimes an explanation for poor athletic performance, failure to learn, and other problems can be reduced to some microcause or a set of microcauses. Genetic researchers, for instance, are finding that certain anomalies predict with fairly high accuracy that their bearer will have certain problems or advantages. But such simple, powerful findings are rare. A genetic tendency, coupled with an environmental hazard, accompanied by a persistent psychological stress produces the predicted problem, but only about 60% of the time. We need the ability to look in multiple places for answers to questions about human health and performance.

◆ Reductionists have often enjoyed less success with their clients. Reductionists act as if they can find cures in one isolated place, such as a chemical imbalance that is generating high cholesterol levels. When they base their treatments on those assumptions, patients may not respond well. The cholesterol problem may be related to human behavior and subjective states, not just to a chemical or genetic antecedent.

◆ There is some evidence that excellent practitioners look in multiple places for clues, and that they favor the larger over the smaller (Coles 1989; Siegel 1986; Weil 1997). These professionals attribute some of their success to their ability to see what is going on in their clients' thoughts, not just their cells.

Philosophic Exercise

See if you can modify the following statements and the case study to eliminate excessive reductionism.

◆ "It's all in the mechanics" (baseball coach to a pitcher having difficulty with control)

◆ "The script for our health and longevity is written in our genes, and we can't change that" (statement by a medical provider to a client with unusually poor health)

◆ "Search for the underlying mechanism; that's all you need to do" (common recommendation to graduate students in kinesiology)

Case Study

A middle-aged woman has come to a personal trainer for help. She is overweight and has poor muscular and cardiovascular fitness. She reports that she seems to have lost her motivation and self-control. She says she wants to look and feel better, but just cannot seem to do anything about it. The more she worries about it, the more she eats and the harder it is for her to get a good night of sleep.

The trainer's thoughts turn to the underlying causes of her problem—perhaps chemical changes brought on by menopause, social barriers to exercise, and new psychological stresses now that her children are out of the home. The trainer orders a series of tests that will provide data related to his hunches.

Physicalism

Physicalism drives home the ethical implications of materialism. If only matter exists, and if the human being is only a complex machine, where is the soul? What is the foundation for value? Why should any one goal matter more than another?

While it may be difficult to see how or why a valueless world is desirable, physicalism can help debunk privileged, self-serving value systems, such as those that favor whites over blacks, men over women, or Christians over Jews.

Physicalism suggests that such metaphysical edifices are erected on sand; nothing substantial supports them.

Physicalism also has a frank, courageous, down-to-earth quality. If nothing but atoms exist, and if we are simply the product of inexorable laws of mathematics and physics, it is better to admit this and forge ahead than it is to hide behind the security of myths. If one adopts a goal of becoming a good athlete, taking off a few pounds, or living a long and healthy life, that is fine, but both the goals and the achievements have a no-nonsense source—atoms bouncing against atoms.

Theoretical Problems

◆ Ultimately, physicalism's claim that values are not real is itself a tenet of faith. It cannot be demonstrated. While it is true that values cannot be measured, it does not necessarily follow that such intangibles do not exist. People react to values, beliefs, and ideas all the time. Because we believe that peace is better than war, we vote for certain candidates and not for others. Because we believe that friendship and love are superior to alienation and loneliness, we develop close connections with others and protect our family members. Ideas and values shape almost everything we do, so we live as if values are objectively accessible and real.

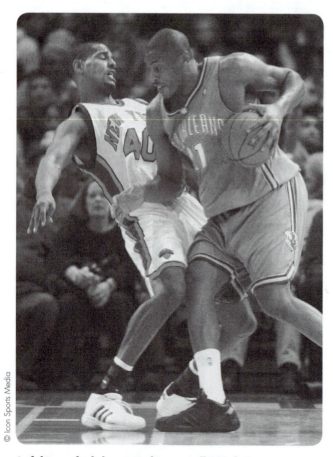

◆Individuals in different cultures, with different religious beliefs, and even from different eras embrace many of the same values. Kidder (1994), for example, argues that the following values are universal: love, truthfulness, fairness, freedom, unity, tolerance, responsibility, and respect for life. The term *universal* means that these values are objectively attractive to people in different social, political, and historical situations. This creates a problem for physicalists, for it is improbable that so many different people who have not collaborated with one another would come up with the same values. Perhaps then values have some sort of objective reality to them, even if this reality is not physical in nature.

© Icon Sports Media

Is faking a foul the same thing as telling a lie?

Practical Problems

◆ Physicalism's skepticism regarding values removes an important implement from our kinesiology toolbox. Many contemporary practitioners acknowledge the significance of attitude and motivation both in learning environments and in health promotion. Optimistic individuals become ill less often and heal faster. Learners who have goals and are passionate about reaching them will learn faster and at a deeper level (American Psychological Association 1995; Niaura et al. 2002).

◆ Physicalists might agree that value commitments need to be treated as if they are valid even though they are not. But this would certainly weaken the power of our ideals and goals as well as the benefits we receive by devoting ourselves to them. How could we trust a coach or fitness instructor who talked about important objectives and the passion needed to achieve them when we knew that he did not believe in these kinds of intangibles himself?

Philosophic Exercise

See if you can modify the following statements and the case study to eliminate excessive physicalism.

- ◆ "Sport is simply a testing ground for the survival of the fittest" (coach who sees sport as merely an evolutionary laboratory)
- ◆ "Might makes right" (skeptical statement about the reality of ideals)
- ◆ "Adapt or be left behind" (recommendation by a hard-nosed instructor)

Case Study

A coach is teaching an eight-year-old basketball player to flop in order to draw a foul. She asks why she should fake illegal contact and accept a foul shot when her opponent did not break any rules. The coach gives a brief cost–benefit rationale. "It pays!" he concludes. "Those who are good at flopping will win more games. Besides, your opponents will do it to you. If you do not adjust to these conditions, you will not survive."

REVIEW

Scientific materialism provides a modern alternative to mind–body dualism. However, while it solves some of the problems of dualism with the mind–body relationship and the tendency to value mind over body, it has weaknesses of its own. In particular it has difficulty accounting for the power of our subjective experiences. Materialism works best when dealing with the physical side of human existence. When questions move toward psychology, philosophy, and spirituality, it works less well. All four kinds of scientific materialism raise theoretical and practical concerns. Like dualism, materialism may not be particularly useful in the classroom, on the athletic field, or in the clinic. We need to modify both our language and our actions if we are to minimize the inaccuracies and excesses of materialism.

LOOKING AHEAD

In this and the last chapter, we have examined two popular perspectives on the nature of human beings, mind–body dualism and scientific materialism. We saw how both embody certain theoretical and practical problems. It is now time to show more specifically how and why these two visions can lead kinesiology astray and put us in a position of professional vulnerability.

CHECKING YOUR UNDERSTANDING

1. *Define scientific materialism and indicate how it differs from mind–body dualism. How does it solve some of the problems of dualism?*

2. *Describe four principal types of materialism and why each one is attractive.*

3. *Describe the theoretical and practical problems of the four types of materialism.*

4. *Indicate how we might downplay negative aspects of materialism by modifying our actions and our language.*

5

Tournaments
of Dualism
and Materialism

Kinesiology has always had difficulty competing in the marketplace even though moving and playing are two of the most universal things that people do. As noted in the preface, it is ironic that in a world where we award multimillion-dollar contracts to professional athletes, we see physical activity as unworthy in many ways. We spend little time on physical education, stereotype athletes as dumb jocks, and see play as more appropriate for children than adults. This raises important questions.

◆ Why is physical activity on a lower rung of the educational ladder? Does it deserve to be there?

◆ If dualism's bias against the body jeopardizes kinesiology, why doesn't materialism give us a solid foundation on which to stand?

◆ Is bias against the body the result of one factor or multiple factors? If it is more than one factor, can we determine what they are?

◆ Might an understanding of our defeats give us insight into how we might portray ourselves in a more favorable light?

TWO TOURNAMENTS

Kinesiology is invited to participate in two tournaments. For both of them, everyone starts together in a single contest on one of two large teams. The losers of each game have to divide up and play again. For the winners of each game, the tournament is over and they reap the political, financial, and educational prizes that go to the victors of that particular round.

The losers, on the other hand, play for smaller rewards with each successive contest. As their status declines, they just try to survive. By the final game of each tournament, the prizes for winning are minimal. Winner and loser alike may find that they are among the educational and social bottom feeders. They reside at a considerable distance from those who swim in the safe waters above—namely,

CHAPTER OBJECTIVES

In this chapter, you will

◆ *review the fate of kinesiology in two tournaments, one controlled by dualism, the other by materialism;*

◆ *learn that our problems stem from multiple factors;*

◆ *see how we run a risk of losing our distinctiveness in our attempt to compete more successfully in these tournaments; and*

◆ *understand what we need to counter the weaknesses of dualism and materialism.*

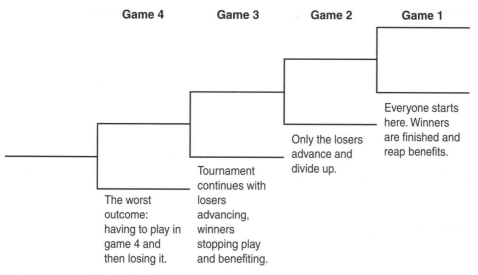

Game 4   **Game 3**   **Game 2**   **Game 1**

Everyone starts
here. Winners
are finished and
reap benefits.

Only the losers
advance and
divide up.

Tournament
continues with
losers
advancing,
winners
stopping play
and benefiting.

The worst
outcome:
having to play in
game 4 and
then losing it.

FIGURE 5.1   Loser's bracket.

the winners of game 1 or game 2 in each tournament. Figure 5.1 is a diagram of
the loser's bracket format.

TOURNAMENT OF DUALISM

Dualism jeopardizes kinesiology for at least a couple of reasons. As we saw in
chapter 3, it separates mind from body and raises a host of difficult theoretical and
practical questions about the relationships between the two, the proper sequence
of attending to mind and body, and the relative importance we give to each one.
It is biased in favor of the mind, relegating the body and thus kinesiologists to
second-class status.

We can examine these two problems in a hypothetical tournament played
in the context of education. Apart from the fact that kinesiologists lose all four
games of this tournament, the rules of the contest present us with unfair decisions
about the teams on which we would like to play. Because value dualism and
several of its offspring tend to typecast us as members of the weaker team, we
are tempted to change our colors just so we can get on the winning team. This
would require us to redefine our profession, largely by abandoning activity. But
most of us remain faithful to sports, games, and other movement forms. Dualism
portrays us as nonintellectual, nonacademic, nonessential, and nonartistic.

Game 1

The first game is about the importance of intellectual understanding. It pits the
theoreticians against the practitioners, the thinkers against the performers—in
short, Team Theory against Team Practice.

Team Theory is devoted to understanding; Team Practice is devoted to skill.

Many of us do not like the way this contest is set up. Kinesiologists are both practitioners and theoreticians, and we believe that there is a multitude of beneficial relationships between theory and practice. Why should these be pitted against one another, and which team shall we play on? But we do not control the tournament. Those of us who see performance at the heart of our field (Newell 1990a, 1990b; Charles 2002) must side with the practitioners. And so the game begins.

Everyone knows that theory without application leaves us uneducated in an important sense. With theory, we can talk about swimming but not stay afloat, describe the biomechanics of a good golf swing but not hit the ball straight, and detail the benefits of exercise but not live an active lifestyle. On the other hand, practice without theory also leaves us with an incomplete education. We may be able to hit a tennis ball effectively but fail to understand the principles that lead to even better play; we can perform a butterfly stroke but we cannot vary the stroke based on our understanding of different competitive conditions.

Both theory and practice score many points, but the game goes to the theoreticians. Understanding, after all, is the hallmark of the educated person. Comprehension of facts, causal relationships, and hypothetical possibilities gives us the ability to plan future practice more rationally, to vary performances, and to be creative. It is better to understand, even if we sacrifice some practical skill, than to be skilled at the expense of understanding—at least, the tournament judges say so.

Those of us who sided with practice are sent off to the second game while the researchers and other theoreticians reap the benefits. The political effect of this defeat is that we are labeled nonintellectual, at least to the extent that we emphasize movement ability and an active lifestyle over understanding the principles of movement and health.

Game 2

In the second contest the issue is not what counts as intellectual, rather what skills are academic in nature. Remember, only practitioners are required to play in game 2. However, skills that largely occur in non-movement contexts, such as writing, are considered mental procedures while those that require motor skill are considered manual or nonacademic skills. Teachers of writing, reading, computing, and all other academic subjects face the instructors of painting, music, acting, dancing, farming, exercising, and all other subjects that can be regarded as physical: Team Academics faces Team Skill.

Once again, we in kinesiology are not pleased with this division because even the most active skills involve critical evaluations, such as strategizing about the next play in football or recognizing a source of error in one's kayaking technique. Moreover, these ruminations can occur in reflective postures, even if they usually take place on the field. Because we are not in control of the tournament, we join those who teach the active skills and end up losing for the second time.

The defeat can be traced largely to two causes. First, physical skills suffer because of their association with manual labor. It is the sign of the free person to be able to work on matters of philosophy and politics rather than toil physically for mere survival (Arendt 1958). Even though our dances and games are not necessarily survival-oriented, they are unmistakably manual. For those who think dualistically, manual means not mental, not reflective, and therefore not academic.

© Jumpfoto

Team Academics is devoted to intellectual skills; Team Skill is devoted to nonsedentary activity.

A second reason for losing game 2 stems from the extraordinarily high value our society places on reflection—the human capacity to recapture lived or imagined experience, produce insightful abstractions, and see something with the mind's eye. Because sense perceptions are always threatened by errors, tournament judges favor logical reflection, which they believe is broader in scope and less prone to error. The movement arts are utterly dependent upon sense perception and thus do not achieve the status of reflective truth. The political consequence of this second defeat is that we are labeled nonacademic.

Game 3

The third game is about the practical worth of movement skills. On one team we find instructors of nonacademic skills that can help make life go more smoothly. Plumbing, sewing, farming, and any other arts that require at least some psycho-motor skill provide various necessities. They take on the title of Team Utility. On the other side are the instructors of skills like drawing, composing music, playing, and other arts that produce the ornaments of life, its delights and refreshments. This is Team Serendipity.

This game throws us into an even more difficult quandary over choosing sides. Because we see ourselves as promoters of fitness, teachers of good character, or stress reducers, we are inclined to join the team that wants to put skill to work for extrinsic ends. Because we hope to promote movement as meaningful and fun, we are also inclined to join the team that focuses on play, recreation, and dance. Even those who think of themselves as health educators and are headed to Team Utility know that their students are less likely to develop active lifestyles if their movement is not meaningful or fun. Some of us compete for Team Utility, others for Team Serendipity.

This game ends in a virtual tie. While manual skills are important, they are typically reserved for those who cannot succeed intellectually. The "vo-techs," "aggies," and "jocks" are disdained by those in academic education. Art and play however, do not fare much better. While the arts have some cultural prestige and people who have the time and inclination to play are often admired, these activities are regarded as extras, things that we pay attention to after taking care of necessities. When hard times come to education, both useful and ornamental physical skills are often cut—driver's education and music, home economics and theater arts.

In this sense, it does not much matter who wins or loses game 3. To be non-intellectual and nonacademic, to have lost games 1 and 2, is to have already lost a great deal of educational stature.

Still, it is a further problem to be seen as ornamental. The winners in this very close game are the useful physical practices. The judges proclaim that if the subject matter is neither intellectual nor academic, it had better be useful. Those who favor art and play are labeled *nonessential* and are required to advance to game 4.

Team Utility is devoted to necessities; Team Serendipity is devoted to meaning and delight.

Game 4

Players in game 4 are those who teach skills more than theory (game 1), who teach active skills more than verbal and numerical skills (game 2), and who focus on the intrinsic values of skill acquisition over their extrinsic, or useful, functions (game 3).

The division in game 4 is between the promoters of art and the promoters of recreational exercise, games, and play. As in the previous three contests, we find ourselves torn. With their deep commitment to aesthetic values, dancers play for Team Art. But coaches, recreationists, and other game and exercise instructors, in spite of claims about beauty and grace in sport, cannot convince the judges that

© Empics

© Photodisc

Team Art is devoted to aesthetic values; Team Play is devoted to the intrinsic satisfaction of joyous movement.

recreational movement is art. Most of the professionals in our field join the team that teaches nonessential physical skills that are not considered art: Team Play.

Having relinquished usefulness, we are faced with some unfriendly comparisons of cultural significance. With ammunition provided by Huizinga (1950) and others, we argue that games and play are as culturally important as classical music, poetry, or theater. But our opponents on Team Art ask some difficult questions. Who contributed more to the advancement of high culture, Mozart or Babe Ruth? Hawthorne or Tiger Woods? Van Gogh or Serena Williams? Judges pick the former example in each case. Games and recreational exercise are still associated with recess, that time when students are on break from real education. It is far easier to invite art than play into the academy's ivy-covered walls. Thus we lose game 4, gaining our final unfriendly label, nonartistic (see figure 5.2).

As the only four-time losers in education's tournament, we are assigned a peripheral role in education. Performance classes are often elective, not required. Students usually do not receive credit toward graduation for such classes, and grading, if it exists at all, is pass–fail. In physical education, things like attendance, proper dress, and good personal hygiene often assure passing marks. When cutbacks occur, we are an early target for merger or elimination. Thus, the four defeats carry significant costs. Dualism creates a tournament in which the cards are stacked against us. We do not have even a chance to compete.

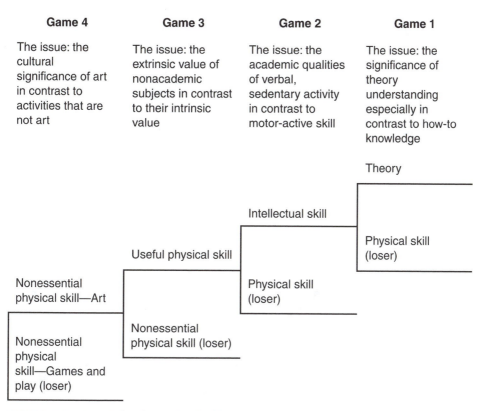

Game 4	Game 3	Game 2	Game 1
The issue: the cultural significance of art in contrast to activities that are not art	The issue: the extrinsic value of nonacademic subjects in contrast to their intrinsic value	The issue: the academic qualities of verbal, sedentary activity in contrast to motor-active skill	The issue: the significance of theory understanding especially in contrast to how-to knowledge

FIGURE 5.2 Loser's bracket under dualism.

Reprinted, by permission, from S. Kretchmar, 1996, "Movement and play on higher education's contested terrain," *Quest* 48:433-441.

Philosophic Exercise

The dualistic tournament affects different kinesiology professions in different ways. For those in public schools, for example, physical education's utility in health promotion may be the most significant issue. For coaches, athletic trainers, or physical therapists, one of the other four games might play a significant role.

Speculate on which one of the four games might have the greatest negative effect on your profession. Give reasons for your decision.

Current Reactions

If this is how the tournament of higher education is run and our record is so dismal, how should we respond? The most radical response would be to refuse to even enter the tournament under its present dualistic framework and with its current judges. However, our behavior has been anything but radical—we believe that we should, must, and will play.

This decision to compete on education's terms has taken us in two directions. First, we have invested much energy trying to gain membership on Team Utility for game 3 by promoting our health and fitness benefits. This is curious because we have seen that, even if we are successful here, the rewards are limited. Even if we win, we still lock in the relatively low status accorded those who engage in nonintellectual, nonacademic pursuits.

In addition, we may lose touch with the joy and relaxation of doing something just for the fun of it. We trade play for work, recreation for survival, and intrinsically motivated movement for just another duty. Movement turns from bright, attractive colors to a gray tone that colors all of our other obligations.

Nevertheless, defenders of this strategy argue that surely it is better to survive under the umbrella of utility than disappear while espousing loftier objectives. If game 3 is the highest game we have any chance of winning, then this strategy makes sense. If utility is our highest commodity, we should double our efforts to bind physical activity to its healthful benefits.

Others claim that our primary allegiance should not be to Team Utility at all. This more aggressive, go-for-broke strategy would have us surprise the tournament organizers by joining Team Theory in the all-important game 1. To make our membership believable, we would have students in gym classes reflect, strategize, and otherwise mull things over while they are sitting and taking notes. We would take time from skill development to lecture on basic information. We would develop academic majors that downplay activity and emphasize abstractions and other facts about time, space, cells, and moving objects. We would recast our pedagogy in the direction of teaching games for understanding (Griffin and Butler 2004) rather than the less cerebral model provided by sport education (Siedentop 1994). Finally, we would call our field something that reflects our commitment to theory and understanding, perhaps something like kinesiology—not sport studies and definitely not physical education.

It is open to debate how well either one of these strategies is working. Some worry that our tactics could backfire. In game 1, we have to downplay actual physical activity in order to portray ourselves as intellectual. If performance shows up at all, it is usually as a means to better theory—that is, as a laboratory experience, not an end in itself. In an effort to gain academic respectability, we may lose touch with our roots and our reason for existing at all.

Conclusions

If our status-elevating strategies do not work, then the dualistic tournament will have had a doubly harmful effect on kinesiology. First, it will have made us four-time losers, putting us in a weak position in education and society, keeping us from having the kind of effect we would like to have. Second, it will have forced us to distort ourselves—to wear certain academic clothes that do not fit. By losing touch with our roots, we lose touch with the activities that gave rise to our passion

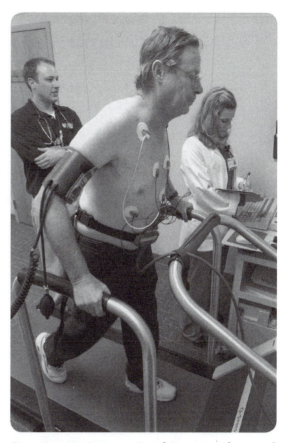

By trying to win games 1 and 3, we may lose touch with activity and play.

for kinesiology in the first place. And by pushing the utility of movement too forcefully, we miss its joys and delights.

The best strategy for kinesiology, as I will suggest in chapter 6, is to get out of this dualistic tournament altogether. As long as we play under these rules, we will either lose or be forced to sell our soul for victory. For the time being, we may have to both work for a better tournament and try to survive by competing in the old one with some degree of success.

There is no question that kinesiologists *are* intellectuals and that our fitness and play activities *are* useful. But to think primarily in these terms is to buy into the old tournament, one that is probably going to defeat us no matter how abstractly and eruditely we present ourselves. Kinesiologists must work to reach a point where society respects the powers of human intelligence both in front of a computer and at the foot of a mountain. We need an educational forum where journeying through literature and negotiating classic problems on a soccer field are equally valued. And finally, we need a place where the sheer delight of play is allowed to simply adorn our sometimes hectic lives.

Philosophic Exercise

How important is experience in physical activity for a college kinesiology program? Should programs require activity classes? Or has kinesiology grown past the stage where firsthand experience is essential? Develop a list of arguments in favor of an activity requirement for kinesiology majors, and then produce a second list of arguments opposing such a requirement. Where do you think the weight of the evidence lies?

TOURNAMENT OF MATERIALISM

We've seen that mind–body dualism jeopardizes kinesiology in a tournament that emphasizes educational values. We competed in a series of games that emphasized knowledge, intellectual skills, utility, and high culture. Under dualism the body is separate from the mind and movement is seen as mechanistic and dependent on guidance from mind, so we activity-oriented players did not fare very well. We ended up being four-time losers, which has had very real and unfortunate effects on our status in education and other contexts.

Scientific materialism would seem to place us in a better situation. As we saw in chapter 4, it involves a more realistic point of view, one that is compatible with the scientific spirit of our times. If we enter a second tournament under this banner, we would expect to do much better.

Unfortunately, it doesn't work out that way. This tournament has different rules, judges, values, and team divisions. We might call this the Tournament of Optimal Health. Optimal health rests on three bedrock values. The first is longevity: People who enjoy optimal health live longer. The second is functionality: People who enjoy optimal health have more effective bodies. The third value is efficiency: Methods with better cost–benefit ratios are preferred over those with lesser ratios.

Why, then, do we have trouble in this second tournament, even though it focuses on the human organism and its material well-being? We are, after all, the activity and health people. Our researchers continually uncover new connections between physical activity and reduced risk of cardiovascular disease, breast cancer, colon cancer, congestive heart failure, depression, gallstone disease, high blood triglyceride, high blood cholesterol, hypertension, lesser cognitive function, low blood HDL, obesity, osteoporosis, pancreatic cancer, peripheral vascular disease, physical frailty, premature loss of various motor functions, premature mortality, prostate cancer, sleep apnea, stiff joints, stroke, and type II diabetes (President's Council 2002). Even the U.S. surgeon general has said, "Physical activity of the type that improves cardiovascular endurance reduces the risk of developing or dying from cardiovascular disease (and other chronic health problems)" (USDHHS 1996). How could we lose in a contest that emphasizes optimal health?

Game 1

The first contest involves those who promote health through behavioral modifications such as diet and exercise and those who promote health through interventions at the physiological, cellular, and subcellular levels. Those who use behavioral modifications are on Team Movement, and those who promote health in other ways are on Team Intervention.

As in the dualistic tournament, those of us in kinesiology have a tough decision to make. Much of our research focuses on cellular effects of health and movement, and vice versa. We often use cellular-level strategies in concert with such behavioral interventions as diet, stress management, and exercise. But we remind ourselves that physical activity lies at the core of our expertise. We know that we must stay focused on movement, on how active living improves life. Ultimately, we aim much of our energy at behavioral change—getting people out of their chairs and moving. We join Team Movement.

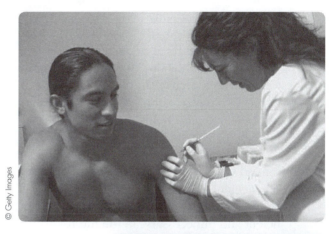

We take an early lead in this game. We cite current research that unequivocally shows the positive effects of an active lifestyle on both longevity and function. We remind the tournament judges that many surgical and chemical interventions are expensive, cause discomfort, or produce undesirable side effects. We ask ethical questions about genetic engineering and creating cyborgs or indefinitely rechargeable human beings. Behavioral change, we conclude, is the best strategy, both scientifically and ethically, for promoting optimal health.

Our opponents, however, are not yet ready to concede defeat. They point out that producing behavioral change is no easy feat. They bring out statistics that show high rates of noncompliance, recidivism, and blatant abstinence. They claim that there is a much better chance of get-

Team Intervention is devoted to biological intervention; Team Movement is devoted to behavioral change.

ting sedentary people to take a pill for high blood pressure than to get them to exercise regularly.

Besides, they continue, exercise is inefficient. It takes time and energy, and for many it can be distasteful and simply not fun. If these folks want to invest their time in more enjoyable pursuits, taking a pill to control blood pressure would be a far better option. Team Movement requires these individuals to spend a valuable part of their day driving to a health club, changing clothes, exercising, showering, and driving home. Team Intervention allows these individuals to take a pill and then do what they really want to do: read a good book, spend time with their children, or do whatever else their heart desires.

We object to this line of reasoning. The Interventionists, we say, have picked too convenient an example. An effective pill for blood pressure might exist, but technology to help the entire organism remain healthy and functional does not exist. Exercise helps the whole physical being, and there is no pill, surgical implant, or genetic manipulation that can do all that.

Our opponents agree that intervention strategies are currently limited. They remind us, however, that with advances in genetic science, smart machines, and other cutting-edge fields, more technology will be available in the future. Wherever technology can provide a safe, comparable health benefit, exercise becomes inefficient and unnecessary. In the future, exercise could become entirely outdated. People could still exercise if they wanted to, but they would do so only because they chose to, not because they had to.

The tournament judges listen intently to this interchange, and then they deliver their verdict. They like the promise of circumventing difficult behavioral changes. They are impressed by the likelihood of future interventionist successes in biochemistry and genetics. And they are swayed by Team Intervention's humanistic argument that people will still be able to run, dance, and swim, but they will not be required to do so.

The victory goes to Team Intervention. They take their prizes, retire from the tournament, and return to their work on more effective, efficient ways to promote health, vitality, and longevity. Those of us on Team Movement head off for game 2.

Game 2

In this game, those who promote movement and behavioral change split into teams according to the different settings in which movement is to take place. The first team's setting takes advantage of all manner of technological support. This is Team Enhancement. The other team's setting is daily life, such as exercise, dance, sport, and work. This is Team Culture.

Those of us in kinesiology see no contradiction in playing on both teams. Many of our fitness facilities and most of our exercise and rehabilitation protocols blend natural movement with the latest technological advancements. We see no problem in enhancing fitness walking with pedometers or heart-rate monitors. However, once again tournament rules do not allow us to compete for both squads. Once

Team Enhancement is devoted to technologically improved forms of movement; Team Culture is devoted to social forms of movement.

again, because we are movement people, and because technological innovations often reduce movement requirements, we choose the side that best reflects a commitment to activity. We join Team Culture.

Team Enhancement quickly goes on the offensive. If we are going to impose exercise on people to promote optimal health, they argue, exercise should be as efficient as possible. Team Enhancement will employ all available technological resources to make sure that every minute of movement bears the greatest fruit. They will use dietary supplements, electrical stimulation, ergonomic exercise machines, artificial motor enhancements, whatever it takes to maximize longevity and function while spending as little time moving as possible. They conclude that exercise professionals owe nothing less than this to their busy clients.

Team Culture has a rejoinder. We argue that we do owe more to our clients. We cite research on the effects of training specificity on motor learning. Artificial, enhanced movements are not likely to transfer well to the actual activities that people encounter in their daily lives. Moreover, we won't find much fun in the kind of clinical environments proposed by Team Enhancement. Dropout rates will be high.

On the other hand, we say, even if the more natural forms of movement we support are slightly less efficient, our clients enjoy being with us. They are more likely to persist. At the end of the day we have a greater positive effect on a higher percentage of clients. Overly artificial environments are for machines. Human beings want to exercise and play in meaningful, enjoyable ways.

Team Enhancement is not impressed by our arguments. Part of their science, they say, is aimed directly at specificity of movement. Their machines and exercises are designed to do exactly what we say is important—provide motor-relevant and task-specific learning. Moreover, Team Enhancement does not leave this learning to chance. Every movement their clients make has been selected for maximal efficiency and specificity.

Team Enhancement admits that their environment is artificial. But their clients, they claim, will not be unhappy there. Because Team Enhancement produces health and fitness more efficiently than we do, they will detain their clients for a shorter time, allowing them to spend a large part of the day on what they really want to do. In addition, Team Enhancement provides the proper stimuli to produce brain states that are associated with good feeling. They provide mirrors, fragrant odors, music, television, and other enhancements. Clients can even choose to have their brains stimulated directly through advanced electrochemical technology. Team Enhancement promises that the clients who choose enhancement services will feel no pain during exercise.

The methodical, efficient, and forward-looking strategies of Team Enhancement impress the tournament judges. They ask us why we refuse to adopt some of these apparently superior techniques. They imply that we might be wasting our clients' time. And they remind us that individuals who benefit from the efficiency of Team Enhancements' methods will still be able to choose recreational activities. In fact, they will have more time to do so. Team Enhancement is declared the winner of game 2.

Game 3

We move on to game 3 along with the other professionals who endorse natural or cultural movement forms. The judges instruct us to divide up on the basis of health efficacy. Professionals who screen forms of movement for their usefulness in promoting optimal health join Team Efficiency, and those who see value in a variety of movement forms with varying degrees of health value join Team Variety.

Even more than in games 1 and 2, we are uncertain about where we belong. Those who take exercise seriously and see our mission largely in terms of health want to join Team Efficiency. But the majority of kinesiologists see that while our mission includes health, it transcends it. In addition to health, we are devoted to skillful movement, the joy of play, creating a balanced life, and so on. We do not want to forfeit all that for the sake of some cardiovascular and movement efficiency. We join Team Variety and begin with our strongest arguments.

We agree with some of the same ends as Team Efficiency. We too want to promote maximal health. But we believe that health should be a by-product of activities that are enjoyable, interesting, challenging, and otherwise meaningful. Research shows that we can achieve many health benefits with only moderate amounts of exercise. It may well be better to endorse recreational gardening, walking the dog, bowling, table tennis, and softball, even if they are not high-intensity activities. When we add the other benefits our clients receive from this kind of activity program—the enjoyment, the relaxation, and the social interac-

Team Efficiency is devoted to maximally effective movement forms; Team Variety is devoted to culturally significant activities.

tions—it is clear we have the superior approach to health and vitality. Humans do not live by efficiency alone!

Our opponents question our professionalism by asking us why we continue to support activities that have minimal health effects. They make fun of the right fielder who just stands in the outfield inning after inning or the poorly-skilled volleyball player who hardly ever gets to touch the ball. They claim that modern FITT principles (frequency, intensity, time, and type) should motivate us to discard old-fashioned activities like softball, bowling, and volleyball. Our opponents claim that we are asking our clients to drive health promotion's version of the Model T. Why not move up to an Acura or even a Ferrari? The ride is much better, and the occupants reach their destination much faster.

We respond that the journey is not just about traveling better and faster. It is about the joy of movement, the intrinsic satisfaction of the trip itself. Efficiency and modernity have to be tempered by history and culture. Movement must be built into *people's* lives. It must be local, personal, and partly idiosyncratic.

From our view, the key to healthful living lies in the heart, not the head. People do not exercise simply out of a sense of duty or just because their movements are maximally efficient. They exercise because they love the activity, and it is part of their lives.

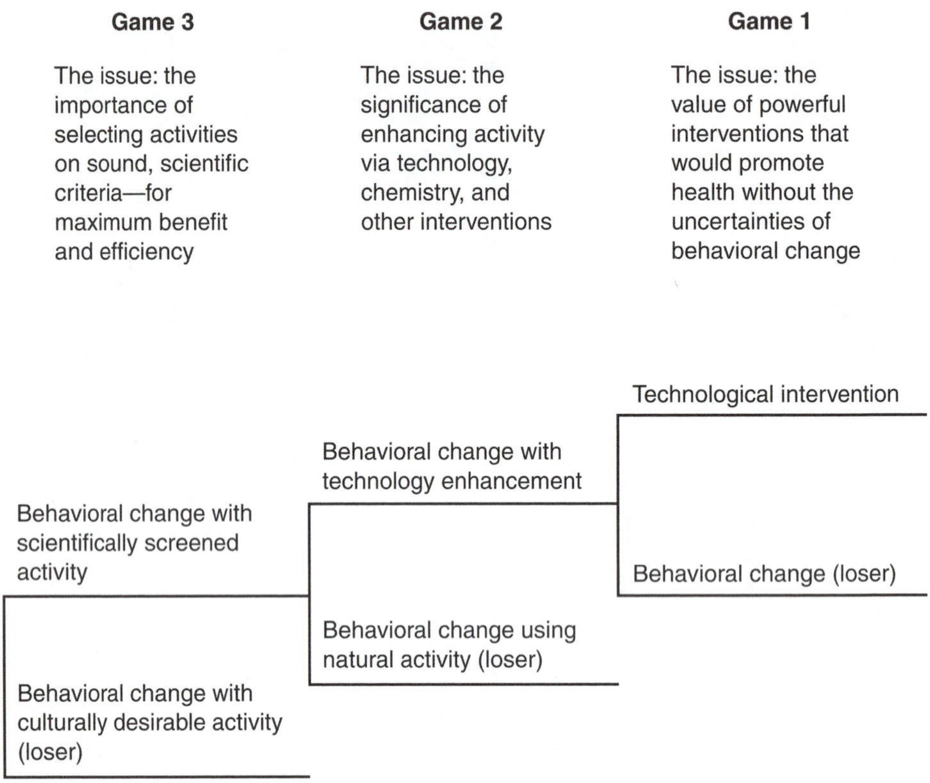

Game 3	Game 2	Game 1
The issue: the importance of selecting activities on sound, scientific criteria—for maximum benefit and efficiency	The issue: the significance of enhancing activity via technology, chemistry, and other interventions	The issue: the value of powerful interventions that would promote health without the uncertainties of behavioral change

Technological intervention

Behavioral change with technology enhancement

Behavioral change with scientifically screened activity

Behavioral change (loser)

Behavioral change using natural activity (loser)

Behavioral change with culturally desirable activity (loser)

FIGURE 5.3 Loser's bracket under materialism.

Team Efficiency responds by arguing that subjective issues like meaning and love can get in the way of progress. Romantic attachments to tradition might actually keep clients from making the changes they desire. When progress is not immediately evident, these individuals lose interest. There is no better motivation than success. In scientific materialism, it makes more sense to aim at physical realities such as organs, muscles, and brains, not at some metaphorical heart. FITT principles address concrete facts of life. Team Efficiency stands by its products, longevity and functionality. They pursue those ends on the basis of science, not a hope and a prayer and definitely not on a blind allegiance to tradition.

The tournament judges award the victory to Team Efficiency. They say that if we are going to require the inefficiencies and inconveniences of movement over simpler and more effective genetic and biochemical interventions (game 1), and if we are going to require natural movement without the benefit of technological enhancements (game 2), then we had better pick movement forms that are maximally efficient. Passions of the heart, if they matter at all, can be pursued after individuals are healthy and fit. We retire from the tournament as the three-time losers (see figure 5.3). Our commitment to natural, culturally significant movement has been judged as submaximally effective and, even worse, as inefficient.

Philosophic Exercise

What do you think about the speculations in this tournament? Is this brave new world of genetic engineering and maximal efficiency just around the corner? Is it 50 or 100 years away? Or is it here already? Try to provide evidence for your answer.

Some argue that we should not fight technology, rather work to make it morally acceptable—in other words, to humanize it. If you were dealing with a sedentary, clinically obese individual who wanted to undergo gastric-bypass surgery, what would you advise? Let's assume that this individual also expresses disdain for activity and hopes that you can prescribe drugs that will lower his cholesterol. What, as an exercise-oriented medical practitioner, would you do?

Current Reactions

Many in the field of kinesiology do not see this tournament as a threat. Their complacency is based on the belief that movement will always be needed, it will always be useful, and it will always play a central role in promoting health. In fact, the research cited at the start of this chapter (on page 90) has breathed new life into everything from activity for older adults to required daily physical education in the public schools. It feels good to be a kinesiologist today.

Nevertheless, we can hardly pick up a newspaper without reading about new behavioral alternatives to exercise, including diet, relaxation, spirituality, holistic health, and technological alternatives, including everything from gastric-bypass surgery for controlling weight to genetic engineering to lessen health risks. Like it or not, we have entered a world in which people can be healthier and live longer than ever before without dramatically changing their behavior and adopting an active lifestyle.

Even if this is not fully a reality today, it appears that it will be relatively soon. Those kinesiologists who have hitched their wagon to movement as an irreplaceable component of optimal health may find themselves tethered to a horse without much power. For all those who do not like to exercise or move in vigorous ways, good news is on the way. They soon will not need to go to the trouble of learning a motor skill, taking precious time to work out, and enduring something that they find boring or even distasteful. They can sit and read a book and listen to music and still live a long and healthy life. Thus this tournament's focus on material health places activity-oriented kinesiology at risk.

Conclusions

In light of this danger, what we need is the kind of radical reaction to the tournament that we looked for under dualism. Perhaps we should refuse to play under the current rules and the current judges. Kinesiology has never been about health alone, so perhaps a tournament that has us pin all our hopes on contributions to health is not a competition we are interested in joining. While we do contribute to health, we also contribute to many more aspects of the good life.

We might also object to the criterion of clinical efficiency that seems to dominate this tournament. This takes the cultural, personal, and subjective out of play, elements that we need if we are to serve our students and clients well. As I will argue in chapter 8, we should see ourselves as caretakers of wonderful playgrounds related to physical activity. If and when we can provide others with the keys to such playgrounds, we enhance the quality of their lives, not just their material health.

Extreme forms of materialism make it difficult for us to go there. We cannot argue for quality of life because this involves subjective judgments about what counts as quality. It is much safer in a materialistic world to confine professional activity to developing functional cells and producing good genes.

REVIEW

The difficulties kinesiology faces under dualism and scientific materialism are many. In the dualistic tournament that features educational dichotomies—theory versus practice, mental skills versus physical skills, extrinsic versus intrinsic values, and high culture versus low culture—we encounter four judgments that often cast us in an unfavorable light. The primary source of our difficulty is dualism's elevation of the mind over the body.

In the materialistic tournament, which values maximal health and efficiency, we encounter three unfavorable judgments: about sites for interventions, technological enrichments for interventions, and efficiency of natural interventions. The source of our difficulty here is the tournament's focus on mechanistic, material efficiency related to health. It removes the humanity from our profession.

LOOKING AHEAD

It is now time to find an alternative interpretation of human beings. If this vision, called holism, turns out to be worthwhile, it will avoid some of the pitfalls that helped us lose the two tournaments reviewed in this chapter. It will also allow us to be true to ourselves while not forcing us against our better judgment to play only for one team or another.

CHECKING YOUR UNDERSTANDING

1. *Describe the four games of the dualistic tournament and try to give at least one reason for our defeat in each one. Which game was most important and why? In which game do we frequently switch teams in an attempt to get on the winning side?*

2. *Identify the dangers of accepting the tournament as is. Why is it dangerous for kinesiology to rely on a strategy of changing teams, particularly in games 1 and 3? Why not get a victory if we can?*

3. *Describe the different criteria of the materialistic tournament. What counts as good or successful in these three games? Why does kinesiology have trouble when it would seem that we would do very well in a tournament that does not acknowledge the significance of mind, ideals, or human experience?*

6

Holism

The vision of people as whole, psychophysical beings was developed many years ago, and at least four generations of kinesiologists have been raised on a doctrine of holism. We have been taught that

◆ the physical aspect of human existence is inextricably united with and influenced by every thought that the mind has;

◆ the thoughtful aspect of human existence is inextricably united with and influenced by body composition, health, and movement; and

◆ human beings are greater than the sum of their parts.

The only problem is that holism didn't take. It did not turn dualistic culture, language, and practices on their head, and it did not dampen the enthusiasm of materialists who see the human being as a complex physical machine. Moreover, the tournaments in chapter 5 demonstrate that we are required, even inclined to compete on the terms of dualism and materialism.

The vision of integrated persons who reflect intelligence in everything from their chemistry to their movement and show traces of embodiment in everything from their attitudes to their values was supposed to create an earthquake effect (Griffith 1970). Instead it barely registered as a tremor. Holism promised to revolutionize the way we think about people—how we educate them, treat them medically, promote their spiritual growth, and help them move—but it did not. This has left us with many questions.

◆ Why has it been so difficult to understand and appreciate holism in our profession?

◆ Is holism really effective in the workplace? If so, why?

◆ Is holism gaining ground today or not?

◆ What do holistic kinesiologists believe?

◆ How does their behavior differ from that of dualist or materialist kinesiologists?

CHAPTER OBJECTIVES

In this chapter, you will

◆ *look at the significance of holism,*

◆ *review four early expressions of holism,*

◆ *encounter a more modern holistic description of human beings, and*

◆ *examine the implications of holism for kinesiology.*

SIGNIFICANCE OF HOLISM

Holism is significant in at least three ways. First, it is important theoretically. As educated body and movement professionals, we need to be able to describe how humanity is tied to physicality. Even though we live this reality day in and day out, it is difficult to articulate our integrated existence. For instance, to combat dualism we may want to argue that mind and body are equally important and that we should devote comparable attention to both. But we are still talking about mind and body as if they were separate entities.

The counterarguments to materialism are no less difficult to find. We may want to put the mind back in the picture and talk about our ideas as if they were independent of mechanics and other physical realities. But this does not quite work because we have to acknowledge that our thinking is tethered to our chemistry and physiology.

So we are stuck with inadequate vocabularies, misleading metaphors, and an incomplete picture of what people are like. We have a hard time describing how cells, body parts, and movement are related. We need this understanding if we are to mobilize holistic strategies for intervention and if we are to generate any passion for this approach to our profession.

Holism's second level of significance lies in its practical usefulness. I suggested in the last chapter that holistic kinesiologists are generally more successful. They teach motor skills more quickly. They get higher exercise compliance. They rehabilitate patients more often and in a shorter period of time. They develop deeper and more meaningful relationships with their students and clients. If this is true, the methodologies of holism have tremendous practical value. We need

Holism does not just fix a motor problem more effectively; it also improves a life more surely.

to identify such interventions and teach them in our professional preparation programs.

The third level of significance in holism is also practical but it is a bit more encompassing. Holism does not just fix a motor problem more efficiently or rehabilitate a patient more quickly; it also improves a life more surely. Holistic educators and health practitioners know that quality of life is always at stake. They know that fixing the part may depend to some extent on treating the whole; conversely, fixing the whole may depend on treating the part. The bottom line is that students of holistic physical educators and patients of holistic health practitioners receive a bonus. They go to the kinesiology professional for help in fixing a bad back, learning a golf swing, or developing better cardiovascular fitness, and they end up improving their overall lives.

EARLY EXPRESSIONS OF HOLISM

Since the beginning of the 20th century, our profession has attempted to describe people in nondualistic terms. Here are four of the most popular descriptions.

◆ *A sound mind in a sound body* (Juvenal in Ferguson 1979). A person is a whole being composed of two closely related elements, mind and body. A healthy mind resides in and therefore depends on a healthy body. Conversely, a sound body is produced under the guidance of a good mind.

◆ *A unity of mind, body, and spirit* (YMCA triangle symbol, created by Luther Gulick). A person is a whole being with three aspects. The human being should be balanced, so no one part should be given more attention than the other two.

◆ *Education through the physical* (Williams 1965). A person is a whole being, and the profession should take advantage of this fact by teaching social lessons through sport, dance, and exercise.

◆ *Education of the physical* (McCloy 1966). A person is a whole being, but the profession should still focus on the physical aspects. Physical education should aim for outcomes like better cardiovascular fitness, strength, and flexibility, even though these outcomes will also affect attitudes and ideas.

Philosophic Exercise

Take the following two phrases and try to complete them using the same verbal pattern as employed in the four previous statements, but using your own ideas.

◆ Education as the physical. A person is a whole being . . .
◆ A sound individual. A person is a whole being . . .

Of the two descriptions you came up with, choose the one you like better. In one or two sentences, explain why you think it may be superior to any one of the four earlier phrases. What is better about your statement? Is it clearer? More accurate? More inspiring? Less dualistic?

Merits and Shortcomings of Early Holism

The four early descriptions of the whole person each contributed to an appreciation of our integrated nature. Nevertheless, each also has shortcomings.

A Sound Mind in a Sound Body

According to this statement, physical education is important because good thinking depends on health. Education should be balanced; the physical should not be neglected for the mental. In fact, the human being is so integrated that complete development is possible only if the whole psychophysical organism is tended to. This statement marked an advance from the belief of some dualists that the mind operates with a high degree of independence from the body and even enjoys an existence of its own.

Nevertheless, there are many problems with this spatial metaphor, which suggests that something called the mind is *in* something else called the body, like a marble in a jar. You already know that this leads to at least two unanswerable questions: How can something nonphysical affect something physical, and how can something that is nonphysical (an idea) be located in something else that is physical (body)?

The very identification of mind and body as human components sets up a dualistic framework. It may imply that the body serves the lesser function in this arrangement, perhaps that the body's health is important as a means to an end (good thinking), not as an end in itself. Notice that Juvenal left the statement one-sided: "A sound mind in a sound body." He could have added, "and a sound body around a sound mind," but he did not.

A Unity of Mind, Body, and Spirit

According to part of the YMCA triangle (see figure 6.1), the activity professions are valuable because physicality is one of three closely related aspects of human beings. In order for people to reach their potential, they must have a balanced education. We should not elevate a single type of learning above the other two. The triangle also eliminates the spatial metaphor of a healthy mind inside a healthy body. Finally, some would argue that adding a spiritual dimension is important. This statement signaled an advance for the activity professions because it gave physical aspects of existence a position of equality with spiritual and intellectual aspects.

Our mind is not in our body in the same way that marbles rest in a jar.

Yet there remains the image of the person composed of three parts that are somehow unified into a single triangle. Moving around the corners of the triangle, the mind fades into the body, which fades into the spirit, which returns to the mind. The problems with this image of personhood are much the same as those of the mind-in-the-body metaphor. If there are no pure sides called mind, body, and soul, there can be no triangle made up of them. And even if there were such sides lying around someplace, how are they related to one another? What happens at those places where one side fades into the others? How can a nonphysical side (mind or spirit) fade into a physical one (body)?

This image also may be misleading because it suggests that mind is a single, uniform thing. It could be that we have multiple intelligences rather than a single capacity that makes us smart. It could also be that we have multiple embodiments—as, for example, we learn new skills, add weight, age, and otherwise change. We will examine these ideas later in the chapter.

FIGURE 6.1   The YMCA triangle.

Author's rendering and interpretations of a YMCA logo and its symbolism represent his viewpoint and opinions and are not endorsed by the YMCA of the USA. YMCA and various Y logos are registered trademarks of YMCA of the USA.

When the body moves, it affects the whole person.

Education Through the Physical

For Jesse Williams (1965), the author of this phrase, the activity professions are important because games, exercise, and play are marvelous laboratories for learning. If people are whole beings, teachers cannot isolate any pure physical element. When the body moves, it affects the whole person. Through the physical the student can, and almost invariably will, learn other things. By manipulating these movement laboratories, teachers could promote socially useful outcomes like the habits, skills, and knowledge related to good citizenship. This statement marked an important advance because it gave physical education stature. Now physical activities were not aimed at merely mechanical outcomes, but were extended to important social and psychological objectives which all educators could identify.

Yet, Williams' language is unfortunately dualistic. His phrase points to something called the physical, and he leaves us with an image of well-intentioned teachers using the physical part of persons as an avenue to achieve more important results. There is an implicit value dualism here where the physical is regarded as a means to more important ends.

Education of the Physical

Charles McCloy (1966), the author of this phrase, believed that the activity professions are valuable because organic contributions to human development and happiness are pervasive and significant. The whole person is biological and every aspect of life is influenced by such biological qualities as strength, flexibility, motor skill, and health. McCloy's education of the physical was not a territorial claim about a physical aspect of the human being that is separate from a mental aspect. Rather it was a nondualistic claim about how our physical nature affects our personalities, goals, values, work, and play. This was an advance for physical education because some dualists felt that physical training, growth, and development were peripheral to human potential. They believed that physical well-being was an optional pathway to success and happiness.

Yet McCloy's language has as much of a dualistic ring to it as does Williams'. The phrase *of the physical* conjures images of fitness instructors working on the bodies of their students much as mechanics work on cars. We are left wondering if there are teachers "of the mental." And like Williams' phrase, McCloy's description suggests that physical education is a means to more important ends. It suggests that education of the physical is necessary for an effective life of the mind, but it is the so-called life of the mind that we really want.

Our physical characteristics affect our personality, goals, values, work, and play.

A Vertical Interpretation

While these expressions of holism helped our field make important advances, they failed to produce much new thinking, speaking, and acting. They caused only a tremor because they still accept a fundamentally dualistic image of human existence. I call this image a vertical interpretation of human beings. It is one that puts mind over body, thinking over doing, and verbal over nonverbal expression.

In the vertical image of persons (see figure 6.2), the human being is still composed of a mental part and a physical part. The superiority of the mental part is symbolized by its place above the physical. The lower, physical part is the foundation, the site of important resources such as health and sensory experience that allow the mind to achieve its full potential.

In these early expressions of holism mind and body are understood to be closely related. They intimately affect one another, and only a fine line separates the two. Yet the line remains because these four interpretations still rely on notions of mind and body and the effect one has on the other.

The arrows symbolize the two-way relationship that exists between mind and body in this vertical model. The up arrow makes Juvenal's point that physical health affects mental functioning; Williams' claim that participation in physical

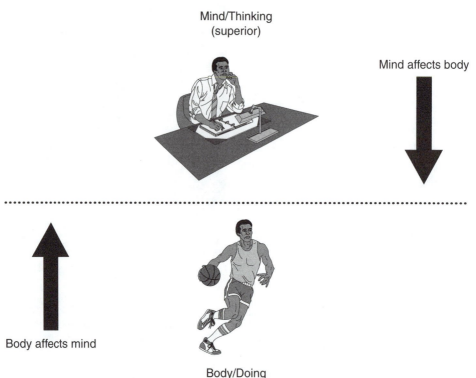

FIGURE 6.2 *A vertical interpretation of human beings.*

games affects the whole person, including personality, hopes, and ideals; and McCloy's assertion that physical strength, flexibility, cardiovascular fitness, and other parameters of physical health play an important role in the achievement of human potential. The down arrow makes the complementary claims that mental health affects physical functioning; theoretical understanding affects the whole person, including posture, skill, and physical health; and knowledge plays an important role in the achievement of human potential.

Nevertheless, with a line drawn between the two and the mind on top, this vertical view of the person still sends the message that the body serves the mind and awaits assistance from it.

FIVE PRINCIPLES FOR A NEW VISION

We need a new, improved vision that does more than replace a chasm between mind and body with a fine line. We need to get rid of the line altogether. In fact, we need to stop thinking of human beings in terms of mind and body, period. From our previous analysis of dualism and materialism, we can now identify five principles that will help us draw a more accurate picture of human beings.

◆ *A more accurate picture will have to show that physical influences are always shaping all that we are and do.* It will have to acknowledge that we are chemical and physical, and that, because we are embodied, we are historical and always act from a certain perspective in time and space. Chemistry and embodied localization affect our every idea and behavior. Genetic inheritance matters; where and when we were born matter; whether we had a fine coach who inspired us when we were young matters. All that we think and do shows that we are tethered to our physicality.

◆ *A more accurate picture will have to show that the influences of consciousness are always at work.* It will have to acknowledge that we are influenced by our personality, ideas, perceptions, and hopes. Ideas are a match for the most powerful chemical. They change chemistry, cell structure, bone composition, and the amount of epinephrine in our bloodstream. Ideas have caused some individuals to dedicate themselves to various causes, even to give up their lives. Everything from our chemical composition to our skeletal structure to our physiology shows that we are tethered to our consciousness.

◆ *A more accurate picture will have to show that these workings are not independent from one another.* It will have to take seriously the interconnection of consciousness and embodiment. Neither can be reduced to the other—ideas cannot be reduced to physical states, and vice versa. Neither retains a separate, abstract character. The footprints of chemicals can be found in ideas; for instance, whether we are more optimistic or pessimistic by nature may be caused in part by our chemistry. Likewise, the footprints of ideas can be found in chemistry. For example, nervous thoughts can increase acidity in our stomach.

◆ *A more accurate picture will have to depict different levels of behavioral intelligence.* It will have to take seriously the fact that some actions are highly adaptable and complex while others are largely inflexible and simple. Solving a complex equation is very different from scribbling simple arithmetic. Making a creative move to the basket is very different from the lower leg moving forward when a rubber hammer strikes the patellar ligament.

◆ *A more accurate picture will have to depict different types of activity.* It will have to take seriously the fact that some behaviors are carried out largely in motor ways while others take place reflectively, often with little or no movement. Kicking a ball and thinking about kicking a ball both involve skill, but one is motor-active while the other is sedentary and thus motor-passive.

The Key Move

We have been trained to think of people as being composed of parts. Dualism divides the person into mind and body, and materialism breaks the person down into cells, muscles, and brain. Both positions harm us, as they hold that movement involves inferior parts—the body instead of the mind, or physical activity instead of theory.

We need to shift our thinking from parts of people to kinds of behavior. Behavior is homogenized, ambiguous, and variable. Some behavior is very machinelike and can be predicted with high degrees of accuracy, such as a simple knee-jerk reflex. Other behavior is more variable and creative. It is learned via instruction and practice and cannot be predicted with accuracy. Improvisation at the keyboard and a creative return by a tennis player are two examples.

The point is this: Once we shift the conversation from the parts of a person to the qualities of human action, we have a chance to compete successfully in any tournament related to well-being. The focus will become *how well* we move, not *what part* of us is involved in the movement. It will require us to describe features of intentional movement that reflect insight and intelligence.

Impressive Intelligence

The shift in focus from parts of human beings to quality of human behavior forces us to redefine intelligence. It could be that merely using our heads, employing verbal symbols, or reflecting in an easy chair does not guarantee intelligence. Rather, it is *how* we use our heads, *how* we employ verbal symbols, and *how* we reflect that determines intelligence. The same applies to physical behavior. It is not merely using our muscles or exerting effort that determines success, it is *how* we do so that makes the difference.

In the photos to the right we see two kinds of behavior that require advanced skills, insight, and years of training. The quality of the behavior is high, even though one individual is involved in motor-oriented behavior and the other in reflective behavior.

Could it be that there are criteria other than "physical" and "mental" that determine the level of intelligence expressed? Could it be that tossing around a ball and tossing around some ideas place comparable demands on intelligence? How could we ever convince our dualistic detractors of this?

Here are some possibilities. The actions of both individuals are partly *unconstrained*—some in close relationship to things, space, time, and gravity, and others in close relationship to numbers and words. Their behavior is *unpredictable*. Their freedom gives them options not available to lesser performers. They can go where they might not be expected to go and do what they might not be expected to do. They are *inventive and creative*. They can *adapt* to new conditions at a moment's notice. Their actions are *complex*. Their skills are based on different habits that no longer require their attention, so they can do many things at once. Their attention is *expansive and distant*. They can take in a considerable amount of information at one time. Table 6.1 highlights these characteristics.

© Photodisc

Impressive intelligence in advanced skills: sedentary . . . and physically active.

TABLE 6.1 Behavioral Characteristics of High and Low Intelligence

Low intelligence	High intelligence
Experiences constraint	Experiences freedom
Acts repetitively	Acts unpredictably
Has difficulty adapting to new circumstances	Adapts to new circumstances quickly
Relies on past solutions	Invents creative solutions
Behaves in a simple manner	Behaves in a complex manner
Has limited or narrow vision	Uses broad perceptual input
Acts in rigid ways; resistant to change	Acts in flexible ways; open to change
Experiences standard, public meaning	Experiences new, personal meaning

Philosophic Exercise

It may be easy to defend this new description of intelligence in the arts. In fact, many universities have performance majors in these areas. At my institution students can even get a master's degree in a program that focuses on skillful activity, such as singing, dancing, or playing the piano. The gatekeepers of higher education apparently see these kinds of advanced motor performance as cultured, creative, and intelligent.

But we have no performance major in exercise, sport, or any other kinesiology movement. When it is suggested that outstanding basketball players should be allowed to major in athletics, muffled laughter ensues. To sort this out, respond to the following questions:

◆ Is this a double standard?

◆ Can advanced athletes honestly claim the eight qualities of intelligent behavior listed in table 6.1?

◆ Could you support a performance-oriented undergraduate or graduate program in kinesiology? If so, list three or four arguments that would justify such a curriculum.

Unimpressive Intelligence

The pictures shown here illustrate actions that require lesser skills, training, and insight. The intelligence on display is not particularly impressive. One picture shows someone trying to solve a movement-related problem, while the other shows someone engaged in a more reflective activity. This suggests that the absence of intelligence in these behaviors is not tied to the part of the person employed in the activity.

Here is a description of behavior that lacks those features we associate with higher intelligence. The actions are highly *constrained*. They are largely at the mercy of things like gravity, distance, numbers, or words. The individuals experience very *little freedom*. Consequently, their actions are *predictable*. They are likely to perform by the book. Because they are overwhelmed by their tasks, they show *little inventiveness or creativity*. They can barely keep track of the basics. Their actions are *simple*. They are in the very early process of building habits that will eventually allow them to do many things at once, but for now they must be content with doing one thing at a time. And finally, their field of attention is *narrow*—the space in front of them, the ball, or the numbers. They cannot take in all the information they need in order to perform well. Table 6.1 on page 111 highlights these characteristics.

Philosophic Exercise

Unimpressive use of intelligence is unfortunate for at least two reasons: It prevents us from being effective and getting things done well, and it makes us feel awkward, uneasy, and even fearful. The pictures and analyses described these two problems in relationship to math (a lack of freedom in dealing with numbers) and ballet (a lack of freedom in moving well).

Unimpressive intelligence in beginning skills: sedentary . . . and physically active.

Try to identify other skill domains where different sorts of intelligence are needed. Can you come up with at least four?

Let us now attempt to improve upon the vertical image of the whole person by creating a horizontal picture. We will eliminate things called mind and body, erase the line that separates the physical from the mental, and find better rules for what counts as intelligent human behavior.

A HORIZONTAL INTERPRETATION

Figure 6.3 is a schematic of behavior, not parts of a person. It does not separate body from mind or discriminate between higher- and lower-order parts of the anatomy.

The vertical axis depicts two poles for all human behavior. At the top is sedentary activity, which includes reflection (the recollection and use of facts and propositions) and intuition (the use of intellectual skills such as computing, writing, and imagining). It is called sedentary because, as intellectually active as this behavior may be, it can be done in a chair with minimal movement. The upper region of the vertical axis is the home for those who win games 1 and 2 of the dualistic tournament. They dwell in understanding and theory (game 1) or they employ the so-called intellectual skills of mathematics, language, induction, deduction, and so on (game 2).

However, a second axis makes another important distinction. It acknowledges that sedentary activity can be done well or poorly. Thinking can be insightful

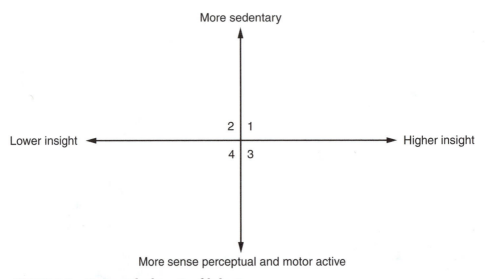

FIGURE 6.3 *Horizontal schematic of behavior.*

and creative (the right end of the axis) or not (the left). The positive qualities listed in table 6.1 (see page 111), in other words, characterize actions toward the right side of the horizontal image of human behavior. The negative qualities lie toward the left side.

Area 1 symbolizes sedentary activity that is done well. This behavior is unconstrained, unpredictable, creative, and complex. Attention is not on the numbers, words, or new ideas, as it is with beginners, but it is expansive and distant. Memory is durable and broad in scope.

Sedentary activity that is done unskillfully and without insight is symbolized by area 2. While behavior here is the same kind of activity found in area 1 and for that reason might typically be called intellectual activity, it is nonetheless primitive, rote, and reflexive. While behavior here also produces oral expressions, mathematical answers, and philosophic statements, they are not worth much. This behavior is constrained, predictable, noncreative, and simple. Memory is short-lived and limited in scope. It involves doing philosophy, math, composition, and history by the book.

The bottom portion of the image symbolizes the other pole of human behavior—the sensuous, perceptual, and motor-active. In this domain human projects involve movement and rely heavily on sensory perception. Art, music, crafts, and athletics come with sound, shape, color, size, weight, and visual illusion. This behavior requires thinking both intuitively (sensing and feeling right moves) and reflectively (considering a proposition or performance tip), but the focus is on intuitive knowing.

As with sedentary activity, physical behavior can be done well or poorly—that is, with high levels of intelligence, insight, creativity, and artistry (symbolized by area 3) or with minimal insight, in a rote, predictable fashion with little or no interpretation (area 4).

Of crucial importance here is the substitution of horizontal behavior for vertical. The winners are those who move toward the right in the diagram, whether they are reflective or physical. Conversely, the losers lie along the left side from top to bottom. Intelligence involves the capacity to move to the right, hopefully at more than one level of the figure.

Finally, with this holistic version of human behavior, the playing field is level. The rules of the tournament give us a chance to compete, and the judges have no reason to start with a bias against us. Kinesiologists, every bit as much as mathematicians, linguists, and philosophers, can teach the quality behavior we all value, such as intuitive and reflective insight, understanding, creativity, and freedom.

Strengths of the Horizontal Interpretation

Let's return to the five holistic principles for improving the image of kinesiology that we identified on pages 109, 110.

◆ The figure must take physical reality seriously. Activity in all four quadrants of figure 6.3 is influenced by chemistry, genes, and physiology. Inferior behavior (areas 2 and 4) is influenced by underdeveloped brains, poor chemistry, biological immaturity, and poor education. Behavior here is constrained; freedom and flexibility are missing. Superior behavior (areas 1 and 3) is also affected by chemistry, genes, well-developed brains, and so on. Behavior here is relatively unconstrained. But all behavior is physically tethered.

◆ The figure must take consciousness and ideas seriously. Insight, ideas, emotions, and perceptions influence behavior in all four areas. Superior behavior (areas 1 and 3) shows purpose, aspiration, ideals, and the like. But even inferior behavior (areas 2 and 4) shows emotion, organization of ideas, and coordination. Thus, all human behavior is influenced by the human capacity to think and perceive, whether this is done well or poorly. Even the reflexive knee jerk shows sophisticated organization that is unavailable to inanimate life.

© Icon Sports Media

The human capacity to think and perceive influences all human behavior.

◆ The figure must show that the conscious and physical sides of people are not independent from one another. In this figure, there is no mind and body. There are only two poles of behavior—the sedentary, nonsensory, and reflective, and the active, sensory, and intuitive (the vertical axis); and there are only two poles of quality for those behaviors—the impressive and the unimpressive (the horizontal axis). The body is everywhere, playing different roles but having an unmistakable influence. The same can be said for consciousness.

Because there is no separate mind and body in this image, it is impossible for one to direct the other. Likewise, it is impossible for one to operate apart from the influence of the other. The mind cannot reflect on ideas without being affected by chemistry, and the body cannot operate simply as a machine.

◆ The figure must show that human behavior differs in character. Some acts are sedentary. They rely very little, if at all, on actual sense perception, muscle coordination, cardiovascular endurance, and so on. They do rely on memory, imagination, and various reflective skills. Others are active in nature. They rely very little, if at all, on reflection, proposition formation, or other reflective skills. But they do rely on effective sight, motor skill, endurance, and the like. The diagram acknowledges the existence of diverse types of behavior.

◆ The figure must show that both sedentary and active behavior vary in their usage of intelligence and insight. There are impressive displays of intelligence that take the form of dance and others that take the form of rocket science. Likewise, there are unimpressive displays of intelligence in both areas. Thus, the horizontal image includes a spectrum of behavior from low to high intelligence (left to right).

Summary

It would appear that the horizontal image of behavior is superior to the vertical image of holism. The horizontal figure honors the five holistic principles we established for the project. All five points provide a foundation on which we can promote an active lifestyle. The fifth point is particularly significant. This vision of intelligence, which places us in both the active and the sedentary domain, forcefully reorients our thinking from vertical to horizontal. Insight and intellectual power are not limited to reflective, sedentary doings. Insight and intellectual power permeate the full range of human behavior from the most sedentary to the most active. We can be involved in acts on the dance floor and in the gymnasium that are just as insightful and brilliant as the acts of the philosopher, mathematician, or writer.

If this image is accurate, what is important is not that we use our mind more than our body, but that we are free rather than constrained, creative rather than unimaginative, and unpredictable rather than patterned. We have new ground rules for what counts as intellectually impressive, and these rules give no advantage to the abstract proposition over the abstract movement.

What determines the quality of behavior is not that we are doing a physical activity, but how we are doing it. The same is true for the supposed intellectual side of life—it matters not so much that we are engaged in a cerebral activity but how we are doing it.

Philosophic Exercise

Recall the three levels of significance of holism on pages 103-104. See if you can describe

◆ why the horizontal image comes closer to getting personhood right intellectually or philosophically (point 1);

◆ how that image can make you a more effective activity practitioner or teacher (point 2); and

◆ how holism might improve your ability to not just teach motor skills, improve fitness, or fix a body part, but to improve the quality of your client's or student's life (point 3).

REVIEW

The vision of people as whole beings has existed for some time, but it has not had the earth-shattering effect that many predicted. Four traditional descriptions of holism allowed physical education to make some progress in arguing for the centrality of movement in human development. Nevertheless, these four visions retained a vertical, somewhat dualistic image of human existence. While they moved us forward, they also held us back by continuing to focus on parts of people, not behaviors.

The horizontal image of people satisfies five basic requirements of holism. This image eliminates entities called mind and body, erases any line between physical and mental activity, and redefines what counts as intelligent behavior. The crucial part of the image is that it depicts free, unpredictable, creative, sensitive, and insightful behavior as both sedentary and active. There might be different forms of human intelligence that merit comparable recognition, attention, and support.

LOOKING AHEAD

You should now be familiar with holism, so you are ready to examine the practical implications of this integrated vision. The discussion in chapter 7 is central to two major claims in this text—namely, that philosophy should affect our professional behavior, and that philosophic insight will make us more effective professionals.

CHECKING YOUR UNDERSTANDING

1. *Why are the four early descriptions of people at least partly holistic, and how did they help our field progress?*

2. *Why are these early descriptions at least partly dualistic, and how did they hold us back? Why is it important to stop talking about parts of people and focus on different levels of intelligence in behavior?*

3. *Describe the five essential aspects of holism in your own words. Which of the five do you believe is the most important, and why?*

4. *Why is the horizontal image of personhood superior to the vertical image? Can you identify at least three improvements?*

7

Holism: From Theory to Practice

The theory of holism lays the foundation for the earthquake of different thinking and practice that was supposed to follow the defeat of dualism and materialism. The implications of a genuinely holistic kinesiology are nothing short of remarkable. In some cases, they almost appear to be counterintuitive, if not utterly scandalous. But such reactions to holism are rooted less in science and more in our habituated ways of seeing things. The biggest challenge we face in moving toward holistic practice may well be tradition, not data. This raises a series of interesting questions.

◆ How exactly would holism change the way we do business in kinesiology?

◆ Is there a holistic methodology? A holistic curriculum?

◆ Why do holistic practices often work better?

◆ Can holism's effectiveness be explained both scientifically and philosophically?

FOUR IMPLICATIONS OF HOLISM

Holistic descriptions of behavior have important implications for our daily work. We may not be ready to accept some of them, and we will have trouble selling some of them. But if our new description is on target, we need to follow it where it leads us.

What Counts As Smart?

In chapter 6, we redefined the nature of intelligence. The old definition was uniform and narrow, focusing on our ability to use numbers and words, follow logic, and understand and remember abstract concepts. Our new definition includes the capability to see and act insightfully. With Gardner (1985, 1999) we came upon the possibility that human beings possess multiple intelligences. Some intelligence has to do with words and abstract concepts, others with sense perception, logic, spatial location, words, or sounds and rhythms.

CHAPTER OBJECTIVES

In this chapter, you will

◆ *examine four controversial implications of holism,*

◆ *discover sites for intervention in holism, and*

◆ *review five holistic strategies for education and health interventions.*

No longer can you encounter philosophy, English, or math majors on your campus and assume that they are intellectual simply because they study philosophy, English, or math. For all you know, they may deal with ideas, words, and numbers in the upper-left portion of figure 6.3 (see page 114). Why should you honor rote, unimaginative philosophy, English, or math just because it is reflective?

No longer can your friends or colleagues assume that you are intellectually impoverished just because you use your cleverness in a mostly nonverbal, athletic world. For all they know you may kick, swing, or pirouette in the lower-right portion of figure 6.3. In fact, many of us were attracted to this field because we were already well on our way to that lower-right area of creative activity. Why should we overlook the intellectual significance of creative, insightful movement just because it is active?

If you wanted to demonstrate your activity IQ, you would not ask others to read what you have written about sport or look at your test scores in classes on the physiology of exercise. You would invite them out to the baseball field, into the dance studio, or into the weight room and say quite simply, "Please watch!" And if somebody asked you if you were intelligent, you would undoubtedly have to answer, "Yes and no." You may have two left feet when it comes to dance but still show a grace and shrewdness on the wrestling mat. You may break out in a cold sweat in the presence of quadratic equations but still make confident, clever discriminations in basketball. Different intelligence, in other words, works in different ways and in different places.

This changes the notion of what it means to be educated. Many educational theorists focus on games 1 and 2 of the dualistic tournament described in chapter 5. They believe that a good education is an intellectual education and that the basic skills of education are reasoning, communicating, calculating, and computing.

Holistic education focuses on the kinds of problems that human beings need to solve rather than the supposed part of the person that does the solving. Holistic

Freedom, both in a chair and out.

© Photodisc

education is guided by the areas where human beings need skills to function freely and creatively. It is not guided by a rigid dichotomy between academic and nonacademic capability.

A holist might be compelled by the tongue-in-cheek argument that there are only two places in the world where people need to be competent and creative: in chairs and everywhere else. The domains of sound, touch, motor competence, and nonverbal expression lie predominantly "everywhere else." A balanced education makes provision for human, embodied freedoms. We do not educate for the life of the mind. We educate, train, and habituate for the life of the whole person.

What Happens to the Activity Professions?

If holism makes sense, there is no reason for movement professionals to feel defensive, act defensively, or even bother to claim (defensively) that they are not defensive. Kinesiologists would no longer need to cloister themselves in schools of health, physical education, and recreation. They would not have to apologize for the fact that their perceptual and motor acuity may be stronger than their verbal or mathematical intelligence. They would find some comfort and peace in their own pattern of intelligence.

Holism helps us arrive at a less compartmentalized view of education.

As we come to a less dualistic vision of human life, we should arrive at a less compartmentalized view of education. Physical educators might form close relationships with other academic departments that use similar forms of intelligence. Foremost among these would be the arts, which place a premium on the ability to move sensitively and correctly in time and space, whether at an easel or on a pair of ice-skates. But new ties might also develop with the language arts when we come to see communication as a whole-person activity that includes posture, sport movement, and dance gesture as much as verbal pronouncement.

What Happens to the Significance of Performance?

Under holism, motor performance is on an equal footing with reflection. Curricular decisions would change in many cases. If sedentary actions like writing and computing are basic skills, then motor-oriented activities like dancing and hiking are basic skills too. If there are compelling reasons to give academic credit for creative philosophic exploring, then it may be right to award academic credit for creative aquatic exploring. If students can be kept out of athletics because of low grades in English, then students should also be kept out of English for low grades in physical education. If there are honors courses in math, there should be honors courses in movement.

Conversely, we might need to change some of our own practices. If it is proper to pass students in movement education because they attend class and take showers, then it may be proper to pass students in philosophy for showing up and keeping a clean notebook. If it is virtually impossible to receive a grade lower than a B in physical education, then it should be impossible to receive anything below a B in Spanish or biology. If it is sound practice to offer beginning sport skills in college, then it is right for university chemistry and physics to present a mostly grade-school curriculum. If it is acceptable to teach two-week units in dance, gymnastics, golf, and weight training, then perhaps it is right for math teachers to give only two weeks of multiplication, algebra, and calculus.

Finally, if skillful movement does not just lead to knowledge but can be itself a legitimate and valuable form of knowing, and if skillful movement does not just rely on previous intelligent behavior but can be itself a form of insightful activity, then why not offer bachelor's, master's, and doctoral degrees in performance (Kleinman 2000)? Students in our field could make a fundamental choice, as students now do in the arts, to emphasize the practice or the theory of movement. Why not award tenure and grant promotions to performance faculty at least in part on their growth and development as performers?

Philosophic Exercise

Do you think these analogies are sound? Are there any good reasons for the different standards for sedentary careers versus movement careers?

See if you can criticize any of the conclusions implied in this section. Provide at least one argument for the validity of different standards where you think they may be supportable. Then see if you can add any more implications for behavioral change. What about faculty benefits, student awards and honors, libraries, study halls, or new kinds of IQ tests?

A Partial Concession

I may well be guilty of drawing some unwarranted deductions from the holistic description of people, thereby committing one of the errors in logic described in chapter 3. As the philosophic exercise implies, there may still be relevant differences between our field and others that justify double standards. But one of the functions of philosophy is to allow us to pull the cobwebs from our eyes, break with convention, and follow ideas with at least a degree of abandon. We may have to pull back to a more conservative position, but we will have given ourselves an opportunity to see the world from a different vantage point based on the force of philosophic reasoning itself.

For instance, the claim about "no pass, no play" policies, where high school students are ineligible for athletic participation when their academic grades are too low, was generated philosophically. In a nondualistic world, logic may tell us that we should think of sport as no more a means for English than English is a means for physical education. But even in a nondualistic world, common sense tells us that there may be good reasons for using athletics to promote better work in such subjects as math, English, and social studies. It can be argued that the inability to speak and write with competence is more harmful than the inability to move well in a game. We live in a sedentary world; in-chair skills, therefore, should trump their out-of-chair counterparts.

Limits to the Concession

Consider the following philosophic argument. Say you are a high school physical-education teacher and coach. Imagine going to an English department meeting and saying that you are working to get a policy passed whereby no student who is flunking physical education will be allowed to continue with their studies in English. You tell them that this is your Motor Affirmative Action Policy, MAAP for short.

We have neglected movement education for so long, you inform them, that until the scales are better balanced, education must compensate in the other direction. Because it is so important for students to see, play, explore, and dance effectively, teachers must threaten them with nonparticipation in English if they do not measure up regarding their movement education.

One of the English teachers objects, "But you can't threaten them with exemptions from English; they don't want to be here in the first place. Some students will intentionally flunk physical education just so they can spend more time with you and less with us."

"All the better," you respond. "Until this lack of balance between writing and moving has been redressed, they *should* be spending more time with me."

You thank your colleagues for their understanding and cooperation. You graciously remind them that once some educational balance is achieved, you will no longer need to use English as a means to enhance movement education.

How Do Kinesiologists Behave?

Materialism and dualism provide one set of clues about how we should behave and what we should do as kinesiologists. Dualism, because it treats the body as a machine, recommends mechanical answers for mechanical problems. Materialism suggests that we should reduce any problem to its root causes and then intervene at that point. The tendency for both dualism and materialism is to find answers for the larger, human problem in the smaller part of the machine or atomic particle.

If someone suffers from lower back pain, the dualistic or materialistic therapist looks for the physical cause of the problem—the pressure point, the misalignment, and perhaps the physiology and chemistry behind it. When the therapist identifies the root physical problem, she recommends the appropriate intervention—surgery, muscle relaxants, rest, or stretching. But the intervention is focused on the back alone and the chemical, neural, and physiological mechanisms that affect it.

Holistic practitioners differ in at least five important ways (also see summary in figure 7.1):

1. Because of the complexity of the human being, they often look more for a group of partial causes than a single cause. Lower back pain may be the result of several factors ranging from genetics to lifestyle.

2. They look more globally for these partial causes. The key to the lower back pain might lie elsewhere in the patient's physiology, not just at the site of pain.

3. They look both at the injured part and at the whole body for partial causes. The pain might lie more in subjective stresses and anxieties than in the patient's local physiology or chemistry.

4. Holistic practitioners often intervene in unlikely locations or in multiple locations. A game plan for the lower back pain may involve discussion and personal decisions about lifestyle and reducing stress rather than surgery.

5. Because holistic practitioners intervene in multiple locations, they need a considerably larger toolbox of methodologies. Low back pain might be alleviated by treating bone, muscle, nerves, posture, or ways of living. The practitioner will need surgery, ultrasound, massage, behavior modification, yoga, and much more in their professional toolbox.

Differences Between Holistic and Traditional Practitioners

Holistic tendencies	Traditional tendencies
1. Look for group of partial causes	1. Look for one or small set of causes
2. Look globally for causes	2. Look locally for causes
3. Look upstream toward consciousness and downstream toward cells for causes	3. Look downstream toward anatomy, physiology, and biochemistry for causes
4. Look in unlikely places for causes	4. Look nearby, rely on categories of disease, look at textbook patterns for causes
5. Need large toolbox; greater use of referrals	5. Need smaller toolbox; referrals used only to expand technical expertise

FIGURE 7.1 *Five characteristics of holistic practitioners.*

FIVE HOLISTIC STRATEGIES

Holistic kinesiologists behave differently with their students and clients, from diagnosis to treatment to follow-up. Holism offers a global mind-set, not a set of isolated techniques. It is an integrated, value-based approach to dealing with other human beings—a philosophy, if you will.

All holistic techniques are part of a single puzzle. The pieces fit together neatly, and missing pieces compromise the value of the whole picture. We will start to build this image of holistic practice with assessment or diagnosis.

Assessment Skills

Holistic practitioners know that every student, athlete, or patient who comes to them is living a unique story. Everyone arrives with his or her own hopes, fears, opportunities, skills, and so on. Holistic practitioners have to make contact with the person, finding out who this unique individual is and what makes him tick.

In recounting his development as a holistic psychiatrist, Robert Coles (1989) spoke for all practitioners in the helping professions. He described one of his breakthrough observations as follows:

> Dr. Ludwig was trying to suggest that what had troubled me was the word "story," that I associated it with literature, with mere reading—not science, not medicine. He remarked that first-year medical students often obtain textured and

Unique people, different stories, individual assessments.

subtle autobiographical accounts from patients and offer them to others with enthusiasm and pleasure, whereas fourth-year students or house officers are apt to present cryptic, dryly condensed, and yes, all-too "structured" presentations, full of abbreviations, not to mention medical or psychiatric jargon. No question: The farther one climbs the ladder of medical education, the less time one has for relaxed, storytelling reflection. And patients' health may be jeopardized because of it: Patients' true concerns and complaints may be overlooked as the doctor hurries to fashion a diagnosis, a procedural plan . . . [Dr. Ludwig] ended with a plea, "more stories, less theory." Err on the side of each person's particularity. (24, 27)

This holistic advice pertains to kinesiologists as well as doctors. When we meet students or patients who are overweight, smoke too much, or have advanced circulatory diseases, we have our own categories of clinical diagnosis and treatment. Yet the most effective intervention may lie well beyond these comfortable categories. Coles seems to be saying that the cardiac-rehabilitation specialist, physical therapist, or coach all have to listen carefully to the stories of the people who come to them. That is, they need to *listen* if they want to move away from dualistic practices that would have them deal with the patient's body as an interchangeable mechanism to be fixed and the patient's mind as an interchangeable computer into which information simply has to be downloaded.

Listening skills are also necessary because the holistic practitioner is looking for clues about the sources of the problem, not just an identification of the symptoms. Overweight youngsters present obvious symptoms; their obesity is hardly a secret. The source of the difficulty, however, is more complex. Is it genetic? Chemical? Physiological? Social and cultural? Psychological? Is it many of these things at once?

Coles, in short, gives us three holistic tips for assessment:

1. Listen carefully.

2. Respect a patient's story.

3. Be wary of theoretical diagnostic categories, and use them judiciously.

Sites for Intervention

Coles' techniques are indispensable for making decisions about forms of intervention, because different interventions may work better for different individuals. Every student or client has intervention buttons, so to speak, that are waiting to be pushed. Some are more or less common to many individuals; some are more idiosyncratic. But where to start? Anywhere and everywhere!

Here is an example of an unusual intervention location discovered by a cardiac-rehabilitation specialist, Jo Packer.

Several years ago, I noticed that many of my female postoperative bypass patients were not healing as quickly as might be expected and consequently were often staying a couple of extra days in the hospital before returning home. I wondered if this might be related to female physiology, a different tolerance for pain, or possibly some social conditioning. The textbooks I consulted did not provide a clear answer.

Because I was still curious about this problem, I went to my female patients and listened to them talk about their operations and their time in the hospital. What I heard surprised me. Most of my patients did not discuss the pain, trauma, or danger associated with the operation. They worried about being away from home. They worried about husbands, significant others, and children who were now fending for themselves during their absence.

This information gave me a clue about a novel, safe, and inexpensive intervention designed to expedite healing and shorten recovery time. The intervention? A simple bedtime telephone call. While most of my female patients were in contact with family members, many of them went to bed without getting reassurance from home. They lay awake wondering and worrying.

From that time on I required all patients with dependents at home to make a phone call immediately before bedtime. Having talked again with their loved ones, and having learned that everyone was doing OK, these patients slept better. Because they slept better, they healed faster. Because they healed faster, they were able to leave the hospital sooner and in better condition. (A paraphrased reconstruction of numerous classroom guest lectures at State College, Pennsylvania)

Analogies in our other fields are not hard to find. We notice a youngster standing shyly by, reluctant to get involved in the activity at hand. In what unusual places might the holistic educator find the keys to getting this child involved? An elite athlete has a tendency to underperform at crucial moments in a contest. In what unusual places might a holistic coach find the keys to getting this athlete over her performance hurdle? A sedentary, middle-aged man has bought treadmills, joined health clubs, and tried all kinds of self-help techniques to develop an active lifestyle, all to no avail. In what unusual places might an exercise specialist find the keys to getting this man into a healthful pattern of living?

Philosophic Exercise

See if you can come up with at least three holistic intervention sites that you could use in your work. Remember, finding interventions that fit the person is important, particularly when motivation is a problem. In addition, think about different sites that may be affecting your client. Even though we deal with many concerns that are physical, we may need to intervene in nonphysical sites that are partial causes of the physical symptoms.

Once you have come up with three techniques, explain to someone else why you think they might work.

Because holistic kinesiologists may need to intervene in many areas, we face a daunting challenge. We need to be familiar with physics, chemistry, biology, biomechanics, physiology, sociology, psychology, philosophy, and everything in between. While it is unlikely that we will be experts in all of these areas, we need to be knowledgeable about the intervention points for each discipline. We may also need to refer patients to experts in these diverse domains. And perhaps most important, we need to respect the power of interventions in all of these places.

Placing Activity in a Human Context

The greatest challenge for movement educators and therapists may lie in the domain of motivation and behavioral change. How do we motivate clients in a sedentary culture? Should we cajole? Threaten? Educate? Provide rewards? Pray for divine intervention?

Two holistic methods appear to be moving to the forefront as tools for motivation and long-term behavioral change. Interestingly, they address very different intervention locations. The first speaks to the importance of personal meaning, the second to the development of habits.

Looking for Meaning

The holistic motivational theory behind the first type of intervention is this: People are not likely to be active if the activity is not personally significant. The million-dollar question is how to get a person to this place of meaning, particularly a person whose current identity has very little to do with movement. The best answer may be to start early, well before schooling begins. But what about those who arrive at kindergarten or first grade already habituated in a high-calorie, low-activity lifestyle?

A holistic educator would say that teachers must "go for the meaning"—that is, develop a curriculum that has a chance of bringing students and clients into a movement subculture. The most powerful meanings show up when students become members of a particular activity subculture.

Siedentop (1994) recommends that physical educators devote part of their curriculum to what he calls sport education. Sport education is designed more to invite students into an activity subculture than to give a quick introduction to the rules and skills of the activity. Among his key recommendations are these:

A holistic educator would say that teachers and health care providers must " go for the meaning."

◆ Spend more time on a single activity.

◆ Make sure that students take some responsibility for organizing the unit and conducting its activities.

◆ Provide a variety of related activities (umpiring, scoring, coaching, record-keeping) to further bring students into the sport culture.

◆ Promote team identity and include spirited but friendly competition.

◆ Keep records.

◆ Make sure that each unit ends with some special, culminating experience such as a tournament, championship, or exhibition.

Where are the repetitions, drills, and rules tests? They are here, in a way, but they are embedded in a human context. Skill teachers become activity brokers (Kretchmar 2000a, 2000b) who create an environment that invites students into various activity subcultures, such as dance, tennis, cycling, and distance running. As a holistic educator, Siedentop knows that teaching machines to move correctly is not what physical education is about. Teaching people to move well in a meaningful context is. For Siedentop and all holistic educators, teachers are not just skill technicians. They are also promoters of movement subcultures.

Good Activity Habits

A more subtle method exists for changing behavior. It has relatively little to do with motivation and meaning, but it gets results. All the American pragmatists from William James to John Dewey understood that positive behavioral change is inextricably intertwined with the development of good habits. They understood that good habits provide a foundation for our most creative, impressive activities. They knew that we like the familiar and that we tend to repeat what we have already learned. Thanks to the emerging science of the late 19th and early 20th centuries, these holistic pragmatists knew that everything from the biochemistry of neural pathways to the positive feelings related to familiarity prepare human beings to develop habits.

The million-dollar question for the holistic practitioner is how to develop good habits of movement. As with the previous kind of intervention, it is undoubtedly best to start at birth, well before school begins. Studies show that one of the best predictors of adult activity is an active childhood (President's Council 2001). But the truth of the matter is that many people enter the workplace with all the wrong habits. How can they change these patterns of behavior that are so firmly implanted?

Anyone who has tried to change a bad habit knows how difficult it is. Strong medicine is surely needed for a serious disease. Providing people with all the rational reasons for exercising does not seem to work. Structuring activity with friends is not entirely effective. Merely making something fun does not do the trick. Removing barriers and improving movement efficacy is not the entire answer (Kretchmar 2000a). While helpful and important, none of these cures is strong enough on its own to change deeply rooted habits of chronic sitting.

While this is unsettling, the solution to the problem is obvious: New habits have to replace old habits.

Consequently, part of the solution lies in encouraging people to act differently over and over and over again, until old habits fade and new habits take their place. Here is what one company did in an attempt to combat an obesity problem that, by their calculation, involved over 50% of their workers (Zernike 2003):

◆ Placed parking lots a considerable distance from offices

◆ Installed slow elevators

◆ Built wide, attractive staircases with windows

◆ Constructed the food court at the far end of the facility and offered better food choices

◆ Provided recreational facilities in a number of locations, not just in the company health club

◆ Set up financial incentives for obese employees to eat better, lose weight, and stay healthier

Our buildings, automobile-favoring public policies, and high-tech gadgets encourage us to spend nearly all of our day in a chair or moving briefly from one chair to another. Then, when we are exhausted from all this stressful non-moving, we retreat to the horizontal chair called a bed (Robinson and Godbey 1997). No wonder we need structured repetitions of behavior to replace these ingrained habits.

It is no problem for a holist to see that going for meaning and going for good habits are two sides of a single coin. Good habits can stimulate enriched meaning. The most creative basketball players, for example, arrived at the pinnacle of their craft by developing excellent habits such as the ability to automatically perform

the basics of dribbling and footwork so they could look up and see opportunities for exciting moves on the court. Conversely, we tend to repeat activities that are profoundly meaningful, resulting in new habits. On the foundation of new habits, new meanings emerge. This cycle between habits and meaning goes on and on.

Good habits can stimulate enriched meaning, and vice versa.

The bottom line is this: Human beings seek meaning, not in spite of being embodied and neurologically wired, but because we are embodied and neurologically wired. We *are* our habits. And we *are* our meanings. For holistic practitioners, habit formation and meaning cultivation are important, mutually reinforcing sites for intervention.

More Patience, Less Talk

Going for meaning and good habits takes time. As human beings, we are built more to dwell on things than meet them on the fly. Brief encounters often have little lasting significance. Merely being introduced to an activity is not usually enough to make it part of our lives. While we romanticize love at first sight, more often than not we need to hold hands for a while, as it were. We need to get to know this new activity if it is ever to have much of an effect on us. Dwelling quietly, respectfully, and patiently in the presence of the activity is a powerful holistic technique for change.

Philosophic Exercise

Getting to know an activity over time is good advice, but in practice it is often difficult to do. Gym classes are crowded and too short. Economic factors limit the amount of time therapists can spend with their patients. And some clients are impatient and demand a quick fix. They are not interested in a long-term program.

Faced with these realities, we can either give up or find creative solutions. Try to find one or two creative solutions to the problem of insufficient time in your kinesiology profession. How can you get those you serve to move more often and more regularly, even if you are not always present?

Zen masters know that change takes time. They understand that it is impossible to tell a pupil how to negotiate the pathway to peaceful and competent performance. At best, teachers can encourage, give advice, and generally point the way. Thus they are quiet and patient while the student slowly moves down the path from movement that is mechanical, stressful, and full of ego to movement that is smooth, effortless, and selfless.

In *Zen in the Art of Archery,* Eugen Herrigel (1971), a German philosopher who traveled to Japan to learn the secrets of Zen Buddhism, describes his journey down this path. He studied under Kenzo Awa, a celebrated archery master. Although Herrigel was impatient and wanted to be verbally told the secrets of shooting well and the related spiritual truths of Zen, Kenzo Awa said little while slowly leading him along the path toward freedom. Lessons during the first year involved relaxation and breathing. Herrigel recounts his progress:

> Though I breathed in technically the right way, whenever I tried to keep my arm and shoulder muscles relaxed while drawing the bow, the muscles of my legs stiffened all the more violently, as though my life depended on a firm foothold

and secure stance. Often the Master had no alternative but to pounce quick as lightning on one of my leg muscles and press it in a particularly sensitive spot. When to excuse myself, I once remarked that I was conscientiously making an effort to keep relaxed, he replied: "That's just the trouble, you make an effort to think about it. Concentrate entirely on your breathing, as if you had nothing else to do!" It took me a considerable time before I succeeded in doing what the Master wanted. But—I succeeded. I learned to lose myself so effortlessly in the breathing that I sometimes had the feeling that I myself was not breathing but—strange as this may sound—being breathed. Now and then, and in the course of time more and more frequently, I managed to draw the bow and keep it drawn until the moment of release while remaining completely relaxed in body, without my being able to say how it happened. The qualitative difference between these few successful shots and the innumerable failures was so convincing that I was ready to admit that now at last I understood what was meant by drawing the bow "spiritually." (40-41)

Kenzo Awa and all holistic instructors understand that words do not translate directly into habits, skills, and least of all, spiritual experiences. A student needs guidance along the path to these objectives, but no teacher can magically transfer these to the learner. The student is not a rational computer that is ready to be programmed by any teacher who has the right formula. Holistic teachers understand the power of patience and the need for time. They also know that some of the best learning occurs when the teacher is quiet.

Posttreatment Assessment

Practitioners need to know if their interventions worked and whether improvements were temporary or more permanent. Data-based tests often provide such answers, and the tendency in a dualistic and reductionistic world is to look only at the numbers. But if our students and clients are affected globally by our interventions, we should be able to see their health and new skills in many different ways. And least of all we will always have to run tests to see if there really is a difference in the underlying mechanisms.

Veteran skill teachers typically gravitate toward holistic assessment. They develop skilled eyes

Some of the best learning occurs when the teacher is quiet.

and ears that can see and hear durable change. Any subsequent generation of numbers, graphs, and profiles is largely redundant.

This is the case, for example, with experienced aquatic instructors. One of the greatest teaching experiences involves beginning swimming. Instructors begin with a young group of frightened and wary children. The children's body language, their overly excited chattering, their reluctance to even approach the edge of the pool—everything shouts out their view of water as unfriendly and dangerous. Eventually a conversion takes place, sometimes gradually, often quickly. The water that moments or days ago repelled now attracts. Everything changes—sounds, posture, facial expressions. It is done. For the rest of their lives, water will no longer provoke fear and anxiety. The instructors don't need tests or surveys to realize this, only trained eyes and ears.

This ability to see the whole through a partial glimpse of the person or the performance is more dramatically exemplified in the parting conversation between Herrigel and Awa. After seven years of archery-based meditation and practice, Herrigel was returning to Germany. He had experienced an unusual harmony between himself, the bow and arrow, and the target. He could now "let the arrow shoot itself." He wanted to continue this art in Germany, and he asked Awa if he could somehow continue to help Herrigel and tell him how he was doing. Awa answered:

> I need not ask you to keep up your regular practicing, not to discontinue it on any pretext whatsoever, and to let no day go by without your performing the ceremony, even without bow and arrow, or at least without having breathed properly. I need not ask you because I know that you can never give up this spiritual archery. Do not ever write to me about it, but send me photographs from time to time so that I can see how you draw the bow. Then I shall know everything I need to know. (92)

REVIEW

Holistic theory leads to potentially controversial claims about the nature of intelligence, the status of activity professions, the significance of performance, and the behavior of practitioners. Many holistic professionals are unusually successful. They use distinctive techniques for diagnosis (e.g., listening to patients' stories), intervention (e.g., going for meaning and habits), and assessment (e.g., looking at a still photograph of a past student).

LOOKING AHEAD

In part III we turn our attention to the subject matter of kinesiology—human movement. We will attempt to understand the nature and value of games and play. Because play is a fundamental human experience, we will begin there.

CHECKING YOUR UNDERSTANDING

1. *Why are some of the practical implications of holism controversial? Can you give at least one example of a holistic practice that could be regarded as unusual or even unacceptable?*

2. *What does holism say about the following three issues: (a)What counts as smart? (b)What happens to the activity professions? (c)What happens to the significance of performance?*

3. *How do holistic practitioners act or behave differently, particularly in terms of diagnosis, intervention, and assessment? Can you give an example of concrete holistic actions in each of these three areas?*

4. *What does it mean to "go for the meaning" and "go for the habits?" Why are these important interventions for holistic practitioners?*

5. *Give one example of a strategy that encourages opportunities to create personal importance. Give one example of a strategy that expedites the development of good habits.*

◆ *Part III* ◆

THE SUBJECT MATTER OF KINESIOLOGY

This section analyzes our subject matter—work, play, games, sport, and other activity forms. However, the focus is on two cultural forms of activity, play and games. These two kinds of movement stimulate personal meaning, an important key to promoting an active lifestyle.

In chapter 8, you will be introduced to play, including deep and shallow play, how we come to play, and how playgrounds are grown. You'll also learn some tips for manufacturing play.

Chapter 9 follows a similar analysis for games. I claim that games are a fundamental human activity and that they have their own distinct value. We will examine differences between shallow and deep games. And once again, you'll learn tips for promoting games.

8

Creating Movement Playgrounds

© Associated Press

Across the centuries, human beings have spent much time, energy, and ingenuity coming up with ways to relieve themselves of difficult physical work. Today we are the beneficiaries of untold numbers of laborsaving devices, machines that supply much of the muscle power that people once spent on everything from harvesting crops to washing clothes. This trend from greater to less physical exertion generally has been regarded as a sign of human progress, even as a requirement for the rise of civilization (Arendt 1958). The benefits of reducing labor are obvious:

◆ Less physical discomfort, less risk of injury

◆ The capacity to get many tasks done faster and better

◆ More leisure time

◆ The ability to choose physical activities we want to do, not ones that we have to do

◆ More time for high-culture activities such as listening to music, reading, tending to spiritual interests

◆ Less time spent on low-culture activities such as finding food, securing shelter, protecting ourselves and our offspring

This trend away from the physically active lifestyle leaves us with several questions.

◆ Is movement still needed? If the answer is yes, how can kinesiologists make the strongest case for its preservation and cultivation?

◆ Is the health and fitness argument the strongest case we can make?

◆ Where does play fit in?

◆ What exactly is play?

◆ Why is it so fundamental in human existence?

◆ And why is it one of the most important tools in our professional toolbox?

CHAPTER OBJECTIVES

In this chapter, you will

◆ *review the argument for health and the active lifestyle,*

◆ *examine the case for play,*

◆ *see why movement playgrounds are grown rather than found, and*

◆ *learn about one set of strategies for producing deep play.*

THE CASE FOR HEALTH THROUGH ACTIVE LIVING

Everyone from the surgeon general to the American Medical Association now agrees on at least one thing: sitting kills. It shortens life as surely as driving recklessly, eating a diet high in saturated fats, or smoking a pack of cigarettes a day (Blair et al. 1996). Chapter 5 stated that activity reduces risks related to everything from heart disease to certain kinds of cancer (USDHHS 1996; Booth et al. 2002). Data indicate that, in spite of a national fascination with sports and an increase in the availability of recreational facilities in North America, three times as many adolescents were overweight in 2000 compared to 1980. A good portion of this increase is related to physical inactivity, not just poor diet (Ogden et al. 2002; Hill and Peters 1998).

Even the most sedentary human being would have to admit that this research is impressive. Even people who fight off urges to exercise by lying down until the feeling passes would have to acknowledge that this lifestyle carries high, unnecessary risks. On top of a mountain of persuasive data we can state our case emphatically and clearly: "Move to live! Move to live longer! Move to live with more energy and vitality!" End of argument.

As a result of this airtight evidence, we should be witnessing a rush to movement. Surprisingly, we are not. The President's Council on Physical Fitness and Sport reports that 33% of the nation's youth are obese, and 2/3 of all adults in the United States do not get even the minimum amount of exercise needed for basic health benefits. The fact is that citizens in many societies are overfed and

Still life—once it referred only to certain paintings; it now describes the habits of many.

thoroughly bound to TV, CDs, DVDs, video games, automobiles, chairs, and beds. In the face of energy-saving devices, choices, and behavioral patterns, what chance do kinesiologists have to motivate the masses to live more actively?

Movement As Work

The message of active lifestyle and health is one of common sense. Ultimately, it is an appeal to rational self-interest. It assumes that we respond to good logic. When we hear a compelling reason to do something, more often than not we will do it.

The health and fitness message also casts movement in the role of a tool. Whether or not individuals enjoy movement or have any other intrinsic attachment to it, they should adopt exercise for extrinsic reasons, namely that movement produces important health benefits. A little discomfort, some costs, and a modest time commitment are well worth it when the outcome is a longer, healthier life. If the activity is fun, all the better, but the central motivation is extrinsic. Movement is a tool that gets people something that they want. Consequently, movement is work.

This method of describing and using our subject matter is powerful. We should and must use it to improve medical education, convince school boards to expand physical education, and inform social policy. But it also has limitations. A philosophic analysis of movement as work will show us these weaknesses.

Limitations of Movement As Work

The major philosophic weakness of movement as work is that intrinsic values, or experiences that are ends in themselves, usually trump extrinsic values, or experiences that are means to other ends. The argument boils down to this: Extrinsic values depend on intrinsic worth. Tools are good only because they build something else. It is not the experience of running, sweating, or lifting weights that people want. It is what the tool of exercise builds: a longer, more productive, and meaningful existence. Where great end values exist, tools that get us there take on greater value. The converse is also true—where there is little end value, tool value declines accordingly. This dependence on end values raises serious questions about putting all of our motivational eggs in the extrinsic basket, even though strategically some of them need to go there.

A second weakness of movement as work is that this argument doesn't affect some of the individuals who need it most—our young people. It is in the formative years that we develop good dietary and movement habits, but young children do not have the intellectual and experiential resources to appreciate the extrinsic-movement argument. They need to be pulled into movement prerationally. Even teenagers and young adults, who have the cognitive hardware to understand the logic of self-interest, are often not emotionally ready to make such potentially sacrificial decisions. They think of themselves as bulletproof. The risks of old age are perceived as too far off to be meaningful. Movement for health reasons

The only reason I put up with this is to get that!

becomes a hard sell, and many youths are not buying. Statistics show that, in spite of ubiquitous messages about healthful living, activity declines as children grow older (USDHHS 1996, 2001).

The statistics for older adults are not much better. Over 50% of mature patients treated for cardiovascular disease return to old patterns of eating and inactivity within one year of the intervention (Dishman 1988, 1994). This is a remarkable statistic for one simple reason: If anyone is ready to take to heart the prudential message, it should be those who have had near-death experiences. But even among these individuals, the success rate of converting a chronic sitter into a daily mover is not particularly good. This raises serious questions about treating human beings as if they were simply, or even primarily, rational creatures. Perhaps we should put only a few of our motivational eggs in the extrinsic basket.

Third, doubts about the force of appeals to rational self-interest have led to strategies to upgrade enjoyment. While the central message in many educational and therapeutic settings is still "activity is good for you," the methods for getting people moving are designed to be pleasant, perhaps even fun:

◆ Fitness facilities have TVs located in front of treadmills so that clients can enjoy a favorite show while putting in the miles.

◆ Most facilities add music to the exercise environment.

◆ Many professionals recommend that cardiac patients walk with friends so they can enjoy one another.

◆ School programs downplay excessive competition, emphasize success, and include a broad range of popular recreational activities, not just team sports.

The problem is that fun wears out. What was novel and pleasant today becomes commonplace and even distasteful tomorrow. When the sugar wears off the pill, the pill is still there and it still needs to be swallowed. Fun helps the medicine go down; it does not turn it into a tasteful meal. While fun may get people moving for awhile, it is typically not enough to overcome deeply ingrained sedentary habits. Thus, it is probably wise not to put all our motivational eggs in the fun basket, though some of them deserve to go there.

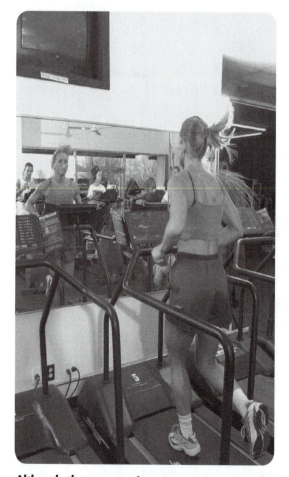

Although the message in many movement settings is that "activity is good for you," the methods for getting people moving are designed to be pleasant, perhaps even fun.

Finally, looking back at the loser's bracket for the dualism and materialism tournaments in chapter 5 reinforces doubts about promoting movement solely or even primarily in terms of utility (see pages 81-87 and 90-96). You will recall that in the dualistic tournament, utility did not become important until game 3. Before we even got to movement as useful, we had already lost two games that speak to quality of life: the possession of knowledge and understanding (game 1) and the possession of intellectual skills (game 2). Even though the structure of this tournament is deeply flawed, it does have a point. Concerns about quality of life often defeat concerns about quantity of life.

Our current analysis of movement as work helps us see that human beings do not live by prudence alone. We are built for play, not just for work. We always have an eye trained on the joy and meaning in our lives, not just on existence itself. Any comprehensive approach to motivation in movement has to speak to all sides of the human equation—the blind love of play as well as the 20/20 vision of careful calculation and work.

Any holistic practitioner who meets the full needs and interests of a client needs to develop skills both as a sober, competent physician and as a loving, playful teacher.

In chapter 5 we also struggled in the tournament of optimal health. Its principles of longevity, functionality, and efficiency threatened many forms of movement, particularly the games we often find most meaningful. Tools retain their value only as long as no other tool can do the job better. While we certainly do not want to overlook the important health benefits of movement, we have to be realistic in anticipating the day when biochemistry and genetic engineering may create health benefits that used to come only with elevated heart rates. The active lifestyle as a prerequisite for longevity, vitality, and overall health could become an antique, a roped-off display in the museum of health promotion. Consequently, we may not want to use health and fitness as our sole justification for existence.

Philosophic Exercise

Educational strategies for improving the behavior of youth and adolescents often rely heavily on extrinsic motivation. These tactics typically involve both sticks (punishment and penalties) and carrots (incentives and rewards). The argument in defense of this tactic goes something like this:

1. Young people understand rewards and punishments. This method gets their attention. It works.

2. Young people cannot immediately appreciate the intrinsic rewards of a behavior. Eventually such appreciation will increase, but in the meantime, extrinsic motivation will get them going.

3. At some point in the future, intrinsic fun and meaning will replace extrinsic rewards and penalties.

What motivation does your kinesiology profession use most frequently to promote behavior modification? Is it common practice to move from extrinsic to intrinsic motivation? If so, does this strategy appear to work? If you were a practitioner who wanted to emphasize movement as play, what would some of the dangers be of relying heavily on extrinsic motivation at the outset of your intervention?

Social Excesses and Human Responses

In the first edition of *Practical Philosophy of Sport* (1994), I made much of three excesses that plague many Western cultures—excess survivalism, rationalism, and individualism. Some 10 years later, the scene has shifted ever so slightly. It is not that these excesses have disappeared; to be sure, all three are alive and well.

Under extreme survivalism we still

◆ have an inordinate focus on health,

◆ use workouts as a psychological fix,

◆ recreate to "recharge the batteries," and

◆ regard winning as a life-and-death necessity.

Under runaway individualism we still

◆ rely on personal, isolated decision-making to improve lifestyle,

◆ recommend individual rather than team activities,

◆ see an absence of community-based values and little group consensus on sport ethics, and

◆ hear clichés such as "go for the gusto" and "do your own thing."

Under oppressive rationalism we still

◆ see a field of kinesiology that is dominated by the findings of science over the traditions of culture;

◆ witness an amoral fascination with higher, faster, stronger;

◆ see more interest in records than heroes; and

◆ see many avenues of life remain unadorned by the spirit and reality of play.

The difference today is that we can better see counterreactions to these excesses. Rather than choosing simply to live long, prudent, and individualistic lives, people are opting for meaning, excitement, quality of life, and community. Individuals are choosing jobs and job locations that prioritize lifestyle over work (Shellenbarger 2004). Strong communities continue to form around a variety of recreational activities, from hunting and fishing to hiking and distance running. Extreme sports are luring people from the moderate, safe, and prudent to the immoderate, high-commitment, and sometimes high-risk domains. Individualistic and opportunistic ethics are being countered by community efforts to develop standards for the common good.

The upshot of these excesses and countermoves is that while play may be shaped and victimized by our society, it refuses to be extinguished. Play is a fundamental activity—genetically, biologically, psychologically, socioculturally, philosophically, and spiritually (Huizinga 1950; Ellis 1973; Ackerman 1999). Additionally, it has been indissolubly linked with sensuality and movement (Sheets-Johnstone 1999). Of course, excess survivalism might discourage the excesses and imprudence of play. Certainly, excess rationalism may force adults to hide their play. And excess individualism may give some play the unpleasant aftertaste of loneliness. However, it appears that play cannot be stamped out. No political or economic system, no religious doctrine, and no rulers have been able to get rid of it, even though some have tried. Play would seem to be rooted in something more durable than the waxing and waning of cultural fancy, religious doctrine, or political ideology.

THE NATURE OF PLAY

Play is freely chosen (Huizinga 1950). It is not the consequence of duty, fear, necessity, or even courageous self-sacrifice. Rather, it is what those who have a light and adventuresome heart *want* to do. For this reason we often associate play with children. They are not the only ones who need to play, but they exemplify the spirit required for play to take over one's life, if only sporadically and for short periods of time. They allow the spontaneous to trump the planned, a pre-rational invitation to beat out a studied game plan. In a flattering sense, players are delightful and unpredictable fools (Cox 1969; Harper 1973-76).

Play is also fragile and temporary (Suits 1977; Schmitz 1972; Fink 1960). It is an oasis of intrinsic meaning and joy in a desert of responsibility and work. Because we are biological creatures who are inclined above all else to protect ourselves, the spirit of play might be broken at any moment by necessity. Even for play-intoxicated children who have forgotten what time it is late on some warm summer afternoon, the reality of dinner, parents, and rules about getting home before dark still looms in the background. Even for the strongest players, this oasis offers but a temporary place of respite in a larger biopsychological journey of need.

If we were to speculate about the evolutionary sequence of events that produced us, we might picture one-celled animals first moving to find food or shelter or to promote reproduction (Sheets-Johnstone 1999). They were hardwired to do these things, and they did them over and over. But along the way they too were distracted by whatever primeval playgrounds meet the fancy of one-celled animals. At some fateful moment, they hesitated, and they played. At some level of primitive intelligence, they enjoyed the movement for its own sake.

Because our wiring is more complex than these one-celled animals, we are less tightly tethered to necessity (Midgley 1994; Pinker 2002; Ridley 2003). We have more room to play, and potential

© Empics

In today's win-at-all-cost sport we sometimes push play off the playground.

playgrounds lie everywhere. We are inclined to trade work for play, and some have recommended that this is exactly the way we should live our lives (Morgan 1982; Lasch 1979; Pieper 1952). We should not play or otherwise recharge our batteries on small oases of play just so we can return to the large desert of work. Rather we should spend only as much time as necessary on small islands of work in order to play as long as we can in the large, open spaces of the world's playgrounds. In our workaholic world, according to these authors, we have turned things upside down.

Even so, and even if we were able to get our priorities straightened out, work still looms. We still share a common fate with our evolutionary ancestors: Eventually we must tend to a variety of biological, psychological, and social necessities. Play therefore involves a periodic reallocation of time, energy, and attention (Suits 1977). For mere mortals, play is temporary and fragile.

Human Resources for Play

Human beings come into the world built to play. In a very real sense, play is at least part of our destiny. This claim is neither a speculative hope about how we would like things to be nor a stipulation from some god's-eye point of view. Rather it is a rough-and-ready description of human behavior.

Plenty of anthropological, sociological, and phenomenological information suggests that across the centuries, whether conditions are good or not, people have danced, frolicked, and moved just for the fun of it. They have done this behind their caves, along the lanes next to their crops, and in the backyards of suburbia (Huizinga 1950; Sheets-Johnstone 1999). Play cannot be snuffed out by concentration camps, war, grinding poverty, or even by becoming adults and receiving a higher education. It would appear that, whether conditions are favorable or not, we are ready to play.

One resource for play comes from our embodiment. We take up space; thus we can encounter physical places we call playgrounds. We live coherent projects across time; thus we can encounter periods in our lives that we identify as playtime. We are social creatures who share lived time and space with others; thus we make contact with playmates. And finally, as embodied individuals we are alternately driven by necessity and temporarily relieved of such requirements; thus, we encounter play opportunities when we can break the means–ends relationships typical of work.

Higher Intelligence As a Foundation for Play

The grounding of play in embodiment runs even deeper. Returning once again to the primeval ooze of the earliest forms of life, we might speculate that primitive intelligence allowed sentient beings to make the crucial distinction between here and there. This distinction is a prerequisite for all intentional movement and thus the foundation of virtually all projects. One could even argue that intelligence developed as an ever-increasing cleverness in getting from one place to another

(Sheets-Johnstone 1999). Certainly this early movement was not self-conscious or reflective in ways that would make sense to us. But neither was it the blind, physics-dominated movement of rocks and other inanimate physical objects. These animals were employing some criteria to move efficiently, effectively, and thus skillfully.

A second major cognitive advance had to do with the connection between moving skillfully and getting what was wanted or needed, such as food, shelter, territory, and safety from predators. This marked the evolutionary dawn of work and prudential behavior.

Then a dangerous thing happened, something that has both blessed and plagued living beings ever since. Primitive creatures began to notice that the journey had its own charms. Simply getting from here to there could be fun, whether or not the work was successfully completed. From this time forward, the intellectual foundation for joy, the risk of being off-task, and the pleasure of following the heart were in place.

What was the basis of this fun? And why did primitive animals get distracted by the inherent joys of the trip? Once again, answers to these questions cannot be separated from embodiment. The trip included sensuous delights, such as tickles, temperatures, and textures. It provided variety and adventure in an existence that mostly involved staying put. It may have added challenge to an otherwise routine existence. As evolution advanced, such trips from here to there may have involved imagination, the taking on of interesting roles. If movement continued after food and shelter were secured, it may have taken the form of primitive celebration.

The development of play has been going on for hundreds of thousands of years, and we biological creatures have been getting better at it. Today, as more capable beings, players and playgrounds have been transformed. Human play is distinctive, reflecting all that we have become and all that we can do. Nevertheless, as the progeny of those ancestral players, we are firmly tethered to our embodied roots, to those advances made by the first creatures that went from one side of a prehistoric puddle to the other and found the journey enjoyable. An appreciation of our rootedness in play, as we will see, should make a difference in how kinesiologists look for play and promote it.

Philosophic Exercise

Do you think that intelligence is a double-edged sword when it comes to the promotion of play? I have portrayed it as a prerequisite for play, but it could also be true that as we have gotten smarter and smarter, play has become more difficult. In fact, we associate play with children and perhaps too with their lesser intellectual sophistication.

See if you can identify two or three reasons why higher levels of intelligence might actually make play more difficult to experience. In terms of promoting play, do you think it unwise to get too smart?

FINDING AND GROWING PLAYGROUNDS

The importance of play has not been lost on practitioners in our field. If youngsters are to develop patterns of active living, they must find activity to be fun. Corbin (2002) noted, "One key point is that children are concrete rather than abstract thinkers and will not do activity simply because 'it is good for them.' Instead, they are active because they enjoy it" (131). Many others have also trumpeted the importance of putting fun back into physical education or the exercise prescription (see Griffin et al. 1993; Kimiecik and Harris 1996; Kretchmar 2000a, 2000b; Scanlan and Simmons 1992; Suppaporn and Griffin 1998; Wankel 1993).

So what has gone wrong? Why are children sitting too much? A philosophy of play can help answer these questions and provide clues for how practitioners can become better playmakers.

Shallow and Deep Play

Play comes in different sizes, shapes, and textures. Because of this, dichotomous thinking that pits work against play is not entirely helpful. We can make more headway by describing variations of play, such as weak play, good play, better play, and deep play. If play is to be the engine that drives an active lifestyle in a world that has powerful disincentives for movement, it had better be powerful. Four-cylinder engines, or all varieties of shallow play, are probably not up to the task.

Is this boy heading toward the open waters of deep play? Will he ever become a soccer player?

Shallow play could be described in any number of ways. Its primary motivation comes from intrinsic sources. After all, it is fun, something we look forward to. But for some reason the activity does not grab us at our core. Thus it tends to be superficial. It does not last long, and it merely diverts and entertains. As I said earlier, it puts a sugar coating on what, for some people, is the unpleasant pill of physical activity. Shallow play does not engage the imagination; it does not inspire; it does not carry us away on wings of delight (Kretchmar 2000a, 2000b, 2004).

Invitations to play that are marked only by fun have a limited shelf life. And such invitations must compete with similar invitations, including those from the computer, the TV, the cell phone, and the chair at the dinner table. Because fun can be had most anywhere, our chances for victory are not particularly good when we compete on those terms. Shallow play is better than mindless repetitions at the gym, but as ammunition for conversions to active living, it often turns out to be too little, too late.

Deep play is personal. It becomes part of who we are and, perhaps even more important, who we are in the process of becoming. We can have fun experimenting with tennis, for example. It can be enjoyable to hit the ball in the center of the racket, to see it fly over the net and land in the opponent's court, to compete, and to win. But it is another thing to *become* a tennis player, to have the game become part of your identity.

Symptoms of advanced stages in this evolution might include the following: sneaking in extra tennis games, purchasing subscriptions to an unreasonable number of tennis magazines, fussing over equipment and protecting it as if it were your own child, planning your day or week around tennis, missing work for tennis, and honoring the game and its rules like a religious canon and respecting the court as a temple. When these or other symptoms show up, improving your game is not a trivial matter. Finding your serve, for example, will be a cause for delirious joy, as tennis player Adam Smith discovered after consulting with a tennis-playing Zen master (Smith 1985).

> We set up an empty tennis-ball can in the corner of the service court. I know, those kids in California and Florida who are out hitting 360 days a year, who hit 500 serves a day for practice, can knock over the empty can a couple of times a day, but weekend players can't even get the ball in the court.
>
> "Slow it down more. More. Please body, send the ball—"
>
> "Please, body, send the ball—"
>
> "Slower. Slower. Make time stand still. No time."
>
> Zank! The empty tennis-ball can went up into the air and bounced metallically.
>
> "Who did that?" I said.
>
> The tennis guru said nothing. He handed me another ball. It went into the corner of the service court, on roughly the same spot. So did the next one.
>
> I began to giggle wildly. I danced around a little, the scarecrow had a brain, the cowardly lion had courage, I had a serve.

Tennis that has become deep play will no longer be a way to simply spend your free time. As Ackerman (1999), Murphy and White (1995), Novak (1976) and so many others have pointed out, altered states of consciousness, or what might be called moments of spiritual transcendence, are likely to occur when your relationship with a movement practice becomes intimate and intense. Over the years, we have developed descriptions for such encounters with ecstasy, including "playing in the zone," "having a peak experience," or simply "flow." Craig Lambert (1998, 124-125) had such an experience while rowing on the Charles River near Boston.

> The boat is perfectly level. Set up beautifully, we skim the surface on an invisible laser beam running from horizon to horizon. There is no friction; we ride the natural cadence of our strokes, a continuous cycle. The crew breathes as one. Inhale on the recovery, exhale as we drive our blades through the water: inspiration and expression. *In. Out.* Row with one body and so with one mind. Nothing exists but: *Here. Now. This.* Rushing water bubbles under our hull, as

if a mountain brook buried within the Charles flows directly beneath us. I have never heard this sound before, but I know it means we are doing something right. Rowers have a word for this frictionless state: *swing*. The experience of swing is what hooks people on rowing. The appetite for swing is limitless.

A game can become a ritual, a ceremony that reminds and inspires more than it entertains and sedates (Lasch 1979). In a sense, game commitments have the surrogate religious function of giving us focus, and showing us what really matters in our development as a human being. Michael Novak (1976, 150-151) once wrote about the potential of sport for spiritual revelation.

> I love tests of the human spirit. I love to see defeated teams refuse to die. I love to see impossible odds confronted. I love to see impossible dares accepted. I love to see the incredible grace lavished on simple plays—the simple flashing beauty of perfect form—but, even more, I love to see the heart that refuses to give in, refuses to panic, seizes opportunity, slips through defenses, exerts itself far beyond capacity, forges momentarily of its bodily habitat an instrument of almost perfect will. I love it when the other side is willing and there are only moments left; I love it when it would be reasonable to be reconciled to defeat, but one will not, cannot; I love it when the last set of calculated, reckless, free, and impassioned efforts is crowned with success. When I see others play that way, I am full of admiration, of gratitude. That is the way I believe the human race should live. When human beings actually accomplish it, it is for me as if the intentions of the Creator were suddenly limpid before our eyes; as though into the fiery heart of the Creator we had momentary insight.

The appetite for swing is limitless.

Sport psychologists may worry about deep play because human beings are prone to what is called "exercise dependence" and to other forms of overdoing it. A playground that becomes too deep, they caution us, could be unhealthy. While we should undoubtedly heed these warnings, in a world of short attention spans and an inability to get past the temporary pleasures of fun, an emphasis on the meaningful and seductive call of deep playgrounds is a risk worth taking. To convert sedentary individuals to a life of activity, it may even be a necessity. To help our students and clients find the better and more captivating varieties of play, we need to become highly skillful playmakers. We need to understand how human beings grow into play.

Playgrounds Are Made, Not Found

Many kinesiologists think of their role in promoting play as one of a matchmaker. Their model for professional activity goes something like this:

- ◆ The statement of faith: We are all born with at least one playground that is meant for us.
- ◆ The empirical observation: Students typically come to us without knowing what their special activity is or where that special playground can be found.
- ◆ The game plan: They must be introduced to as wide a range of activities as possible in hopes of finding one or more of these playgrounds.
- ◆ The outcome: When the students and this special movement playground meet, the students will play happily ever after and will, from that time forward, embody an active lifestyle.

According to this model, different playgrounds are items on a smorgasbord, each one with a different texture, flavor, and aroma. The professional arranges these entrées on a long table and clients queue up at one end, grab a plate, and start down the line. Postcardiac patients get lists of activities that produce safe and helpful heart rates, such as walking, biking, exercising in front of the TV, hiking, swimming, gardening, and square dancing. Schoolchildren are introduced to numerous activities, usually two weeks at a time. Tennis, golf, jogging, weight training, volleyball, off-road biking, in-line skating, skiing, and others make up an attractive menu of possibilities. Health-oriented vacationers have various options, including white-water rafting, mountain climbing, horseback riding, skiing, golfing, snowboarding, and hang gliding. In all cases it is believed that we will find a movement that suits our tastes. Once the activity moves from the table to the plate, the hidden playground will have been revealed. Activity for a lifetime will be the happy result.

This approach of putting people in touch with their movement playgrounds has worked for some. But this mode of thought about players and playgrounds has enjoyed very limited success if current statistics on inactivity can be traced to its doorstep. Even if this empirical claim cannot be substantiated, philosophically the notion of playgrounds as places in the world that are simply discovered is fundamentally flawed. Neither players nor playgrounds are fixed entities, and neither players nor playgrounds develop independently of one another (Merleau-Ponty 1962; Torres 2002).

The player–playground relationship works more like this: Would-be players, exhibiting certain qualities of play capability, meet would-be playgrounds that exhibit certain kinds of play possibilities. While there may be an initial attraction, this is not essential. It is what happens after the first encounter that determines the fate of the player and the potential playground. The player might have some fun on the playground and then go his separate way. Or the player and playground may spend time together, eventually transforming one another during their lives together. Playgrounds are grown more than they are found. Rich play relationships develop. They do not show up full-blown and eternally durable.

If this idea of play approaches the truth, we should focus more on growing, not finding, playgrounds. If we are to be powerful agents for change for our students or clients, we need to be play cultivators rather than matchmakers.

Philosophic Exercise

With all the varieties of dance, sport, games, and recreation, we have an almost limitless number of potential activity playgrounds. We are a little bit like English teachers who are the educational custodians of a library full of wonderful books. We are the custodians of a library full of marvelous movement opportunities. It would be wonderful if our students could get behind the covers of a good number of the movement classics.

This idea runs somewhat against the notion of patiently growing playgrounds. If we patiently grow the mountain-biking playground, there may not be enough time left to make square dancing, weightlifting, and waterskiing into deep playgrounds for our students or us.

What do you think we should do here? Is a compromise in order? Does the mix of in-depth experiences and superficial introductions depend on the situation? Develop a coherent position on this and then try to defend it to a colleague or classmate.

GROWING PLAYERS AND PLAYGROUNDS

The process of developing players and playgrounds is more suited to apprentice forms of education than didactic approaches. We can see this by examining what occurs as playgrounds and players are grown.

How Places Become Playgrounds

First encounters with potential playgrounds are not always full of great fun or excitement. In fact, at first blush the environment may not appeal much at all.

© Photodisc

On the first date, some playgrounds do not look particularly attractive.

The playground just sits there and does not issue any invitation whatsoever. Sometimes it may even intimidate the would-be player. The formidable cliff, the significant running distance, the choppy body of water, even the stationary golf ball may evoke beads of sweat, not goose bumps of joy.

Short introductions usually will not do. Sometimes they just reinforce fears or confirm reasons for disinterest, particularly if the playground requires skills, knowledge, and attitudes that we do not yet possess. Brief introductions that are supposed to provide love-at-first-sight partnerships too often produce boredom or anxiety instead (Csikszentmihalyi 1975, 1990).

Urgings by a physical-education teacher, cardiac-rehabilitation specialist, or kinesiologist are also unlikely to work. While verbal enthusiasm and good body language can be contagious, ultimately our students have to find and make that place *their* playground. While we can ask would-be players to repeat after us, "This is a cool place to be," such mantras do not usually produce a playground. Those who come to us looking for interesting movement cannot be talked into deep play.

Rather, they begin to take the first small steps, ideally with someone who is familiar with the playground as their guide. A skill gained, a fear overcome, some knowledge transmitted—would-be players rub shoulders with this new environment, watching the mentor who is so comfortable there, trying, testing, venturing a little further out. Eventually, the playground begins to talk; it starts to come alive. Almost magically, it begins to morph into a special, personal playground for this individual. Such converts can hardly believe that this vibrant playground is the same one to which they were first introduced. And, in truth, it is not.

A playground is not a fixed thing, then. It is not simply a physical place full of toys or other neat objects. Rather, it is a partner, a constantly changing companion that may not be lovable at the start of the relationship but can eventually become so. In fact, it can become so tightly tethered to the player that life without it becomes unthinkable.

How People Become Players

When would-be players first visit a playground, they may not know what to do. No personal challenges or interests have anything to do with this place. No individual habits or skills allow the players to engage the environment. But this does not necessarily mean that their current incapacities cannot be overcome. It simply means that requisite muscles and attitudes for this particular playground have not yet been developed. The player inside lies dormant, waiting to be awakened.

Once again, a mentor can be helpful. Potential players need to touch the playground to become play-grounded. They need to develop the capabilities required by this domain to become play-skilled. They need to connect their ongoing life story to the challenges of this location to become play-motivated. They need to care deeply about the achievements that hang in the balance on this terrain to become play-valued. The master teacher knows all this and can point would-be players in the right direction.

Little by little the playground transforms the players. The players take on an identity forged by repeated encounters with this place and its requirements. The breaststroker who finds deep play in watery environments *is* a swimmer. He is not someone who just happens to trifle with water. The mountain biker who finds deep play on the seat of her two-wheeler *is* a cyclist, not just someone who experiences momentary fun out in the wild. Values change, worldviews change, skills change, spaces and distances change. Hard becomes easy, far becomes close, the mechanical becomes expressive, someone else's challenge becomes your challenge. The playground has become part of the player.

Consequently, the same things can be said of players that were previously claimed about play-

© Photodisc

Players are grown, not found.

grounds. Players are not fixed entities. Players change constantly as skills, attitudes, and values grow little by little. In the process of discovering that special playground, individuals become discriminating players by cultivating the play potential they possessed from the start. And as long as the partnership endures, players will continue to add new and interesting chapters to their story.

Growing Playgrounds: A Case Study

Several years ago Bane McCracken developed a novel outdoor education curriculum for his high school students in West Virginia (Pennington and Krouscas 1999). In many ways his program followed the principles of Siedentop's sport education, a brand of holistic physical education that I described in chapter 7. Like Siedentop, McCracken was on the lookout for play. And like Siedentop, he knew that this required more than simple, short-term introductions. McCracken patiently led his students into the subculture of different activities. He got them past the front gate of fun and at least a few steps into the kingdom of deep play. He literally grew a playground for the majority of his students. How did he do it?

First, he selected a group of outdoor activities that were popular and readily available in the area—mountain biking, skiing, hiking, and camping. This was crucial for at least two reasons. His students would, at minimum, be familiar with them, so he would not have to start from scratch. But more important, McCracken had an available set of out-of-school opportunities. He knew that in-class time would not be enough. From the start, the curriculum included recreational activities (and portfolio accountability) for weekend and after-school involvement.

Second, he set high standards. He challenged his students to get fit, lose weight, and learn how to negotiate long distances and hills on bike rides in the mountains. At first students complained. But when they realized they were developing new bodies, and when the mountain biking became easier, attitudes changed to delight and gratitude.

Third, with the use of portfolios, he helped students enter the subculture of outdoor life. They learned the values of ecology, principles of safety, information about the weather, and some of the lore associated with these popular activities. Many students reported buying new outdoor equipment or asking for it at the first Christmas or birthday opportunity. Some indicated that they now spent time with friends, parents, or grandparents in one or more of these outdoor pursuits.

Not everyone in McCracken's class tasted the fruits of deep play. Some were entertained, had a bit of fun, but did not progress much beyond that. Some did not like the hard work. But many of his students clearly began to grow a personal playground, one that promised to distract and delight them for a lifetime.

REVIEW

We can present movement to our students and clients as work or play. While both are important, play has an advantage, particularly when we are trying to promote an active lifestyle. Human beings are built to play. We are drawn to the intrinsic over the extrinsic. We pursue delight. However, play comes in gradations, and the level of involvement called deep play holds the greatest promise for conversions. In order to reach this level of deep play, we need to patiently grow playgrounds. Kinesiologists and physical educators have developed techniques that can expedite this process.

LOOKING AHEAD

If play is a fundamental tool in our professional toolbox, so are games. Some literature confuses games and play, talking about them as if they were the same thing. But, as we will see, games are quite different. Anyone who wants to become an expert at promoting an active lifestyle must understand games and shrewdly employ them.

CHECKING YOUR UNDERSTANDING

1. *Explain how movement can be portrayed either as work or play. What are the key differences between the two approaches?*

2. *Identify two or three disadvantages of selling movement as important and useful. Why is it not entirely effective?*

3. *Describe play. What is the difference between shallow and deep play? Why is it important to make this distinction?*

4. *What is the difference between finding and growing a playground? How does this distinction change the way kinesiologists deal with clients and students?*

5. *Provide at least three practical tips for growing playgrounds. Why do these tips seem to work?*

9

Understanding Games, Competition, and Winning

American philosopher John Searle (1999) once poked fun at his own discipline by suggesting that common sense has consistently won out over the theories of famous philosophers. But he went on to say that there was one notable exception—the public acceptance of mind–body dualism, the idea that people are composed of separate mental and physical parts.

Kinesiologists could offer a second common misperception: the belief that games are trivial. It is difficult to find anyone who thinks that games should occupy any seat of honor in the good life. Such phrases as "It's only a game" are deeply ingrained in our language and psyche. We've also heard people ask, "Are you serious, or are you playing some kind of game with me?" Like play, games tend to be associated more with childhood than later life. Participating in games is fine for youngsters, particularly if those activities have some educational value, but for adults, games come after work and even then must be "kept in perspective." While we spend considerable passion rooting for favorite teams and devote much energy to winning games, we eventually come back to reality and remember that none of this is "a matter of life and death."

This common take on games is consistent with the unhappy fate we faced in the dualistic tournament in chapter 5. There we saw that games are associated with low culture. In game 4, games and other forms of physical play faced the fine arts. Motor skill on the soccer field was pitted against motor skill at the keyboard. High culture trounced low culture, resulting in our fourth and final defeat in that poorly conceived tournament.

In spite of this liability, many vigorous movement opportunities come in the form of games. As noted in chapter 8, laborsaving devices have made work-related physical activity unnecessary for most industrialized societies. If people are going to move in any vigorous way, games are one of the major avenues for doing so. Consequently, any disrespect shown to games, whether merited or not, has serious consequences for us in kinesiology. This leaves us with a number of puzzling questions.

CHAPTER OBJECTIVES

In this chapter, you will

◆ *review the nature of games and see how they differ from play,*

◆ *begin to appreciate the power and significance of games,*

◆ *consider the value of competition, and*

◆ *determine whether winning is overrated.*

◆ Would it be wiser to disassociate ourselves from games and emphasize movement or exercise?

◆ Should we rally a defense for games and keep them near the front of our professional portfolios?

◆ If games have redeeming features, do they include competition? Or should we support noncompetitive game playing?

THE NATURE OF GAMES

Suits' (1972) definition of games is one of the clearest and most accurate available:

> To play a game is to engage in an activity directed toward bringing about a specific state of affairs, using only means permitted by specific rules, where the means permitted by the rules are more limited in scope than they would be in the absence of the rules, and where the sole reason for accepting such limitation is to make possible such activity.

Put more simply, "Playing a game is the voluntary attempt to overcome unnecessary obstacles" (22). Games are artificial tests. Because these activities are not natural problems and have to be constructed, they need rules. Game rules perform at least four functions (see figure 9.1).

1. Game rules establish the problem, or the challenge. This, of course, is the heart of the game. The problem involves something to be done (a goal) against a set of means (allowances and disallowances). If the modulation of these two factors is done well and the resulting challenge is neither too hard nor too easy, a provocative problem is the result. Game players encounter an "opposition by cut" (Kretchmar 1975) and experience the delicious uncertainty or "sweet tension" (Fraleigh 1986) that goes with it. Valid opposition by cut has players thinking, "Maybe I can do this thing; maybe I can't."

Because the goal and means make a game intelligible, they need to be calculated together. If the goal is particularly ambitious, the means may need to be relaxed. If the goal is not hard to achieve on its own, then the means may need to be more restrictive. The rules of the game establish the relationship between means and ends. They produce an artificial problem by stipulating what counts and how players are allowed to pursue the goal.

2. Game rules indicate when and how testing starts as well as when and how it comes to an end. The two methods for determining test length are clock time and event time. All games last either for an agreed upon amount of time, such as two 20-minute halves, or until a certain number of events have occurred, such as 18 holes in golf. Soccer, football, and basketball are clock-regulated games. These

Questions	Purposes of the rules
1. What is this game about? What's the goal? What are we allowed and not allowed to do in pursuing the goal?	Define the game.
2. How does the game start and stop? What counts as a complete game?	Indicate the length of time or number of events during which testing occurs.
3. What happens when a rule is violated, equipment breaks, unusual weather conditions intervene, or other extraneous events interrupt the game? How do we get a compromised game back on track?	Stipulate penalties, contingency plans.
4. How would two or more people share this game?	Describe how contests proceed, how winning is determined.

FIGURE 9.1   Four kinds of game questions, four kinds of game rules.

games permit testing literally until time runs out. By way of contrast, baseball, golf, track and field events, figure skating, gymnastics, skiing, and horse and automobile races are event-regulated. They require a certain number of events or tasks to be completed before the testing comes to an end. Testing lasts until the slalom skier negotiates a certain number of gates and crosses the finish line, or until the winning side in baseball has gotten the opponents out 27 times, or until the gymnast has completed the routine.

3. Game rules provide contingency plans for when the activity goes awry. Game rules are violated both intentionally and unintentionally, so games need additional rules to get things back on track. Penalties preserve the integrity of the test against accidental illegal advantages or cheating. A foul shot is awarded in basketball; a penalty kick is taken in soccer; a repeat offender is thrown out of the game. Contingency rules cover a host of other possible occurrences—for instance, when equipment fails, when fans interfere with play, when a player is injured, or when weather conditions prevent valid testing. We might call these guidelines optional or secondary constitutive rules. They are employed strictly on an as-needed basis, and they exist only to serve the purposes of the game.

4. Game rules provide a method for sharing tests and competing. Tests are not contests. Tests provide a problem and produce a score. They do not require more than one party to take the same test, nor do they require two parties to try to outdo one another to produce a winner. Of course tests can be taken repeatedly, and individuals can improve their scores. Some call these improvements "victories" and claim that they "beat themselves," but this is a very different use of the word from its normal employment in reference to actual contests. In short, rules that create the test do not indicate how players will share that test in competition.

In a contest at least two individuals or teams take the same test so that a comparison of scores is meaningful. In addition, all parties must commit to taking the test in a superior way—that is, they must promise to do their best. This too is necessary to make the comparison of scores meaningful. The result is what I have called "opposition by degree." The sweet tension and uncertainty result from trying to do the same thing as one's opponent, only a little bit better.

Rules indicate how the test is to be shared and how players are to pursue this "little bit better" performance. In skiing, for example, rules indicate the order of taking the test—who goes first, who goes second, and so on. Rules also indicate how many times skiers must negotiate the slope before scores are tabulated. These rules might be called regulative rules because they do not stipulate a new problem. They merely formalize pragmatic and ethical understandings related to sharing the test and competing fairly. Like contingency rules, they are optional and used as needed.

Regulative rules are optional because tests do not need to be contests. Testing oneself by going down a ski slope as quickly as possible can be an exciting, meaningful, and otherwise valid human project. Contesting with another skier may embellish the testing project, but it is not required. Later in the chapter we will need to look at the significance of competition, the drive to win, and the ethics of this behavior.

Evolutionary Resources for Gaming

Just as human beings come into the world built to play, so too do we come ready to participate in games. And just like our tendency to play, our curiosity about games did not simply occur to us one day as a logical conclusion. Both play and games are primordial. Both are rooted in our biology and our long evolutionary journey to our current condition.

Darwin showed us that from the beginning of sentient life, all creatures have had to meet challenges. Those who could solve their problems survived and passed on their genes. Those who avoided challenges or were not able to meet them did not fare as well, and their genes died out. Consequently, over time our genetics inclined us toward an interest in problems, attitudes that allow us to persist in solving problems, and intelligences, habits, and skills that are needed to solve these problems. In short, we have been built and rebuilt from the

© Martin Shumway

The human species has been built to take tests successfully.

start of life to take tests successfully. The evolutionary process has selected in favor of better and better problem-solvers.

This side of biological tendency is much different from the one that led to play. You will recall that the speculations in chapter 8 suggested that one-celled animals stumbled upon play by beginning to enjoy the journey for survival. Not much intelligence is needed to encounter intrinsic satisfaction, the satisfying sensations that may accompany satisfying movement. Play, therefore, came into existence in the process of solving natural problems, not artificial ones. Playing preceded gaming. The conversion of natural tests into artificial ones came later.

This evolutionary sequence from play to games makes sense because gaming is the more intellectually demanding of the two. It requires two subjective advances:

◆ An interest in embellishing a challenge—that is, the ability to appreciate that an unnecessary problem may actually be a good thing.

◆ The intellectual ability to connect the means and ends of this artificial test—the capacity to see, for instance, that achieving the end by alternate means does not count.

The first advance is the capacity to appreciate gratuitous logic—to see a value in inventing a new problem or artificially fortifying an old one (Suits 1972; Morgan 1994). The second is the capacity to appreciate constitutive logic—to enter an artificial world where rules stipulate meanings and relationships.

Perhaps this first advance came about something like this. A precocious amoeba sensed two directions that it could take across a puddle to secure the same bit of food, route A and route B. This animal's advanced primitive intelligence allowed it to sense that route B was slightly more dangerous—let's say variable temperatures made it more difficult to reach the food. For hundreds of thousands of years, this amoeba's ancestors were hardwired to take route A. Not a single amoeba was interested in B. And, in terms of survival, this was probably a good thing.

This was not true, however, for this particularly precocious amoeba. Its intellectual capacities rose to the level that permitted an appreciation of gratuity. Route B beckoned, and it beckoned specifically because it presented *more* problems than route A. These were the kinds of problems that might be solved by a clever amoeba, and this one wanted to see if it could do it. So, off the amoeba went on route B.

Not long after moving in the direction of B, our bright amoeba came upon route C. This was a shortcut that led back to the safety of A. By taking this route, the amoeba knew that it was virtually guaranteed access to the food that lay across the puddle. What to do? When it departed, the other amoebas were impressed with its courage and determination. It was, after all, a special amoeba. Perhaps they would not see it take route C. If so, this amoeba could have both fame and fortune without facing any of the risks of route B.

However, our hypothetical amoeba, again somewhat surprisingly, chose to stay on the more difficult route. It sensed that the food would not taste as good if it were gained by defecting to route C. This creature knew that, by choosing route B, it had entered a convention. The rules of this convention would not allow the amoeba to secure the food any old way, but only by fully honoring the requirements of route B. In other words, cheating would not count, even if the food was reached. Happily, this amoeba negotiated the trials of route B and arrived at the food, albeit thoroughly exhausted and somewhat battered and torn. It feasted. The food never tasted so good before.

We might further speculate that this move to gratuitous and conventional logic eventually benefited survival. These creatures were tested in superior ways compared to their duller compatriots. They faced tougher problems; they developed a stronger attachment to the problematic; they gained superior strength, better skills, and more discriminating sensations. When real problems came their way, they were better prepared to compete. Consequently, attraction to gratuity and the ability to enter conventions turned out to be adaptive.

Our precocious ameba was the stronger for the experience. The next time it took route B, it made the journey even faster. During its life, it divided many times. Its offspring, all of whom carried its genes, likewise tended to select route B over route A. While some perished because of their imprudence, many survived and were better for purposely committing to the more difficult path to the food.

Contemporary Resources for Gaming

Our situation is both different and similar. We are obviously not as hardwired as the amoeba; we are less predictable and our lives are not as dominated by survival activities. In many ways we face fewer natural problems. We can fill our days with activities that we want to do, not that we have to do. Suits (1978) suggests that our world is becoming more and more like utopia, a place where all natural problems have been solved.

This turn of events is both fortunate and unfortunate. The fact that we are not consumed by survival and that we have more free time would seem to be a good thing. But with fewer challenges and more time comes something that human beings do not handle very well, and that is boredom. Boredom is excruciatingly painful in a psychological sense. Nothing to do, nowhere to go, nothing of

Boredom, a disease that comes with intelligence.

interest to attend to, nothing meaningful to address—it's better to be asleep or drugged than chronically bored.

This is so because during the course of evolution, we became the best problem-solving creatures that ever walked the face of the earth. As abstract-thinking, tool-making, language-using beings, we are far more inventive, flexible, and thus adaptive than any of our ancestors. We show up on this planet well-prepared to solve incredibly complex problems. We are so good at it, in fact, that we have solved many natural problems related to shelter, nutrition, disease, and procreation. But we face a different problem—too strong a predisposition to solve problems and too few problems that need solving. Enter boredom!

Philosophic Exercise

Based on personal experience, can you validate this claim about the relationship between boredom and games? Can you describe an experience where you turned an otherwise tedious task into a game?

Is it possible to take a relatively boring activity like driving home from work and turn it into a game? How would you do that? Look back at earlier sections of the chapter and see if you can identify the kind of rules you would need to create a game.

1. Establish the game problem—the goals and allowable means.

2. Determine how long the test would last, either by time, such as 20 minutes to see how far you can get, or by event, such as pulling into the driveway.

3. Indicate what happens when the game goes awry, say you encounter a detour.

4. Describe how to share the game in a contest, say your sibling wanted to drive home in her car at the same time to see who would arrive first.

Without challenges, our problem-solving abilities atrophy. Without exercise, our skills decline. Unfortunately, we may be worse off with flabby capabilities than if we had never developed those capabilities in the first place. It could be that, in an evolutionary sense, we are overbuilt for the world in which we now live.

However, this was also the case, at least hypothetically, for our bright amoeba. This little creature got too smart. Repeated trips via route A became too easy and thus tedious. The amoeba experienced boredom, or at least what counts as boredom for an amoeba. Fortunately, intellectual access to gratuity and convention presented route B, and games were born.

In some ways, then, we are not so different after all. We are still finding, inventing, and taking our own route Bs. The roots of our interest in games run deep, perhaps to the core of who we are as intelligent human beings. Nevertheless, as is the case with play, we can learn as much from looking at types of games as from observing the structure of games themselves. Games come in different shapes and sizes, and they perform different functions. As kinesiologists, it would behoove us to examine the varieties of gaming that are the most gratifying.

Deep Games and Shallow Games

All games present an artificial challenge that includes a goal and a specified set of means for achieving it. We understand that if we violate the means accidentally—or even worse, if we cheat—there is a sense that we can no longer achieve the goal. We know too that we undertake the game project just so we can experience the problem that it gives us. In seeking out games, we are looking for challenges. Yet, within this framework, some games satisfy deeply and others do not (Hardman 1999). Some games grab hold of us and fascinate for a lifetime, and others soon wear out and are quickly discarded.

Shallow Games

Shallow games are activities that have little staying power. They attract our attention for a time, the problem they present is provocative, and we take them on with energy. If we cannot solve them, or cannot solve them well, we are upset. If we play these games well, we experience a degree of closure and satisfaction. But we are not compelled to return again and again. We are not driven to take lessons, subscribe to magazines, or take out memberships in the organizations that support these games. In fact, shallow games often lack the institutional support that accompanies deeper activities. Where few people are durably interested in a game, institutional support makes little financial or cultural sense.

Shallow games tend be rigid and simple. While their problems initially attract, they quickly lead to anxiety if they are too hard or boredom if they are too easy. Some brainteasers and interlocking-ring games have these characteristics. Sitting on the couch trying to get two pieces of twisted metal apart can be a good challenge—for awhile. However, if we don't make progress, we may become frustrated and set the rings aside. If we find the solution, we can usually repeat it without difficulty. The rings no longer offer a challenge and again, we set them aside.

Sometimes shallow games lack sensuous variety. We are not challenged to hear, touch, smell, see, or feel with any discrimination. We never have delicious encounters with perfect timing, utter exhaustion, or sporting implements that almost magically become part of our own bodies.

Sometimes shallow games are only about chance, like rolling dice or spinning a roulette wheel. They do not touch skill and insight, the

Games come in different shapes and sizes, and they perform different functions.

other two wellsprings of game playing. Some of these games are so lacking in engagement that we have to fortify them with gambling. Spinning a roulette wheel soon becomes tedious unless there's money riding on it.

Shallow games do not have much voice. They do not speak to us. They do not become part of our personal stories. Shallow games can be considered pastimes, in the literal sense of the word. They help us pass time in an agreeable way. This is an important function, and we should undoubtedly spend some of our time in the company of shallow games. But they do not have the clout of their deeper counterparts.

Deep Games

Deep games have tremendous staying power. They can be addictive. They should be required to carry a warning label: "Dabblers beware! Contents can be habit-forming." People who thought they were merely going to fill up a couple of hours on a long weekend may end up getting hooked for a lifetime.

Deep games present a durable problem. Unlike the once-solved-always-solved nature of some puzzles, the difficulties of deep games will not go away. A weekend golfer who pars three holes in a row never brags that he now has a golf swing. He is, as the old joke goes, only borrowing it. The challenges of golf will be back to haunt him soon enough. Runners who reach a personal goal of running a marathon in 3 hours are not done. The running problem is still there. What about 2 hours and 55 minutes? Or even 2:45? Improved skill poses no threat to durable games. They only present challenges that are ever changing.

The durability of deep games may be due to the fact that their problems are rich and complex. Typically these activities require all three fundamental means for solving the difficulty at hand—good fortune, skill, and insight. This makes them more interesting. Sometimes Dame Fortune asserts herself and the game takes on a flavor of the arbitrary. Sometimes flashing skill wins the day. At other times shrewd strategy will turn the tables. We never know, and consequently we are less likely to tire of the activity.

Many deep games are also sensuously interesting. They provide a multifaceted sensory journey including sights, temperatures, sounds, textures, and those all-important smells. As Hall (1990) has argued, olfaction is the sense most tightly tied to memory, and many

Deep games tend to engage us more completely than shallow games.

of our deep games have distinctive aromas—a new leather glove, the grass and earth, a wet track, wintergreen, a clean uniform, sweat, fresh oranges at halftime. Deep games tend to engage us more completely. The abstract game plan influences concrete sensations. Concrete sensations influence abstract game plans. Smelling and thinking, feeling and reflecting come together in a pleasant blend of fully human behavior.

Deep games are meaningful. Some games fit their culture. They send messages about a particular ideology or such concerns as success, freedom, justice, individualism, and community. They can reinforce certain political or religious views. They can bolster a people's sense of history, or what a given community wants to believe about itself and its destiny. Deep games, in short, are usually a good fit with the prevailing culture or with what the citizens of the prevailing culture hope to become.

But deep games transcend culture as well. Individuals have their own resources for meaning, and deep games tend to fire the individual imagination. They attract individuals and invite them to become members of that activity community. Such games become high-cost, high-demand, high-commitment affairs. But the rewards are commensurable. In such challenging activities we often say that we find ourselves. We are reminded of who we are and what we want to be. Deep games take on functions of meaning usually associated with religion and ritual.

Philosophic Exercise

The power of deep games to evoke and shape meaning carries liabilities as well as assets. Neo-Marxist philosophers have argued that unjust societies use sport in hegemonic ways—that is, as an intentional and unintentional tool to placate and socialize us into being more or less comfortable with the status quo. For instance, competition can be used to teach the lesson that "we get exactly what we deserve." If we don't play well, in sport or in life, we lose. When this logic is turned around it sends a debilitating message that goes something like this:

1. All the losers must not be playing well.
2. Their repeated defeats are their own fault.
3. They are getting exactly what they deserve.
4. Life is fair.

Based on your own experiences, do you believe that games are manipulated to send potentially harmful ideological messages? For example, do a majority of game forms favor the generally taller and stronger male physique and thereby reinforce stereotypes about lesser female athletic ability? Or, are contemporary sporting spectacles akin to the "bread and circuses" of ancient Rome? Do they debilitate more than they refresh and empower? (For further information on either of these topics, consult Morgan 1994; Sage 1990; Gruneau 1983; and Simon 2004.)

THE VALUE OF COMPETITION

We have learned that games need not be competitive. Artificial problems can be durable, complex, sensuous, and culturally and personally meaningful without a single contest taking place. Why, then, have our games so regularly made this move from test to contest? Why would we trade an activity that guarantees an informative test score that everyone receives for a competitive project that promises up front that one side will get nothing?

In philosophic parlance this is called moving from a non-zero-sum to a zero-sum activity. It works like this: Your getting a good test score does not prevent me from getting a good score. Your improving on the test does not prevent me from improving on the test. There is no zero-sum relationship between testing scores. But that is not the case with contesting. When the test becomes a contest, your victory means my defeat. You get everything, I get nothing. This is a classic zero-sum relationship. Why would people want to trade a potential win–win testing arrangement for a win–lose competitive project? Let's look at some potential reasons.

Cooperation and Mutual Gratification

Sporting contests are inherently cooperative enterprises that we voluntarily enter into. Opponents get together and promise to play the same game, at the same time, and under the same conditions. Opponents also promise to try their hardest to win, not just to do well. Thus, near the end of close contests, an opponent who is barely behind will use risky strategies if such strategies might produce victory, not safer techniques that would preserve a good test score. In contests, both opponents agree that getting a good test score does not matter as much as getting the best test score.

Overall, this is a very civil arrangement. Opponents agree to call fouls on themselves or submit to the will of an objective third party called an official, umpire, or referee. Each side needs a comparable opportunity to produce the better score, so equipment is standardized and other controllable factors are monitored to produce a level playing field. Unlike

Sport should embrace civilized competition.

all-out war, people voluntarily submit to these controls just so that they can have a good contest and see who played best on a given afternoon.

We typically make these civil and cooperative moves voluntarily. We are saying we want contests, not just tests. We will be edified more deeply by playing a contest than by experiencing a test. We want to venture into an environment that promises to be zero-sum. We know beforehand that one of us will get nothing, but we are willing to take that risk.

But are competitors thinking clearly, or are they reverting to a behavior that is base or retrograde? Perhaps this desire to defeat others is an unfortunate side of our evolution, one that is making a last behavioral stand before human beings become wholly loving, noncompetitive creatures.

Doubling Our Pleasure

Contests can be regarded as enriched tests. If tests provide an opposition by cut (maybe I can solve this problem; maybe I can't), and if contests provide a second kind of opposition, difference by degree (maybe I can solve this problem better than you; maybe I can't), then contestants reside in a richer land than those who remain in the territory of tests alone. If human beings enjoy and seek out tension, uncertainty, and dramatic resolutions, then it stands to reason that we would prefer a project that offers two sources for these desirable experiences than an activity that offers only one.

Our thirst for "sweet tension" is not difficult to see. Imagine three friends who climbed the same mountain day after day. They were flower children from the 1960s who disavowed any interest in achievement or competitive success. Climb-

ing the mountain at a leisurely pace, smelling the daisies, enjoying good conversation, and having a group hug at the top was all they wanted. Indeed, this satisfied them for years.

However, eventually the activity grew a little stale. After all, you can smell daisies only so long before the fragrance no longer satisfies. The three friends wanted a little more stimulation, some way to put more spice into their climbs. They decided to turn the climb into a game. They established a goal—reaching the top of the mountain—and they settled upon restricted means. They would have to walk rather than use their off-road vehicles; they would not be allowed to use well-known shortcuts; and they would have

Contests are enriched tests.

Competitors love performing the skills of the test, but they also love competing at these skills.

to reach the destination before a set amount of time expired. Thus they introduced opposition by cut to a previously nonoppositional activity. They also added a delicious uncertainty to the climb. This set up the possibility of a number of dramatic outcomes—making it, not making it, making it three times in a row, making it today faster than yesterday, and so on. This group-testing activity proved very stimulating, and the three friends climbed this way for several more years. But eventually, the group felt that the game was growing old. Just as smelling the daisies can become tiresome, so can taking a test over and over again.

The group decided to spice up their game by sharing it in a competitive way. One of them remarked that by doing this they "could have their climb and enjoy it too." They could experience the climb (exercise); they could enjoy the challenge and work for self-improvement (the game); and now they could experience the new tension of seeing who could climb the best on any given afternoon (the contest). The game doubled the pleasure first experienced when the activity was only exercise; the contest doubled the tension of the game. They added two levels of sweet tension to the experience without sacrificing the delights of the original exercise.

In competition, the primary relationship is still with the exercise, the activity itself. Competitors are always members of a testing family, not the other way around. Baseball players love hitting, catching, and running above all. Secondarily they love competing at these skills. Great runners are not competitors who just happen to run; they are runners who also happen to compete. The foundational love affair is with a concrete activity that requires endurance, skill, determination, and cleverness. Competition just adds frosting to the already tasty cake.

Some worry that the move from exercise to games to competitive games might not be an entirely good thing. For all the sweet tension that it adds, competition may also result in alienation. Might not the friendship among the three climbers be jeopardized if the climb became too competitive? What about the move toward zero-sum outcomes, where presumably only one of the three climbers, the winner, would be satisfied?

Competition and Zero-Sum Logic

Zero-sum outcomes are not entirely bad. It is precisely the zero-sum nature of opposition by degree that promotes the desired uncertainty. Only one side can finish ahead. Only a small degree of skillful difference or good fortune can make all the difference in the result. A courageous move at the end of a game that results in just one more point or just 1/100th of a second less time could turn the participant from a loser into a winner.

We can't have it both ways. We can't have everyone win and still retain the tension of contesting. There have to be losers, and losing has to matter if the drama is to engage us. So, zero-sum structures are good in that they provide a more biting drama for us to experience as players and enjoy as spectators.

Such exclusionary outcomes are also good because they are temporary and repeatedly put up for grabs. We might call this a civilized deployment of zero-sum logic. The current winner graciously allows the loser to try again. There is always hope in sport; there is always next year.

Friendships between competitors have a good chance to be sustained in this kind of environment. We gratify one another by playing hard. We enjoy the process of trying to win. We want to do this again and again, so it makes no sense to destroy an opponent who has been beaten. We count on them returning full of energy. In warlike activities, on the other hand, zero-sum relationships are often terminal. They signal the end of hope. Survivors on the losing side experience alienation at the hands of the victors.

Zero-sum contests also produce at least two outcomes that are *not* zero-sum. That is, in the process of generating a winner and loser, contests also manufacture two desirable outcomes that are shared by winner and loser alike. We've already discussed the first one, enjoyment of the fray. Because most competition is voluntarily sought out, both sides may feel that, in spite of a potential loss, it is still gratifying to be in a good contest. It is more fun to compete, whatever the outcome. Thus, it is not illogical for both winner and loser to report that a given competitive experience was enjoyable.

Competition also adds a set of skills that can be shared by all. Losers can compete well. They can make moves at just the right time, they can employ just the right strategies, they can retain their composure under pressure—they can do all this very well and still lose, particularly if the opponent is more

A mixture of testing and contesting excellences.

skillful. It is logically possible, and indeed often happens, that the superior performer shows fewer competitive excellences during the contest than the loser, particularly when the underdog makes a futile but valiant effort to prevail.

In addition to these contesting excellences, those who lose can also show testing excellences. Take two world-class runners in the Olympic Games vying for the gold medal in the 100-meter dash. The favorite defeats the underdog by 2/100ths of a second, and both runners break the old world record. The loser in this race still reaps two non-zero-sum rewards:

◆ The excellence associated with testing: He confronted the challenge extremely well, with a good start, good form, and a world-record test score.

◆ The excellence associated with contesting: He had never come this close to the world's best runner before. His quick start surprised his opponent. He ran a brilliant race.

Here, then, are two additional sets of goods that are *not* zero-sum. Even losers can play well against the game test and compete well in relation to the opponent. Zero-sum competition paradoxically increases opportunities for non-zero-sum benefits.

Philosophic Exercise

An evolutionary approach to understanding human behavior might suggest that men and women relate differently to competition. For example, ethicists who see moral decision making as tightly tethered to biology claim that the two genders approach moral dilemmas in different ways (Gilligan 1982; Singer 1995). Could the same be true for competition? Does competition mean different things to men and women? Do men and women compete in different ways for different stakes? How much of the difference in competitive interest can be attributed to nature (genetics, biology, evolutionary history) and how much to nurture (cultural influences that systematically discourage women from playing competitive sport)? Where do you think the truth lies? Why is it dangerous to suggest that durable, biologically-tethered differences exist between the genders?

OTHER FORMS OF MOVEMENT

In chapters 8 and 9 we have devoted much attention to movement as exercise, play, games, and sport. This alone covers a great deal of movement territory. Should we choose to move, we often do one of the following:

◆ Exercise for good reasons
◆ Perform some intrinsically satisfying play activity like biking or walking
◆ Engage in an artificial test
◆ Compete

But other movement is both needed and desired.

The Significance of Work

Even in a push-button world, much movement can be understood as work. We have daily chores at home, including raking, cleaning, lifting, walking, and balancing. While perhaps not as attractive as play, these activities are tremendously important for good living. Our independence hangs in the balance. Many elderly people are forced to leave their homes for a long-term care facility, not because they can no longer function cognitively, but because they can no longer move. Freedom and dignity are attached to our ability to stand upright, move from one place to another, clean ourselves, and use our body skillfully. From a holistic viewpoint, our significance does not just lie in our eyes, our head, or our thoughts. Everything plays a role, including our ability to complete simple chores.

Many elderly people have to leave their homes for a long-term care facility, because they can no longer move well enough to complete the daily chores of living.

Work movement outside the home is also significant. We walk to the car, drive it to work, and climb the stairs to our office. Even at a computer we have to employ motor skills. If we don't have a desk job, movement plays an even more significant role. Most of the skilled trades require eye–hand coordination, artistic judgment, creativity, and other forms of activity cleverness. And we should not forget that some very important work requires high levels of physical fitness. Finally, we saw in the last chapter that exercise is a kind of artificial work; we can sell movement as a duty for the promotion of health. Accordingly, we emphasize the extrinsic merits of exercise and other physical activity.

Our sedentary world is still full of work-related movement, even if it has decreased in magnitude and intensity over the centuries. Our capacity to perform basic human chores is based on a phenomenon as old as animate life itself—the ability to move purposefully and skillfully. When that goes, much of us goes with it.

The Significance of Dance

If kinesiologists are movement people, we cannot ignore dance. In many ways it is as fundamental as play. Some books on play cite dance as a basic recreational activity, perhaps the most pure type of play that exists (Keen 1990; Neale 1969).

When human beings achieve a great success, when their stomachs are full, when their week of work is complete, they kick up their heels and celebrate. In short, they dance.

When people are having trouble forgetting their worries, they often go out on the dance floor and begin to move, whether erotically with another person, under some intoxicating rhythm, or lost in a favorite song. They dance their way into the intrinsic world of play and away from the domain of duty.

Dance also transmits cultural values and traditions. Folk dance tells a story about a people, a way of life, events that are idiosyncratic to them and events that are common to human nature. This kind of dance is a ritual that reorients, reminds, and even inspires. It provides a comfortable, culturally important place to return to.

Expressive or modern dance carries out yet additional functions. When words fail, we may need gesture, mime, or modern dance. The same frustration with the limits of verbal or numerical communication also leads us to draw, write sonatas, sculpt, and seek out the imagery of poetry.

When human beings have something that is difficult and important to say, they move. Even passionate speakers cannot help but get their body into the action. Arms flail, hands appeal, shoulders shrug, fingers point, the torso leans. We even joke that the best way to shut some people up is to tie their hands to their sides.

Modern dancers are artists who have something to say. They take the hand gesture and elevate it to a coherent kinetic expression. Excellent choreography is delightful because it is rich with intrigue. Polanyi and Prosch (1975) suggest that artistic dance has at least three sites of intrigue. First, the dance itself is interesting to watch. The forms, the athleticism, and the rhythms are fascinating in their own right. Second, the symbolic meanings evoked by the dance—freedom, suffering, hope, whatever the dance is about—are interesting. Finally, the dance and its symbolic meanings point back to us. Through the symbolism of the dance, we gain a new perspective on these human experiences. The dance stirs us. Our story intermingles with the story of the dance, even to the point that we are moved to tears.

© Associated Press/Herald Times Reporter/Tim Swoboda

When words fail, gesture, mime, and dance may be required.

SCIENTIZED MOVEMENT AND CULTURAL ACTIVITY

We have paid much attention in the last two chapters to cultural movement, including work, play, exercise, games, sport, competition, and dance. This reminds us that human beings do not move in the abstract. We do not move in terms of identical mathematical spaces and regular clock time. While science can graph, measure, and otherwise abstract human movement, such conversions of movement from the subjective, lived experience to an objective, not-lived abstraction come at a cost. These shifts produce a distortion that must be kept in mind when using numbers and graphs to represent human activity.

From Play Experience to Dose-Response

Some literature (e.g., Bouchard 2001) talks about doses of activity and how the person as machine responds to them, instead of talking about play and how it changes our personal stories. The differences between the two approaches are striking. A dose is a measurable quantity, like a pill composed of a known number of grams. Its attractiveness lies in its presumed precision. Slightly different doses of medicine produce better and worse effects. Slightly different doses of movement undoubtedly follow the same pattern.

But distortions here are significant. Human beings do not simply "take" activity as if it were a uniform pill. For example, meaningful activity, as we have discussed, is very different from boring exercise. Yet in terms of dose measurements—say, kilocalories for amount of energy expended against a period of time like a week (kcal/week)—joyous play is absolutely indistinguishable from tedious work. Each could produce 1,000 kcal/week. Each presumably would be equally valuable for reducing mortality rates (Corbin, Pangrazi, and Franks 2002).

This idea, however, eliminates the subjective. If the subjective has a causative role in human health and well-being, this is an extremely unfortunate elimination. Such reductions of experience to kilocalories, while they may be helpful, are not definitive (Midgley 1994). They provide only part of the story.

This means that talk of doses is misleadingly precise. In human terms, an expenditure of 1,000 kcal/week is not like another expenditure of exactly the same amount of energy. One expenditure could inspire, refresh, and empower, while another could deflate, deaden, and weaken. The hoped-for precision is thereby lost as the picture becomes far muddier than the purveyors of kilocalories would hope.

At the end of the day, conversion of human movement to doses, while helpful, is insufficient. When its lack of precision is misunderstood, it becomes dangerous, leading kinesiologists to dispense activity as if it were a fail-safe pill. When the focus falls on kilocalories rather than meaning and fun, activity becomes too clinical, and vitality is drained from many forms of otherwise enjoyable activity.

From Play Experience to Movement

Some literature (see Newell 1990a, 1990b) talks more about abstract movement than about specific, cultural human activities. The advantages of this are not hard to find. Movement is a more inclusive concept than sport, dance, or games. Conceptually, our field should rally around the active lifestyle in all its forms, not just a few of the more popular ways of moving. It is also probably better to call our field kinesiology than physical education or exercise and sport science. In the halls of academe, the abstract and inclusive usually win out over the idiosyncratic and specific. For instance, we do not have a department of trombone, rather a department of music. Likewise, it may be politically astute for us to say that we are a department of movement science, not a department of sport.

With this helpful generality, however, comes some loss in particularity. Human beings do not fall in love with movement in the abstract. We are culture-embedded, and culture is carried in play, games, sport, folk dance, and exercise forms. These specific activities carry particular cultural meanings. These meanings resonate with students and clients. Because they resonate, students and clients become more fully engaged. Because they are more fully engaged, our interventions work better, and our students and clients learn, grow, and heal faster.

At the end of the day, we need to balance the logical, conceptual, and political advantages of dealing with movement in the abstract with the pragmatic, embodied, holistic mandates to address activity in its popular cultural forms. We are as much scholars of play as we are kinesiologists. In terms of the effectiveness of our professional interventions, we are undoubtedly more practitioners of play, games, and dance than of abstract movement.

When the focus falls away from meaning and fun, power and value of movement are reduced.

From Play Experience to Utility

Some literature focuses on the utility of physical activity, and not its intrinsically satisfying qualities. This may stem from a deeply embedded defensiveness about our subject matter, a kind of intellectual inferiority complex that undoubtedly finds at least some of its roots in mind–body dualism. The harsh treatment we continue to receive among intellectualist educators and practitioners tends to make us anxious and defensive. As we lose games 1 and 2 in the dualistic tournament (see chapter 5), we retreat to game 3 and dig our defensive trenches under the banner of utility.

Of course, there is nothing wrong with being useful. But there is something wrong with thinking of ourselves as worthwhile only because we are useful. We trade the intrinsic value of movement for its extrinsic value. We move from play to work, from promoting movement as meaningful in its own right to regarding activity as duty.

Things can get even worse if we become desperate to show that we are useful. When this happens kinesiology becomes a chameleon, quickly and sometimes thoughtlessly changing its color to suit the times and presumably survive. While no discipline is immune from social influences that would define what it is good for, an anxious discipline with a poor self-concept may be too ready to please. Indeed, we are currently making strong utility claims for the following outcomes—all of them are hot buttons in many cultures:

Let us focus not on the utility of physical activity, but on its intrinsically satisfying qualities.

◆ Improved health, specifically a longer life span (CDC 1997)

◆ Stronger self-confidence (Whitehead and Corbin 1997)

◆ Reduced obesity, particularly in overweight children (USDHHS 2001)

◆ Elevated academic success (Blakemore 2003; CDE 2002)

◆ Improved ethics; reinforced fair play, respect for the rules, teamwork, and leadership (Gough 1995; Clifford and Feezell 1997)

The issue is not that we embrace these ends, nor is it our attempts to achieve them; it is how we go about it. English teachers, for example, know that reading Shakespeare or memorizing poetry has any number of useful benefits that transcend the sheer joy of reading, such as facility with language. But they do not pin their self-worth as English teachers on this. Reading good literature is not something we put up with in our schools just because it helps people read the bills that will come in the mail when they become adults. A love of literature improves quality of life and provides a resource for repeated encounters with good books in the years ahead. With this belief in the value of literature for its own sake, claims for the usefulness of reading stay in perspective.

REVIEW

Physical activity should be both enjoyed for its own sake and put to work for other ends. For both purposes the roots of games run deep into our biology. Just as we are built to play, we come into the world ready to solve problems. In a sense, we do not choose to play games; we are born to play games. Games that are competitive events have unique merits, as zero-sum activities actually add non-zero-sum benefits. In addition to games, other movement forms such as work and dance are important. All forms of movement have both personal and cultural significance, and their intrinsic meanings should not be lost to doses, abstractions, or preoccupations with utility.

LOOKING AHEAD

In part IV we examine our responsibilities as moral agents, as professionals who help people and make the world a better place. The general term for such concerns is ethics. We will begin by looking at notions of moral responsibility and ethical decision making.

CHECKING YOUR UNDERSTANDING

1. *Describe the difference between play and games. What sources support games and play? What two kinds of logic are required to negotiate a game?*

2. *Why are games valuable? Can you describe a valuable game experience that is not also play? Conversely, can you describe a play experience that is not also a game?*

3. *What advantages exist in converting a game into a contest? Describe the experiences available at three different levels: exercise, test, and contest.*

4. *What is the human significance of other forms of movement, particularly work and dance?*

5. *Describe the dangers of turning human activity into doses, abstractions, and useful tools.*

Part IV ◆

ETHICS, VALUE CHOICES, AND THE GOOD LIFE

Chapters 10, 11, and 12 draw our philosophic analysis to a close. You will be asked to draw conclusions about ethical behavior, the kind of values that promote the good life, and how kinesiology can best contribute to good living.

Ultimately, you will wrestle with the question of whether the good life is based on the active lifestyle. Can a person lead a good life and be sedentary? In chapters 11 and 12, we'll discuss principles that will allow us to answer that question. In chapter 12, you will examine four activity-intensive profiles of the good life. The chapter concludes that human beings are built for movement and that we are always ready to find significance in our movement activities.

10

Developing Sound Professional Ethics

© Corbis

Everyone who works in a kinesiology profession or who hopes to do so in the near future faces important choices about personal standards of behavior. Such groups as the American Medical Association, the American College of Sports Medicine, and the American Alliance for Health, Physical Education, Recreation and Dance have adopted codes of conduct that provide some guidance. But no code can produce good conduct on its own. We also have to rely on upbringing, role models, and teachers who treat people fairly and respect the products or services for which they are responsible. Some organizations conduct ethics seminars, and many use some form of test that is designed to distinguish potential employees who can be trusted from those who cannot. Surveillance systems, audits, penalties for wrongdoing, and incentives for good actions can also help employees stay on the straight and narrow.

But we are not just products of our moral environment. We are free to make our own decisions. Personal moral habits may lead us to act in unusually good or bad ways. We develop a moral signature; a typical way of behaving that may earn us deep respect or a reputation that is far less flattering. Either way, we will be held accountable.

In spite of what has been written about selfish genes and the supposed human inability to move beyond narrow personal interest, hardly anybody wants to be immoral. Surveys consistently show that people regard integrity as more important than success. Most people regard themselves as better than the majority of their peers (Josephson Institute 2002). While it is impossible for everyone to be ethically above average, people want and need to see themselves this way. Ethics is somehow deeply important to people, and being seen by others as having integrity is a prize that almost nobody is willing to trade away.

Given these data, it might seem surprising that professional ethics faces severe challenges today. High-profile corporate scandals have sent CEOs to jail; absenteeism and employee theft have cost corporations billions of dollars annually; and reputable institutions of higher education have broken NCAA rules to produce winning teams, fill stadiums, and benefit from lucrative TV contracts. This leaves us with some interesting questions about professional ethics.

CHAPTER OBJECTIVES

In this chapter, you will

◆ *review the nature of ethics,*

◆ *examine foundations for good professional ethics,*

◆ *examine the basis for good sport ethics, and*

◆ *address a case study and speculate on possible resolutions.*

◆ How can people say they care about ethics and still act unprofessionally?

◆ What causes bad behavior? A defect in us? A defect in our culture?

◆ If we want to improve professional standards and behavior in kinesiology, how should we go about it?

INTRODUCTION TO ETHICS

In this chapter, I use the terms *ethics* and *morality* synonymously. They have to do with making decisions where right and wrong are at stake. These terms define an area of human responsibility and, by themselves, are value-neutral. All human beings have ethics and morals, but not everyone has good ethics or high morals. The issue for professionals, then, is not simply to have ethics but to develop a morality that is praiseworthy. Good ethics involves at least two things: identifying intelligently and discernibly what is worthwhile or valuable, and finding ways to distribute that good fairly (Frankena 1973). Promoting good has often been associated with beneficence. Looking for fair ways to share the good has typically taken place under various rules of distributive justice.

The history of ethics provides a record of the messy struggle to make life better for humankind. This process of developing good ethics began many years ago. As our predecessors became more intelligent, began to use language, and started to reflect on their impulses, needs, and interests, they encountered what may

Better and worse choices lie at the heart of ethics.

be the generator of all ethics—conflict (Midgley 1994). Different choices raised questions about what to do. Realizing that there might be some principles that could provide reliable guidance when such conflicts arise, early humans began to formalize a distinction that remains with us today—the difference between how people *do* live and how people *ought* to live. Ethics, if nothing else, is about how people ought to live, about preferred values and behavior.

The search for ethical guidelines that describe how we ought to act involves a great deal of trial and error. We are still in that process today. For instance, some argue that ethics is largely an individual issue, a matter of personal choice. Others claim that ethics is corporate, a product of human consensus. Some think that ethics must be grounded in theology, in the will of God or some authoritative scripture. Some believe that ethics is a product of reason. Such intellection produces social contracts that protect everyone. Others argue that ethics involves emotions, habits, body, and will, and that virtue, not contracts, motivates good ethical behavior. Finally, some argue that good ethics dignifies humankind by radically separating us from animal life, while others disagree and say that good ethics is tethered to our biology and our evolutionary past. While humans are, in general, ethically superior to animals, they are also in many ways similar to other biological creatures.

These kinds of disputes have often given ethics a bad name. In the face of such seemingly irreconcilable points of view, we may well want to throw in the towel and retreat arbitrarily to one of the positions just described or some other philosophy of life. We might well conclude that ethics is a personal matter, one that involves a series of essentially groundless choices that you must make for yourself.

Surely this is too pessimistic a conclusion. In our daily lives we do not operate this way, and we certainly count on others to behave with at least a degree of ethical consistency. Our commitments to our friends or spouse, our passion for various causes, the fact that we finish every day without pillaging and plundering—all of this seems to rest on something more solid that our own arbitrary preferences. But what is the foundation for these common experiences and judgments?

A holistic, pragmatic ethic can provide at least some partial answers. They are not always comfortable answers, but that is not the point of scholarly inquiry. The point is to get closer to the most useful explanations, even if they challenge us to the core. We take the first step in this journey when we see that moral confidence is needed for good ethics and realize that this is a trait that is slowly developed and earned, not intuited or bestowed.

DEVELOPING MORAL CONFIDENCE

How can we get our "moral legs" as kinesiologists in the face of so many different opinions about what is right and wrong? Actually, it should not be that difficult. Most of the time we perform very well as moral agents. We try to be fair, we help our neighbors, and we leave the world better at the end of the day than we found it at the beginning. When we slip up, we notice it. We either rationalize the wrongdoing, or we promise ourselves not to make the same ethical mistake again. This is the day-to-day moral life that most of us live, not one where we flounder about in a moral fog, unable to tell better from worse or selfishly pandering to ourselves at the expense of everyone else.

But lack of moral confidence is real in our personal and professional lives, and it is worthwhile to examine ways to bolster a trustworthy moral compass, one that we consciously pull out of our pockets and consult day in and day out. While most of us have a fairly good compass already in hand, three common problems may undermine the trust we place in it.

Looking for the Wrong Kinds of Answers

If we look for clear-cut answers to moral dilemmas, we will be disappointed. Answers to moral dilemmas aren't always obvious.

Holistic ethics suggests that answers to moral dilemmas are often messy. This messiness includes the possibility that there is no good answer to a certain problem, or that there are multiple good answers, or that an answer is a shade of gray instead of the more comfortable white or black. Those who do not accept this feature of ethics use it to undermine our confidence. Here is an example that presents a frustrating moral conundrum.

Nearly all athletes honor the principle of trying one's hardest. This is a worthwhile principle because the integrity of the contest and its outcome depend upon such effort. If one side is playing down to the other team, the outcome may not reflect the actual differences between the sides, and the determination of actual differences is what the two teams are looking to establish. You will recall from chapter 2 that this is one of Dixon's arguments for running up the score.

It is also true, however, that nearly all athletes honor the principle of not rubbing it in against an overmatched opponent. This is a worthwhile guideline because athletes do not want to embarrass their opponents in any significant way. Even less do they want a lopsided contest to be a source of alienation between teams

Go for the gray: the right thing to do.

and the occasion for a negative spiral that produces new harms. Consequently, it is common practice to scale back strategies that are likely to expand an already wide margin. Baseball teams that are ahead in the ninth inning by 12 runs do not steal bases or try suicide squeezes. Football teams that are leading by 40 points in the last few minutes of play do not throw "bombs" to wide receivers. Each sporting culture has mores for decency in these awkward situations.

These two contradictory principles lead to a moral dilemma. What should athletes in embarrassingly lopsided games do: try their hardest at the risk of running up the score, or limit their strategies out of genuine concern for the welfare of their opponents? Either way, they compromise one of these sacred athletic principles. Some moral commentators would lead us in the direction of skepticism. No good answers exist, they say. There is no way to get out of this mess. This is just the way it is in ethics; it all boils down to personal opinion.

However, alternative conclusions are available and, in many ways, they are more plausible. First, most moral dilemmas are not like this one, in which two apparently solid moral principles are in conflict. Day in and day out we tell the truth, avoid harming our friends, and do things the right way without facing similar ethical brainteasers. It is simply inaccurate to suggest that these kinds of conundrums are the norm.

Second, the fact that we are somewhat stumped by this problem is actually proof that our moral compass is in hand and functioning well. After all, we would not even be able to see the dilemma if we did not recognize the validity of the two conflicting principles. The fact that we are torn presupposes that we are seeing two attractive moral directions. Noticing that we cannot follow both at the same time suggests that we are thinking well. Thus, falling into occasional moral conundrums should actually reinforce confidence in our moral sensibilities.

Third, and most important, if we do not expect white and black answers from our moral deliberations, our confidence will not be undermined if no slam-dunk insight drops out of the heavens and into our laps. The lopsided-contest dilemma might involve some kind of gray answer—perhaps a compromise solution of some sort. A coach could pull her basketball team to the side, after already having substituted freely, and tell them to run plays that they only began to work on the previous week. She tells them to try their hardest and score if the opportunity presents itself, but only under these more restrictive conditions.

This creative solution to a potentially harmful situation splits the difference between the legitimate right to play hard and the right not to be unduly shown up. Compromises may not be pretty, but on occasion a well-functioning moral compass requires us to go for the gray as the right thing to do.

Looking for Simplistic Answers

If we look for simple answers to the dilemmas of life, we will be disappointed. Good living is complex, and it can be achieved in countless ways.

Holistic ethics is comfortable with pluralism, the philosophy that many things are good and many combinations of good things can lead to a satisfying life. This is not grounded in skepticism (everything is good because we cannot tell good from harm), nor is it grounded in nihilism (nothing is better or worse, so we might as well behave as if everything were good). Rather, it is grounded in a cautious pragmatism that believes that many ways of living work well and many ways do not.

However, we typically have two problems with this conclusion. First, human beings like simple answers. We gravitate toward books that promise 10 easy steps to total happiness. We like to package things, get them under control, and then deploy them in fail-safe programs. On the other hand, if we saw a book that promised 100,000 alternative pathways to well-being, we would likely wonder about the competence of the author. We would be inclined to say that surely the writer could boil it down to something more straightforward. Complexity tends to bother us.

Holistic ethics is comfortable with pluralism.

© Digital Vision

Second, professionals often make a basic logical mistake when confronting pluralism. They confuse the claim that many things are good for the assertion that anything can be good. The first claim requires discrimination and judgment—weeding out the good from the bad and prioritizing the more valuable above the less valuable. The claim that anything can be good trades careful thinking for indiscriminate personal preference.

Imagine pluralists as visiting a grocery store that is full of mostly good food but also some that is not so good. Such bounty does not mean that shoppers can pick out any tomato without checking it for freshness or eat as many candy bars as they desire. They need to balance their diet, complement bland foods with a bit of spice, and look for variety. They need to avoid things that may look good on the shelf but actually lead to an upset stomach or even poor health.

While no two people fill their baskets with exactly the same foods, both can have successful shopping experiences. They will eat differently but well. The existence of many good foods and the influence of their own taste do not relieve them of the responsibility to be skillful, principled, and discriminating shoppers.

The fact that 100 people around the globe argue for 100 slightly different interpretations of the good life does not have to mean that nobody is right. Nor does it mean that only one person is right and the other 99 have to be wrong. It could be that all 100 interpretations are good. A person would do well to follow any one of them. In the process, this person would be avoiding possibly 800 other interpretations of the good life that are seductive but defective. As professionals in kinesiology, we want to zero in on a group of values that promote good living. We don't want to insist that only one vision of the active lifestyle has to fit everyone.

The existence of more than one sound answer to moral questions need not shake our moral confidence. In a pluralistic world, responsible moral agents still need to carefully choose and prioritize. In the next chapter, we will take on this task as we try to determine what role movement plays in the good life.

Ignoring Points of Consensus

If we dwell on the differences among interpretations of the good life, we are likely to miss similarities. Without similarities we may lose confidence in our ability to identify common points of interest—agreements that cut across culture, religion, politics, gender, age, and history.

Holistic ethics recognizes that we are all human beings who live in a common temporal and spatial world. Across the centuries we have faced similar problems of sharing scarce goods, organizing ourselves for common ends, and developing the trust that is needed for such arrangements. Consequently, it would be odd indeed if people developed radically different rules to live by in different parts of the globe. Holistic ethics expects to find similarities in moral principles.

The existence of different levels of consensus across time and culture is not difficult to document. One study conducted by Kidder (1994) included interviews with respected leaders from radically different walks of life around the world. He asked them to talk about the nature of the good life and recorded their answers. These wise individuals from different cultures did not paint an identical picture of excellent living, which is not surprising—we already know that American Indian, Buddhist, Catholic, Hindu, and materialistic values are not the same.

But significantly, Kidder noted that a rough consensus did exist on certain issues. He

© Associated Press,/Anat Givon

All human beings live toward a common temporal and spatial world.

concluded that societies around the world honor seven common values: love, truthfulness, fairness, freedom, unity, tolerance, responsibility, and respect for life. Amidst differences, considerable agreement exists. Such consensus would seem to warrant a degree of confidence in our abilities to reason ethically. Our own speculations in chapter 11 about satisfaction and the active lifestyle will rely similarly on our roots as embodied creatures with very different attitudes, traditions, and languages, but also with a common humanity that leads us to some consensus about movement.

Philosophic Exercise

Do you agree with Kidder and others who argue that people can come to at least a rough consensus on good living? You can test this out empirically by jotting down your ideas of good sportsmanship. How should we treat opponents, officials, fans, and coaches? What obligations do we have regarding game rules? How are we to deal with winning and losing?

Do you think you can get a rough consensus on this? If you are in a classroom setting, share your principles with others. Then negotiate, argue, listen, learn, and negotiate some more. See if a majority can agree on a single set of principles for good sportsmanship.

DEVELOPING GOOD MORAL ATTITUDES AND HABITS

We develop moral attitudes and habits gradually. As Aristotle well understood, developing good ethics takes practice—repetition, feedback, and time.

According to many modern ethicists, we do not begin this process from scratch. We come into the world ready for caring and loving. By nature, we are social animals who are built to cooperate (Wilson 1993; Midgley 1994; Singer 1995). Mothers care for their children; fathers love their families; people have strong feelings for their kin, their favorite sport teams, and their countries. This does not mean, however, that we are predestined to walk through life interested only in the good and beautiful. We know ourselves too well for that! And we see far too many examples of blatant selfishness in our daily lives for anyone to conclude that we are thoroughly kind and noble. But it does mean that in a deep biogenetic way we are ready to be good and join hands with fellow human beings to make the world a better place for everyone.

Our ethical destiny, while promising, still very much hangs in the balance, a balance that is affected by training and environment in addition to biology. If we develop strong virtues, habits, and skills related to beneficence and justice, we are more likely to survive the moral firestorms that will come our way. If we lack these things, we are more likely to be blown by the winds of self-interest, economic pressure, and other influences that have us occasionally do things that we later end up regretting.

Growing Moral Calluses

The process of moral development can be likened to developing calluses on our hands and feet. To an extent, calluses are good. They protect us from the wear and tear of life. They keep blisters from developing so we can continue to use the tools that are part of our job. But when calluses get too thick, they become a problem. They keep us from feeling what we need to feel. They prevent us from sensitively dealing with our tools, and our performance declines.

Similarly, we need a degree of insulation from the many moral imperatives of life. We cannot respond to every need; we cannot afford to hurt along with everyone who is hurting; we cannot personally right every wrong. Thin moral calluses allow us to operate with a degree of sanity in a world in which millions of people are politically oppressed, victimized by economic hardship, dying of AIDS, or losing their lives in war. But just as we lose physical sensitivity when calluses on our skin get too thick, we lose moral sensitivity when calluses grow around our hearts. We become less able to see, need, and experience personal responsibility. We can see this pattern in sport.

It is quite a distance from a spontaneous gesture of concern for an opponent to some of the acts of intimidation and general insensitivity we witness in the play of many athletes. How long does it take for young athletes to become sophisticated players who exhibit rough play and think little or nothing of an opponent's injury or discomfort?

Holistic ethics suggests that we become what we practice. If young athletes learn that winning is the only thing that matters, and if they watch their coaches disrespect the rules, cut corners, lose their temper, talk poorly of the other team, and react to both victories and defeats without composure, then they begin to grow the calluses that go with these attitudes. The more sporting days that are filled with these kinds of experiences, the less young athletes are able to feel the things good moral agents need to feel. By the time they reach high school, the calluses are in place, perhaps permanently.

Habits and attitudes are resistant to change, so the development of these negative qualities is no trivial matter. Those who have a bad case of moral calluses cannot easily soften them in order to restore full moral functioning. Many who walk around the world with a callused heart are morally challenged and are forced to make do with what amounts to a disability.

We can develop a tender heart or moral calluses by observing those we look up to.

PLAYING WITHOUT CALLUSES

Setting: A girls' soccer game
Participants: 7- and 8-year-old girls
Coaches: Volunteer parents
Officials: Two male high school soccer players

For most of the girls in this contest, it was their first soccer season and, for many, their first experience with organized competition of any sort. Their soccer skills were primitive, and they had not yet been socialized into any contemporary soccer ethic. These young girls were not so much soccer players as youngsters who happened to be playing a game that vaguely resembled soccer.

Except for the two goalies, the players traveled in a pack chasing the elusive ball. It was as if they were all tied together. Had they not been wearing different colored shirts, it would have been difficult for an onlooker to tell one team from the other.

Often the ball became trapped in the middle of this mass of players, with those closest to the ball kicking furiously to dislodge it. On one of these occasions, one player contacted the ball solidly and sent it about 2 yards squarely into the stomach of an opponent. There was an audible thud, and the victim dropped to the ground gasping and sobbing. No whistle was blown, but spontaneously and instantly the action stopped. Girls from both teams gathered around the temporarily injured player, some of them asking if she was all right, others watching with interest and concern. The soccer ball, still officially in play, lay motionless and unattended somewhere around midfield.

The two officials, never having been told what to do when play stops while time is *in*, looked genuinely nonplussed, but one of them finally blew his whistle. The officials retrieved the ball and walked over to the huddle of girls. The injured player had nearly regained her breath and was rising to her feet.

She wiped away the few tears that remained and told her coach that she still wanted to play. Shortly, the game resumed and once again the girls, as if a single unit, began following the ball around the field (Kretchmar 1990).

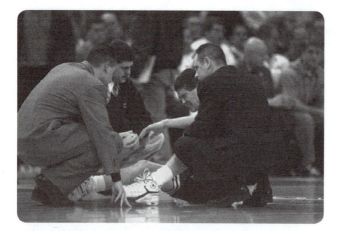

How long does it take for young athletes to exhibit rough play and think nothing of an opponent's injury or discomfort?

The most popular way of coping with this handicap is to rationalize behavior. Rationalizing does not make the behavior in question any less wrong, but it does make it feel better. Following are a few common rationalizations.

◆ "Everyone is doing it." Usually this statement is false. Everyone is not doing "it"—taking drugs, intimidating officials, or whatever "it" may be. And besides, ethical right and wrong cannot be decided by common practice. Nevertheless, the "everyone is doing it" rationale provides some salve for those who are habitual sport offenders.

◆ "It's just part of the game." Athletes often point to the existence of penalties in rulebooks to argue that such violations are expected. Because penalties for X are in the official rulebook, X must be part of the game. Of course, such reasoning is fallacious. Penal codes for robbery do not make robbery right. Least of all do such penalties suggest that robbery should be a normal part of life. But again, suggesting that some misdeed is just part of the game can help individuals live more comfortably with their moral calluses.

◆ "It's just good strategy, particularly if it works." We often hear sport commentators make these kinds of inane statements. For one thing, nobody wants to live in a world that mindlessly equates successful strategies with good ethics. But for those with particularly thick moral calluses, almost anything that produces a win can be rationalized. The ends justify the means.

◆ "If you don't get caught, it isn't wrong." Again, this is a common comment on television when, for example, an instant replay shows blatant cheating that was not detected by the referees. No penalty was paid for the illegal advantage gained, so the behavior becomes "good."

The existence of common rationalizations for wrongdoing provides some evidence for the validity of two claims made earlier in this chapter. First, people want to be good and want to think of themselves as good. Accordingly, they use rationalizations to cope with misbehavior. Second, calluses are difficult to remove. Misbehavior tends to become habitual. Individuals need a ready stock of justifications that they can use when the workings of their own conscience or the reactions of other people raise questions about their behavior.

The bottom line is that even professionals who habitually act badly do not see themselves as immoral. Invariably, they have reinterpreted their behavior through a rationalization process to be normal, the way everybody acts, or maybe even a little better.

Philosophic Exercise

Two of the most pressing ethical issues in the workplace today are employee theft and absenteeism. According to government studies, American companies lose over $30 billion annually to absenteeism and another $64 billion to employee theft. Both are complex problems, and sometimes corporate exploitation of workers contributes to these behaviors. Nevertheless, breach of contract and theft are usually unjustifiable and require the salve of rationalization.

For the following two relatively common behaviors, speculate on five rationalizations that employees would use to justify their actions.

◆ An employee calls in sick even though she is healthy. It is just before a holiday, and company will be arriving in a few days. She has much shopping and other preparations to tend to, and too little time to take care of them. This person has sick days remaining and will be paid for this day. (What rationalizations might this person use to soften what is basically a breach of contract and a lie to her employer?)

◆ An employee has gotten into the habit of padding his expense account after out-of-town trips. When he attends various conferences, nearly all meals are taken care of. Their cost has been built into the original registration fee, which is paid by the employer. During the conference, the employee has virtually no out-of-pocket food expenses. Company policy, of course, requires that this be reflected when requesting reimbursement. Nevertheless, when the employee returns home and submits his expenses, he always claims the full $67 per diem for meals. For some lengthy trips, this amounts to several hundred dollars beyond actual expenses. (What rationalizations might this individual use to gloss over breach of company policy, falsification of records, and theft?)

The point of this exercise is to show how easy it is to justify wrongdoing. Rationalizations lie almost everywhere, and using them may become habitual. Such thinking can be a warning signal for the existence of questionable behavior. Where rationalizations abound, poor ethics is probably not far away.

Avoiding Calluses and Finding Good Ethics

The previous discussion would suggest that good ethics is not simply an intellectual achievement. People do not reach the age of reason, figure ethics out, and then become saints. Ethical growth is better described as a process of habituating, refining, and developing the requisite virtues and skills (Meilaender 1984). It is a lifelong process of cultivating sensitivity and insight as well as mustering the courage to act accordingly.

If we see good ethics as a natural process and as something for which the human species is prepared, we can gain some clues about good behavior by observing ourselves at our best and our worst.

Natural Ties

Charity starts at home. This is as much a biological statement as it is a philosophic or religious one. Animals naturally care about their offspring. Likewise, human beings care deeply about family members.

It is almost as if we are born with concentric circles of diminishing duty around us. The strongest, innermost circle includes immediate family. The ties here are extremely tight, and all manner of inconvenience and even sacrifice are borne for the sake of blood kin. The next concentric ring might be extended family, then our circle of good friends, then perhaps our countrymen and women, or those who share the same faith, or people who work in the same company or profession.

We are likely to care more about those we know and with whom we have some important ties than strangers (Glover 2000). While good ethics cannot stop with friends, our natural tendency to behave better with those we care about can help foster better professional ethics. This requires us to "expand the circle" (Singer 1981) of those we care about to include more occasional acquaintances.

Steps can be taken to build family ties in sport, the workplace, the neighborhood, and across the globe. Some athletic leagues generate a great deal of respect between competing programs. Belonging to the league is a source of pride, and member actions reflect the respect they show for the organization. Some athletes in a given sport generate a great deal of respect for competitors. The fact that they are all committed to the same activity is an important tie between them. In a palpable sense, they are members of the same family and need to act accordingly.

Corporations, schools, and businesses would all like to find formulas to help them build a family atmosphere at work. They can conduct workshops, train managers, and establish policies that work in what might be called a family direction. When employees feel strong personal ties to the workplace, they are much less likely to take the sorts of liberties that are associated with questionable professional ethics.

While biological families do not always provide the most idyllic settings for high ethics, family ties are typically strong. "Family feeling" offers a foundation on which to build good behavior between colleagues, teammates, or even opponents. If we are naturally inclined to take care of our own, we should take advantage of this tendency by fortifying family ties and by expanding the family circle, even to the workplace.

Some athletes generate a great deal of respect for competitors.

Philosophic Exercise

Is it realistic to think that a strong sense of family can be created in sport or in the work-place? If you were in charge of a team or a company, what policies, traditions, and practices would you employ to build a sense of family? Be specific about the setting, the age of the individuals involved, and the chance of success for each of the strategies. You may be able to find some tips on the Internet by searching for themes like "employee loyalty," "employee morale," "teamwork," and "good sportsmanship."

Trust

A hypothetical game called the prisoner's dilemma has provided much material for moral theorists. One version of the problem is the farmer's dilemma (Singer 1995).

Farmer A needs help harvesting a crop before bad weather comes. He asks a neighbor, Farmer B, for assistance. This neighbor agrees in exchange for help next year when he puts a new roof on his shed.

From a self-interested point of view, the best option for Farmer A is to get the help he requested from Farmer B and save his crop. Then next year, when Farmer B asks for help, he should refuse to honor his promise and use the time for another personal project.

If these kinds of broken promises occurred very often, trust would be hard to come by. Next year if Farmer A once again asked B for help, the latter would probably refuse, simply to protect himself. While Farmer B would forfeit any chance of getting help on his roof, at least he would not also lose the day of work.

Many people, like Farmer B, end up not helping one another in order to protect themselves from the worst possible outcome. Without trust, all parties forfeit a much better future in which everyone benefits with only a moderate amount of sacrifice. With trust, Farmer A harvests his crop and Farmer B gets a repair job completed, outcomes that neither one could have pulled off alone.

The dilemma resides with Farmer B. He has to choose first, and he does not know if his neighbor is going to keep his promise. Does Farmer B have any rational way to decide that cooperation is the best choice when this exposes him to the worst possible outcome? The important part here is not the game theory behind the dilemma, but its practical implications for our behavior and how we create a workplace that generates trust, collaboration, and superior outcomes.

Singer (1995) argues that we can do five things to improve trust between individuals.

1. Start by cooperating. Positive spirals beat negative spirals in ethics, and the two kinds of spirals tend to perpetuate themselves. If Farmer B refuses to cooperate, this is likely to leave Farmer A with a bad taste in his mouth. When Farmer B later asks him for help, Farmer A will undoubtedly refuse. Conversely, when Farmer B cooperates it improves the odds of a positive response from A at some future time. A positive spiral has been initiated.

2. Cooperate as long as your partner cooperates. If these two farmers continue to live near one another and continue to have needs that require reciprocal help, back-and-forth cooperation will make both of their lives better.

3. Defect as soon as your partner defects. Anyone who selfishly defects must learn that such behavior carries a cost. Anyone who defects without negative consequences may take this as positive reinforcement. It is not ethically wise to be a sucker, not only for yourself but also because it perpetuates selfishness on the part of others.

4. Be ready to forgive. Negative spirals need to be turned in positive directions. If your neighbor shows signs of remorse and readiness to cooperate again, be receptive. Don't hold grudges. Move back to a cooperative attitude.

5. Promote stability in relationships and transparency in cooperation and defection. The first four steps work in stable relationships and where any defections are immediately known.

As noted, if Farmer A and B are going to live next to one another for a long time, they have good reason to develop trust and the reciprocal cooperation that trust allows. Each year Farmer A will be sure to get his crops in, and each year Farmer B will have help with a project that would be difficult to accomplish alone. If each one wants to continue to reap these benefits, they need to maintain the cooperative cycle. And if either one reneges on the arrangement, it will be immediately evident. The guilty party could be made to pay by the instant withdrawal of the other farmer's assistance.

In real life, however, such stability and transparency are not always available. Coaches sometimes act like selfish farmers, coaching a team, breaking rules, and then leaving for a different job. Employees may not honor their contract but then, before facing the consequences, move on to a new position and start the process all over again. Likewise, it is not always clear when a defection takes place. A fellow worker may act like she is cooperating when secretly she is not. Only later is it discovered that she has been defrauding the company or otherwise not doing her job.

Philosophic Exercise

Picture yourself as a head coach in a high school basketball conference of eight members. The coaches in this league do not particularly trust one another. Rumors abound, for example, that several coaches are breaking state rules by recruiting players into their school district.

Some coaches are also known to exaggerate home-court advantage by placing pep bands directly behind opposing team benches, providing poor locker-room facilities, and allowing raucous behavior in the stands. Because angry coaches are responding in kind, a negative spiral of behavior is dominating league competition, and trust is very hard to come by.

You would like to get a positive spiral started, if only in a modest way. How would you go about it? Could you use any of the principles listed on pages 197-198? How could you begin to replace distrust with trust?

Finding Freedom, Making Choices, Promoting Altruism

The recommendations related to family ties and building trust focus on our biological tendency to care for our kin and to seek out favorable reciprocal relationships. This by itself does not take ethics very far. Nor does it give us credit for our full range of human capabilities. To put it bluntly, it does not take us much beyond the two minimalist maxims of "Charity should start at home," and "If you scratch my back, I'll scratch yours."

To be sure, humankind is morally situated on the two powerful bases that shape all of us—biology and sociology. We are our genes, and we more or less grow into cultural traditions that give us a potentially parochial perspective on right and wrong. But the constraints of language, parental upbringing, religious bias, gender differences, and genetic endowments do not determine our moral actions. We still have choices. We can struggle to pull ourselves up by our moral bootstraps, look at things more or less objectively, go against the grain of common practice, and do the right thing even when it is not in our own personal best interest to do so. This is called altruism.

This tendency to seek the good without calculating personal gain or loss is grounded in unique human capabilities. They are not unique because animals are unable to put their own interests below those of their offspring or species; altruistic behavior in lower forms of animal life is well documented (Wilson 1993). But we humans can reason our way to altruism because we can step back and think more or less impartially (Singer 1981). We can examine our life as a whole and make what Singer (1995) calls the ultimate choice about how we want to live. We have the intellect to appreciate an altruistic life as a meaningful existence, one that is dedicated to important causes and improvements for a broader circle of sentient life, for our fellow human beings, and for ourselves. Consequently, human altruism is more deliberative, thus carrying a greater potential for the heroic.

Deliberation that moves us from narrow self-interest to concern for others involves several dimensions. Intuitively and experientially, all of us have met these dimensions on many occasions. But ethicists have given them names to help us recognize them and appreciate their pull in the decision-making process. To examine these dimensions, we will review an actual case that invites but does not require altruistic sacrifice.

An Olympic pole-vaulter is one of two favorites for the gold medal, but he breaks his pole while practicing for the final round. He has already snapped the only other pole he brought to the competition, and the particular brand of pole he uses is quite rare. He will either have to forfeit or use an unfamiliar

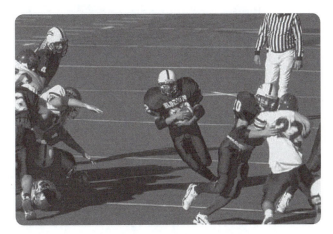

Altruism carries a greater potential for the heroic, such as when we put ourselves in harm's way for the sake of others.

pole, a tactic that would put him at a tremendous disadvantage. However, the other favorite for the gold medal uses exactly the same equipment, and he has a spare pole available. This individual, whom we will call Jim, cannot believe his good fortune at having been virtually handed the gold medal. Nevertheless he quickly realizes that he faces an unsettling moral dilemma, one that invites an uncommon level of altruism on his part. Should he offer his spare pole to his longtime adversary?

The direction that Jim's deliberations will invariably take can be traced out along three dimensions that constitute what I call Kretchmar's Kube of Moral Space, even though the ideas here have been borrowed from common ethical theory. This cube, shown in figure 10.1, will help us see the places Jim needs to go in order to carefully reason out his decision.

Three Dimensions

The horizontal dimension (axis A–B) represents two emphases in making moral decisions. The A-end of the spectrum emphasizes the utility of rules. In other words, when making decisions it may be wise to consult existing principles, such as common rules of good sportsmanship. Rules are useful because moral dilemmas tend to repeat themselves. Moral agents do not need to reinvent the ethical wheel each time they need to make a decision. In addition, many common rules

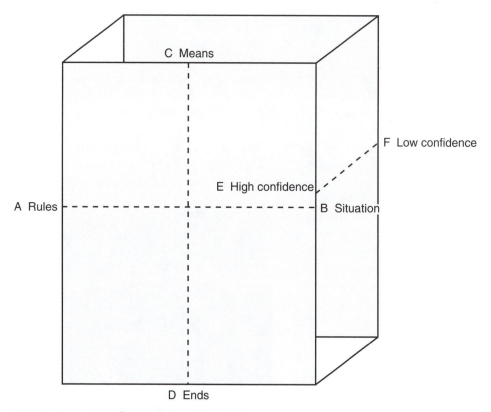

FIGURE 10.1   Kretchmar's Kube of Moral Space.

have stood the test of time. Their usefulness across the centuries gives them a certain authority. Consequently, Jim will need to consider relevant rules before he makes a decision.

The B-end of the axis speaks to a weakness of rules, particularly if they are thought to be a sufficient basis for moral decision making. No two moral situations are exactly alike, and moral agents need to consider those differences. This drives individuals to examine the facts of their case and look for unusual circumstances that might affect moral duty or opportunity. If a situation were radically distinctive, a person might conclude that common moral rules are utterly useless in this case. And some individuals have argued that, even without unusual circumstances, moral rules are unhelpful. Regardless of which position Jim holds toward the utility of rules, he will need to examine the specific facts of his situation for additional guidance.

The vertical dimension (axis C–D) identifies two additional elements of moral space. When we move toward the C-end of the spectrum, we are impressed with the human obligation to do the right thing regardless of consequences. We realize that we need to take our responsibilities to other people very seriously—for example, our duty to keep promises or to tell the truth. It is here that we see how dangerous it is to use other people. At the top of the vertical axis, we see that the ends typically do not justify the means. Jim will consider these notions because his unlucky opponent is, of course, a human being with his own rights and interests.

The D-end of the axis outlines another valid concern, one that complements the thinking at the top of this axis. If we need to take other people seriously, we also need to take the promotion of the good seriously. Good moral agents need to not only tell the truth, but to look at the consequences of that action, the amount of good or harm that their act of truth-telling creates. This thinking leads us to conclude that, at times, the ends do justify or at least influence the means. Jim will need to consider the consequences of his actions, the good and harm that they will produce.

Finally, the third axis, which runs from the front to the back of the cube (axis E–F), depicts another important set of considerations that lie at tension with one another. Near the front of the cube at E we experience a high degree of confidence in the information we have, the clarity of our thinking, the strength of the rules we have employed, or the amount of good that our actions will produce. This is the high certainty area of ethics. From this position, Jim would be inclined to trust his thinking and charge ahead in the direction that he identifies as morally superior.

The area near F forces us to entertain skeptical thoughts. Perhaps our "facts" are merely convenient conclusions that support what we wanted all along. Perhaps we've chosen the wrong rules or incorrectly applied them to our situation. This is the space that acknowledges the fact that ethics is hard work and that solid ethical conclusions are hard to uncover. In this area of the cube, Jim might hesitate in making a decision, or he might conclude that there is no best answer in this situation.

Some ethicists have argued that each of us tends to favor one end of each of the three axes over the others. While this is probably true, it is also useful to see that all six points are attractive and may contain elements of truth. Even though we gravitate toward different comfort zones in the cube, we also entertain thoughts that take us left and right, top and bottom, front and back.

Philosophic Exercise

What do you think Jim should do in this situation? Try to identify at least two arguments from points A, B, C, and D. Based on this, identify the best course of action for Jim. Then speculate on where this places you on axis E–F. Do you have much confidence in this recommendation? Why or why not?

In the following section I will visit the first four sites and make the argument that John has no moral responsibility to share his pole. See if you can take the opposite point of view at each of these four sites and find arguments for the moral superiority of choosing to share his equipment.

An Example of Kube Reasoning

The claims made at the various areas of the kube are not the only ones that would work in those places, but they do exemplify the kind of reasoning employed at each site.

◆ Position A. Certainly nobody would blame Jim if he chose not to share his spare pole. Rules about playing fairly do not require us to go that far. We all know that chance events intervene in sport from time to time. A ball takes a bad hop; the sun gets in someone's eyes; a piece of equipment breaks. Rules of sportsmanship do not require opponents to make up for these so-called acts of God.

◆ Position B. When examining the situation, we see that typically athletes are responsible for their own equipment. Bike riders need to have extra bike frames, tires, and helmets because these things can break. Tennis players always carry a bag full of extra rackets in case strings or frames break during competition. Perhaps the unlucky pole-vaulter is responsible for not taking all the required prudent steps. He brought one extra pole, but he should have brought two.

◆ Position C. When Jim considers his obligation to his opponent, in particular his promise to compete fairly, he might well conclude that sharing his pole is not required. He promised to complete fairly, and he has done that. The rules allow his opponent to find another pole, and Jim will fully honor that rule.

◆ Position D. Objectivity on the promotion of the greatest good is difficult for Jim. He has lived the better part of his life for this one moment—winning the Olympic gold. A great amount of good is likely to come to him, his family, his team, and his country by taking advantage of this unexpected intervention of fate. But to make this less personal, it might be better for the sport in general if such accommodations as sharing equipment did not become the norm. If athletes were expected to compensate for every intervention of luck, competitions would be continually interrupted for purposes of voluntary compensation. And Jim has a further unsettling thought about promoting the greatest good. What if he gave away his spare pole, and then his own equipment broke? How would justice be served in this situation? The greatest good, he concludes, is served by allowing fate to play its role, even though at times it is regrettable.

Jim decides that he is under no moral obligation to share his equipment. If asked by his opponent, he will express regrets but indicate that his extra pole must be kept as a backup for his own jumping.

What do you think about Jim's decision? Is it possible that he is under no moral obligation to share his extra pole but at the same time could reach a level of moral excellence if he were to do so? The arguments I presented have a flavor of ethical minimalism, a position that allows us to adopt the least demanding moral requirement. Jim performed acceptably in an ethical sense, and his reasoning was not off. Nevertheless, he missed an opportunity to reach for a more altruistic solution. He was not able to find the reasons—or muster the will and the courage to find the reasons—that would justify the more heroic act of giving an opponent a second chance when such an opportunity is not required.

"Facts" can be selectively gathered to support what we want.

REVIEW

Ethics involves a messy search for how we ought to behave and what kind of life we ought to live. It is important to develop a healthy confidence in ethical reasoning. Some of this confidence is built by having realistic expectations for ethics, by not expecting too much or too little of these evaluative capabilities. Ethics is also complex in that it involves the development of good habits, attitudes, and virtues, not just insight.

While human beings are biologically built to cooperate and participate in good ethics, other forces will often combine to produce moral calluses that reduce the capability to behave well and seek superior values. Good ethics comes from many sources:

◆ From caring for family and loved ones

◆ From trustful, reciprocal arrangements where a positive spiral of cooperation makes life better for everyone

◆ From the human powers of reason that can negotiate the difficult terrain of rules, unique situations, obligations to do the right thing, and interests in maximizing the good, all while keeping selfish interests at bay

Athletes and kinesiology professionals are capable of acts of selfless altruism, but this level of behavior is often difficult to achieve.

LOOKING AHEAD

We can now begin to apply our moral reasoning to professional circumstances. We learned that, as moral agents, we can distinguish between how people live and how people should live. As kinesiologists, we need to be intelligent about how we deliver our services and toward what ends we direct our work. In chapter 11, we will develop a method to make such evaluations.

CHECKING YOUR UNDERSTANDING

1. *What is ethics? Why did Midgley say that conflict is at the heart of ethical reasoning? Why is the difference between "is" and "should" so important?*

2. *How do we develop confidence in ethical reasoning? What are some of the unrealistic expectations that tend to shake this confidence?*

3. *What are moral calluses? How do they develop and what are their consequences?*

4. *What do family ties, trust, and altruism have to do with avoiding excess calluses? How can we apply each one of these to professional practice in order to improve behavior at the workplace?*

5. *In moral decision making, what is the difference between rule ethics and situation ethics, doing the right thing regardless of consequences and promoting the greatest balance of good over evil, and high moral confidence and low moral confidence? How did these six considerations influence Jim's decision on whether or not to lend his extra pole to his opponent?*

11

Physical Activity
and the Good Life

© Empics

In previous chapters we entertained the unsettling notion that movement that requires a high heart rate and use of the whole body is becoming outdated. In other words, our health-promotion services may not be required for something called the good life. In our brave new world of technology, biochemistry, and genetic engineering, nobody would have to move—at least not in the more or less vigorous dog-walking, leaf-raking, stairway-using, game-playing ways that kinesiologists currently recommend. Only people who *wanted* to exercise, dance, or engage in vigorous gardening would put on their sweats and lace up their sneakers.

These speculations, however, may strike many of us as unduly pessimistic. At minimum, they raise some interesting questions.

◆ Is this portrayal of modern medicine too positive? For instance, don't people risk harmful side effects when they substitute artificial interventions for physical activity?

◆ Isn't exercise still an indispensable part of healthful living, and won't it retain this status for the foreseeable future?

◆ Can we find some way to argue that activity is necessary to the good life without playing the health card?

◆ Are sedentary people not only taking unnecessary health risks but also missing out on an important part of life?

THE GOOD LIFE

The good life refers to the experiences and conditions of living that we regard as desirable. While most people aim for good living in one sense or another, we disagree about what exactly it entails. For some the good life includes things like owning a home in a nice neighborhood, having two cars, being happily married, raising healthy and well-adjusted children, and enjoying a successful

CHAPTER OBJECTIVES

In this chapter, you will

◆ *define what values are and see how they contribute to the good life,*

◆ *encounter four traditional values of physical education,*

◆ *understand the dangers of blindly promoting traditional values,*

◆ *learn why it is important to distinguish the significance of different values, and*

◆ *discover a technique for doing this.*

career. For others there are fewer criteria; for them the good life is being healthy and happy, or perhaps rich and famous. Some describe the good life in more philosophic terms. They think that it includes loving and being loved, having a close relationship with God, or dedicating themselves to important causes like world peace or protection of the environment.

As noted in chapter 10, there are many ways to achieve the good life. As discriminating philosophic shoppers, one person might emphasize excellence, another adventure, another friendship, and yet another achievement. All of these choices can be satisfying.

Values and the Good Life

The good life is not produced by magic or any other mysterious process. It is built value by value. In other words, the good life is a composite of individual values that are woven into a person's life.

Two classes of values exist. Moral values are certain motives and personality traits. They describe what we often call a moral person. These are traits like honesty, conscientiousness, affection, prudence, love, and courage. Nonmoral values are things we desire from life. Rather than describe a person or a person's motives, nonmoral values identify items that people want, such as pleasure, knowledge, wealth, security, excellence, and friendship.

Both kinds of values are important to the good life. For example, it might be difficult to live well without the moral values of integrity and good reputation and the nonmoral values of security and friendship. Kinesiologists, of course, are interested in the relationship between these patterns of good living and the roles that embodiment and movement might play in achieving them. Is it possible or likely that people can live a good life without exercising or otherwise moving?

Philosophic Exercise

How would you define the good life? Following is a list of values from Frankena (1973, 87-88). First, try to reduce this list to the five values that you believe are most central to the good life. See if you can rank those five choices from the most to the least important. Finally, take another look at the entire list and mark those that you believe your movement profession can directly and reliably promote.

◆ Life, consciousness, and activity
◆ Health and strength
◆ Pleasure and satisfaction of all or certain kinds
◆ Happiness and contentment
◆ Truth
◆ Knowledge and true opinion of various kinds, understanding, and wisdom
◆ Beauty, harmony, and proportion in objects contemplated
◆ Virtues

- ◆ Aesthetic experience
- ◆ Mutual affection, love, friendship, and cooperation
- ◆ Just distribution of good and evil
- ◆ Harmony and proportion in one's own life
- ◆ Power and experiences of achievement
- ◆ Self-expression
- ◆ Freedom
- ◆ Peace and security
- ◆ Adventure and novelty
- ◆ Good reputation, honor, and esteem

It is not hard to find good values; if anything, it was probably difficult to narrow the list to five choices. It should also be easy to see how your vocation can foster any number of these values.

The Contribution of Kinesiology to the Good Life

Kinesiology can contribute to many of these values, perhaps even to all of them in one way or another. Our predecessors made several attempts to articulate who we are and what we do best. While they may not deserve the last word on this, we should benefit from their insights and stand on their shoulders, so to speak, before moving ahead.

Kinesiology has shown a great deal of consistency in describing its primary values. This section explains three formulations. One was popular as long ago as the early 1900s (Hetherington 1910), another has been written to lead us into the 21st century (NASPE 1992 and 2004), and a third identifies the root values in the other two formulations.

Formulation 1: The Four Ends of Physical Education

Hetherington was an American physical educator who argued that our contributions fall under four objectives.

- ◆ Organic ends are biological objectives. Examples are fitness, health, longevity, life itself, strength, power, endurance, lack of pain or discomfort, and ease in moving.
- ◆ Cognitive ends are knowledge objectives. Examples are understanding, facts, wisdom, freedom, insight, and truth.
- ◆ Psychomotor ends are skill objectives. Examples are skill, effective action, competence, freedom and expression, participation (in cultural forms of sport and dance, for example), and creativity.
- ◆ Affective ends are attitudinal, experiential objectives. Examples are character development, appreciation, meaning, enjoyment, and fun.

Formulation 2: The Physically Educated Person

A physically educated person

- ◆ demonstrates competency in motor skills and movement patterns needed to perform a variety of physical activities;
- ◆ demonstrates understanding of movement concepts, principles, strategies, and tactics as they apply to learning and performance of physical activities;
- ◆ participates regularly in physical activity;
- ◆ achieves and maintains a health-enhancing level of physical fitness;
- ◆ exhibits responsible and respectful personal and social behavior in physical activity settings; and
- ◆ values the benefits of physical activity such as health, enjoyment, stimulation, self-expression, and social interaction (NASPE 2004).

Formulation 3: Four Prime Values

In many ways formulations 1 and 2 point in the same direction. The best terms I have found to capture these values are activity-related health, knowledge, skill, and fun. In my judgment, these nonmoral goods have been and continue to be the four most significant values in our profession. They constitute our central contributions to the good life.

To make sure we know what these values are, and to be clear that these are four different goods, each one needs further explanation.

Health Our profession places high value on health and fitness. This value shows up in our concern for such matters as organic well-being, aerobic and anaerobic fitness, strength, flexibility, weight reduction, youthful appearance, and lower blood pressure. Our commitment to biological health

© Digital Vision

Sport knowledge and skills enable one to reach places others cannot find.

and to life itself is promoted by the President's Council on Physical Fitness, AAHPERD's Physical Best program, exercise and diet programs, courses in aerobic dance and jogging, and a multitude of self-help books and other products. This value is supported by recent shifts in emphasis from physical fitness to health, from sport to a physically active lifestyle, and from vigorous activities to less demanding but regular movement experiences.

Knowledge   The high value our profession places on knowledge shows up in our concern for research, attaining academic respectability, and promoting learning about human movement. Kinesiologists not only lead people into healthful movement activities and teach them the skills to move well but also explain the scientific basis of good health, in particular relationships between activity, obesity, cardiovascular fitness, and overall health. We see knowledge values in cognitive approaches to learning, academic kinesiology programs, and efforts to make sure that students learn principles related to play and not just motor skills or movement habits.

Skill   The high value our profession places on skill shows in our concern for motor skill development; the learning of dance, exercise, play, and game skills; the acquisition of general movement habits and skills; and the achievement of athletic excellence. This commitment to practical wisdom is reflected in curricula dominated by skill development. It can also be seen in countless books, films, and coaching tips devoted to improving movement skills.

Fun   The high value our profession places on fun shows up in our concern for meaningful involvement, self-development, excitement, and aesthetic satisfaction. These values, and more fundamentally a commitment to satisfaction, are reflected in program emphases on play, self-improvement, and safe challenges. Siedentop's sport education curriculum (see pages 129-130), the proliferation of pedometers, and virtually all modern approaches to teaching physical activity acknowledge the significance of the affective. Movement must be fun!

Philosophic Exercise

Identify some alternatives or additions to these four values and then look for ways in which these value commitments show up in our profession. For example, are excellence, winning, moral development, or artistic expression values that physical education can promote? Can you find ways in which kinesiology already promotes them?

WHY PRIORITIZE VALUES?

If the movement professions are comfortable with the four values just identified, why is it necessary to rank them? Would it not be reasonable to pursue goals in each of these four directions? After all, most activity professions seem capable of producing all four values to one degree or another. And without question all four are important elements in the good life. Why can't we keep health, knowledge, skill, and fun side by side?

There are at least three reasons for not caving in to this temptation, as reasonable as it may seem:

◆ Value choices make a difference.
◆ Prioritization is unavoidable in life.
◆ Prioritization provides focus for professional and political purposes.

Value Choices Make a Difference

Value preferences are powerful things, and they are not to be underestimated. Why did Martin Luther King, Jr, fight for racial equality? Was it something he ate for lunch, or a principle in which he believed? What causes political tension in the Middle East? Is it a chemical in Arabs and Israelis, or a different vision of what fairness and justice demand? Why do some athletes and dancers dedicate themselves to their craft well beyond any reasonable call of duty? Is it the physiological structure of their right knee, or a dedication to excellence?

A holistic answer to all three questions would be both yes and no. Inspiring thoughts are influenced by lunches, brain chemicals, and the anatomy of knees. Likewise, ideas influence metabolism, chemicals, and anatomy. Both the tangible and intangible are involved in the causative chain of events that leads to action.

However that may be, the critical point is what we learned in chapter 5: Our interests and commitments cannot be reduced to physical causes. We can't dismiss values just because they are not physical. Wrestling with ideas and making judgments on values have a tremendous effect on what we plan, where we go, and what we do. Value choices make a difference!

Let's take another look at the four traditional values to see how dramatically different our professional focus would be if we were to give priority to one over the others.

Health-Oriented Philosophy

This philosophy holds that the focus of kinesiology should be on human health and well-being. What is more important than life itself? What allows people to enjoy life more than overall health and physical fitness?

A profession committed to health is on firm footing, for scientific evidence on the beneficial effects of exercise is mounting. Teachers, coaches, and trainers can have a measurable effect on people's weight, appearance, and overall health. This evidence is timely because North America and much of the world needs preventive health-related practices now more than ever. Leading causes of death are more related to unhealthy behavior than to infectious disease. Many adults lead sedentary lives. And high health care and insurance costs present

Health: A powerful tool for everything we want from life.

a clear economic danger to our society. Sedentary living is epidemic among youths as well, with childhood obesity now a national health problem.

There has never been a time when people have been more concerned about their health and conscious of their appearance. Our profession should take advantage of this fact and make sure that its members provide the expertise needed for the growing demand for fitness and health. The reputation of our profession is damaged when untrained practitioners present themselves as wellness, fitness, or exercise specialists.

An emphasis on health need not produce programs that are devoted exclusively to exercise. Many sport and dance activities, for example, have cardiovascular benefits. The goal is to promote active lifestyles that maintain a reasonable degree of health.

Finally, there is no value in our field that we can sell as well as health. A good portion of the public is concerned about it; school boards are interested in it; even the United States Senate has supported it (2003). Some people unfortunately associate kinesiology with fun and games and think of its contributions as trivial. But there is nothing trivial about enhancing the health of a nation and helping to extend the lives of its citizens.

Knowledge-Oriented Philosophy

This philosophy maintains that the focus of kinesiology should be the development and transmission of knowledge about the human body, health, sport, exercise, play, and games. Physical education has been held back because it has refused to consider itself an academic field. The profession is top-heavy with practitioners who want to coach not think, teach not theorize. There is nothing wrong with activity itself, but an overly pervasive anti-intellectual tone has produced generations of gym teachers who are far more trained than educated and who operate more on intuition than on solid information. The field of kinesiology has an obligation to generate knowledge about human movement and to share it with others.

A profession dedicated to the development and transmission of knowledge is on firm footing because society recognizes that science and technology hold many of the keys to the future. Elite athletes cannot afford to ignore the fruits of research any more than practitioners working on pollution, world hunger, or other complex issues can. As kinesiology heads into the 21st century, we must aggressively study its potential to alleviate such problems as chronic disease, rising health care costs, childhood obesity, and debilitation in an aging population. We must also communicate the results more clearly and put them to use.

We need to reemphasize kinesiology as an academic field. First, there is a general mood that supports a return to the basics, and the basics are generally understood to be academic skills and knowledge, not health and recreation. Second, if teaching, professional preparation, and research are to survive in colleges and universities, they must present an academic image. Teaching Games for Understanding (Griffin and Butler 2004), for example, should replace rote, drill-oriented approaches to skill and health instruction. Knowledge and understanding should lead or accompany every objective our field endorses and every program it offers.

A field that focuses on the generation and transmission of knowledge need not abandon the practices of

© Getty Images

The field of kinesiology has an obligation to generate knowledge about human movement and to share that knowledge with others.

sport and exercise. These are important, too, but they must not dominate the field. Good practice follows from good science. Practice should not precede science or take its place.

Finally, there is no value we can sell as well as knowledge. People spend millions of dollars on how-to books and literature ranging from topics like diet and exercise to stress reduction through sport. People want to know how to live longer, how to stay young, how to win Olympic gold medals, and how to dance and play better. Ours is the profession that can and should provide the answers to many of those questions.

Skill-Oriented Philosophy

This philosophy holds that kinesiology should focus on skill development in physical activities. This is what the profession does best. Professionals must stop trying to be something they are not. They must stop jumping on the health and academic bandwagons just so they can say that they are important and respectable. They should stop trying to be like everyone else and start being themselves.

To help individuals participate successfully in their culture, teach them how to perform the movements, play the games, and dance the dances of their people.

A profession devoted to skill development is on solid ground, for skills are the foundation of so much that people do. Movement capabilities are basic skills every bit as much as reading, writing, and arithmetic. People who don't move well are afraid to play, dance, and engage in sport. More than that, their very ability to explore the world and express themselves is limited. When asked to exercise, learn, or recreate in physical ways, they participate reluctantly or simply decline the invitation. Literally and figuratively, they remain victims of fear and ignorance and as a result remain on the sidelines of life.

There has hardly been a time when the teaching of skills has been more important. Our society is movement-crazed. People seek spiritual experiences in yoga and tai chi. They spend billions of dollars on everything from club memberships and athletic equipment to golf and tennis lessons. While large numbers of people participate in vigorous activities on a regular basis, there is an even larger number who might like to do so except for the lack of physical skills. It's a small wonder that there is so much obesity and so many who do not participate. People without basic movement skills find little enjoyment in physical activities. The clientele is there, and so is the need. The only question is whether or not our profession will answer the call and provide sound skills education.

A focus on skills is crucial for yet another reason. When instructors teach dances and games, they teach culture. They prepare individuals to enter a society complete with its values, stories, and myths. It has been said that if you want to understand a people, you should study them at play. It can also be said that if you want to educate individuals to participate successfully in their culture, you should educate them to play the games and dance the dances of their people.

An emphasis on skill development will not produce programs that exclude physical fitness, knowledge, and fun. These values are by-products of skillful behavior, and to some extent skill acquisition depends on health, knowledge,

© Associated Press/Herald Times Reporter/Tim Swoboda

and pleasure. But this must not derail our profession from its unique function in society—instruction in movement skills with an emphasis on sport, dance, exercise, games, and play.

We can successfully promote skill development to individuals, school boards, and corporations. However, we will have to show that our profession can make a difference. Physical educators can no longer roll out the ball and expect skill to magically appear. They can no longer tolerate gym classes that are more recreation than education. They can no longer spend excessive time on theory and repetitive exercises. Kinesiologists do not need to be like everyone else, for teaching movement skills and preparing students to take part in their culture need no further justification.

Fun-Oriented Philosophy

This emphasis suggests that kinesiology should focus on pleasure. When people say that our field is the toy department of service, business, and education, we should accept that as a compliment. People have always wanted to lead fun-filled lives. As members of this profession we should be delighted that we have been identified as major contributors to that end.

A profession committed to fun is on solid footing, for much scientific evidence suggests that people are suffering from many work- and stress-induced diseases. Play may not be simply a good value but rather a necessary one. People are realizing, sometimes too late, that much that is valuable in life is not related to fame, fortune, and extra hours on the job but to the ability to relax and enjoy themselves.

In a workaholic culture, people need help slowing down their frenzied lives and recapturing the ability to play. Kinesiology professionals should take advantage of this fact and present their activities as valuable in their own right, not as a means to a longer life or as a

© DigitalVision

Play is not only valuable; it is also necessary.

laboratory for theory. Whenever sport, dance, and games are made to do work for other values, instructors risk making them less enjoyable. By presenting them as important and useful, kinesiologists suggest that participation in activity is rational, even obligatory. They snuff out spontaneity, exploration, play, and much of the meaning and fun that can be found there.

People who have fun when they move will be motivated to return to the playground. And because they are actively involved, they will gain fitness, develop their skills, and pick up some knowledge. Thus, a program that is oriented toward fun does not stand in opposition to these other values. It may even be good from time to time to directly promote the values of fitness, skill, and knowledge in order to make participation in an activity even more fun. Problems emerge, however, if these and other serious values are introduced as the real goals of activity. When this happens, physical education and recreation become work, not an interlude in which to smell the daisies.

Why is it that so many school-age children report unsatisfactory experiences in their physical-education programs? Perhaps it is due in part to the fact that kinesiology has been too structured, too drill-oriented. At the same time, professionals may have been too little concerned with making their teaching and service environments what they tend to be in the first place—playgrounds.

There may be no value that sells as well as fun, for it is a key element in almost everyone's definition of the good life. In a culture that is fascinated with productivity and achievement, it is particularly useful. In a culture that is also fascinated with enjoyment, it is attractive. The best thing teachers can do with their subject matter is simply let it be, because kinesiology is the home of fun and games.

Philosophic Exercise

Review the four value choices and rank them from most to least important. What does this say about your value system? What does it say about the way you view life?

Now that you've identified your value choices, can you also defend them? Try to give at least one justification for your choices. See if your colleagues or classmates have similar rankings and reasons for their choices.

Value Choices Are Unavoidable

You may have realized from the preceding exercise that you have already made some value commitments, whether or not you set out to do so. Perhaps one or more of the four philosophies hit home. It had you saying to yourself, "Yes, yes! That's it!" Others may have been attractive in lesser degrees, and one or more may have even left you wondering why anyone would want to aim their professional activities in that direction.

If this was the case, then you are not a novice at committing yourself to some values over others. Even if you had no particular reaction to any of these statements, you undoubtedly have made thousands of value decisions in your life. Because all human beings naturally prefer home runs to strikeouts, a graceful and expressive plié to an awkward and mechanical dance movement, and good physical fitness to poor health, it is impossible to honestly claim that you do not make value judgments.

The only question, then, is whether or not you have given careful attention to these commitments. Have you forfeited your right to make further choices by choosing to follow the crowd? Are your decisions automatic, emotional, and based only on what feels right at the moment? Or are your decisions more deliberate and thoughtful?

Value Choices Provide Focus

Even though you have already made value decisions and probably favor one or two of the four values over others, it is likely that you found all four values to be worthy of at least some support. The 2004 NASPE Standards printed on page 209 feature each one. Who of us wants to speak out against health, knowledge, skill, or play?

But you still do not have to promote them all equally. You can say that, while all of these values deserve attention and support, one or more of them should be emphasized over the others. The problem is that many professionals have been reluctant to make these tough decisions. They have tried to be all things to all people. This prevents them from having a clear professional focus, which has serious consequences. Some of these consequences affect professional activities. Others have broader implications.

Professional Problems

Time spent with whomever you are serving in your professional role is limited. Classes are large; equipment and other resources are frequently in short supply; the motivation of students and clients is finite. Given these limitations, you must plan your interventions carefully.

Kinesiologists are not unique in this regard. All teachers, managers, medical personnel, and leaders face limitations. All of them have to target their energies and prioritize their values to make sure that what is most important gets done and gets done well.

In our profession we have a pressing need to convince others that we can accomplish what we promise to do and to carefully document our successes. Too often we have been satisfied with getting people moving and trusting that this alone will produce positive results. But in avoiding a prioritization of values, we have not been careful in deciding *how* people should be moving. Our unwillingness to focus our energies has contributed to our lack of accountability.

One of the goals of the National Association of Sport and Physical Education (NASPE) Justification Project (Seefeldt 1986) was to gather scientific evidence that showed that kinesiologists can and do achieve various outcomes. Vogel (1986) identified 23 areas in which physical education makes concrete contributions to healthful living. More recently the Task Force on Community Preventive Services (President's Council 2003) made similar claims. The areas identified by both studies run the gamut from aerobic fitness, strength, and agility to social gains, perceptual motor development, and knowledge. The problem, of course, is that pursuing more than 20 objectives without any prioritization virtually guarantees that none of them will be accomplished well. Accountability and credibility again suffer.

Political Problems

In a world where we need to court the support of taxpayers, boards of education, investors, and clients, it is strategically foolish to swim aimlessly in a sea of competing values. It could appear to these important supporters that we do not know what we are doing. Before these people invest in us, most want to be assured that we have direction and that clear values provide compass points for moving one way and not another. They want to know whether we embrace fitness over skill instruction, enjoyment over knowledge, good character over strong bodies—and why.

The answer, of course, depends partly on your specific profession. Many physical educators support all four values, but this does not absolve them from the responsibility of showing clients and supporters what their most significant missions are. Anything less sends mixed messages.

A recent study showed a significant relationship between physical fitness and academic achievement (CDE 2002). In some ways this is unsurprising. Healthy

Is there a solid link between physical fitness and academic achievement?

people should be able to do many things better than their less healthy counterparts, including perform better academically. It is also possible that children who are more fit come from parents who enjoy a superior socioeconomic status. Regardless of the validity of claims about activity and academic achievement, it was surprising to observe the giddy, almost euphoric reception of this study among some kinesiologists (Blakemore 2003). Finally, we seemed to be saying, we have an academically respectable purpose. We manufacture intelligence; we produce better capabilities in math and language. We deserve respect!

It is almost sad to see this anxious latching on to whatever society wants. Of course, we need to research the relationship between movement and academic achievement. As holists, we already acknowledge that moving well requires a kind of intelligence. Skilled movement *is* intelligent behavior. Whether it also affects our abilities to deal with numbers, words, and abstractions is another question, one that deserves to be answered. But in the meantime, we need to keep our philosophical composure. What are we about? What should we be about? If we are unsure, we will look professionally immature as we hop on every attractive cultural trend that rolls by.

It has been said that those who value everything in fact value nothing. While this appears to be a contradiction in a strict logical sense, it contains an important truth. Professionals who fail to prioritize their values are often seen as lacking

- ◆ insight (they do not know what they stand for),
- ◆ energy (they are too lazy to come to grips with their commitments),
- ◆ interest (they are in kinesiology simply to make a living),
- ◆ direction (they flip-flop unpredictably), and
- ◆ courage (they have commitments but lack the fortitude to stand behind them).

Such perceptions, whether accurate or not, can have devastating effects on our profession and on individual careers.

MAKING VALUE CHOICES

We need a method that will produce persuasive reasons for our value choices. Such a procedure should not allow us to impose personal values and parade them as if they should be everyone's values. But it must be sufficiently discriminating to keep us from concluding that people can value anything they choose. This method must balance the need for prescriptions about what is good for everyone with tolerance for individual choices.

Tolerance deserves special attention because objectively prioritizing movement values results in prescribing what is best for others as well as ourselves. We will be claiming that we have some idea about how movement should lead to better lives for *all* human beings.

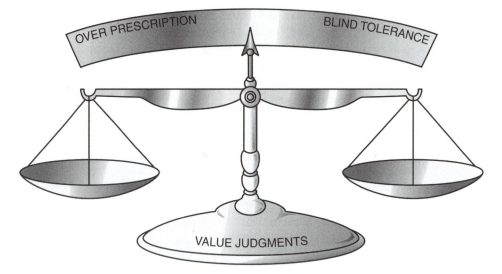

We need a method that balances prescription and tolerance.

Reasons for Tolerance and Caution

There are at least three reasons for being cautious in making judgments about values in different lifestyles:

1. *Sound values show up in many different ways.* The same values wear different costumes around the world. Yet because these costumes are strange to our eyes, we may not recognize the familiar values that lie beneath. Many Americans, for example, do not appreciate the slow British game of cricket, or they think that the practices of Zen archery are strange, or they see traditional African tribal dances as too emotional and somehow inferior. But could these activities include familiar and objectively sound values like patience, excellence, meaning, and tradition? Might they even support some important values that we have missed or underemphasized, such as honoring wisdom and the aged? If so, as we look for the best values we must realize that they will not always look as we expect. And we must be open to the likelihood that other cultures emphasize values that extend, provide alternatives to, or complement our own traditions.

2. *Sound values can be emphasized to different degrees.* Different life circumstances warrant emphasis on different values. In some cultures and for some individuals, health should take priority. For instance, in some developing countries basic health and nutrition are major concerns. In other cultures or for other individuals, health concerns should be more in the background. Because we may have difficulty seeing others' perspectives, there is always a danger that we will be insensitive to the goodness in different value patterns. While we look for the best values we must allow for considerable variation in our prescriptions.

3. *Sound values are difficult to prioritize.* We may well make some mistakes in carrying out our analysis. We can be wrong about the significance of given values. And we can be wrong about which values should receive specific attention. For instance, if we end up ranking fun over fitness, how will we be sure that this judgment is correct? Will our arguments be so strong that we can confidently claim that we are right? And will we be able to tell what needs people really have? What if society has partly programmed people to think and say that they have needs that actually should not be supported?

In any case, there is more than ample cause for caution in prescribing our conclusions for others.

Reasons for Intolerance and Boldness

Even though we need tolerance and caution, we should not be intimidated into blindly affirming that anything goes. Traditions alone do not merit tolerance, affirmation, or even basic respect. Only good traditions do.

It is possible to see variations of the good, the bad, and the uncertain. Sport can foster such values as friendship, freedom, and personal expression. This is undoubtedly good, and these practices deserve our support. But sport has also reinforced traditions of racism, by expecting football quarterbacks to be white, for example. Sexist practices, such as the suggestion that women should not participate in certain rugged sports, remain. These patterns of behavior and so many others do not merit our support.

The third category of traditions is probably the broadest one. It includes activities that may be both good and bad, such as the emphasis on winning, early specialization for the sake of excellence and college scholarships, and health and safety risks that Olympic athletes take for the benefits of elite participation. Are these the practices of a healthy society that values

© Photodisc

Rough sport: the practice of a healthy society that values individual excellence and achievement, or the traditions of a society gone astray?

individual excellence and achievement? Or are they traditions of a society gone astray? We cannot be sure.

It is easier to be bold in supporting traditions that are clearly sound and to condemn practices that are clearly misguided. It is harder to be bold in making the more difficult decisions on ambiguous cases. Nevertheless, our emphasis on tolerance does not relieve us of the responsibility to think boldly about what is right and wrong, to report our conclusions, and to incorporate them into our actions.

RANKING VALUES

Baier (1958) suggests that we must take at least two steps in order to rank values effectively. The first requires us to survey the facts and the second requires us to weigh the reasons.

Surveying the Facts

Surveying the facts involves cataloging the characteristics and benefits of each value, including

- short- and long-term benefits,
- benefits for ourselves and others, and
- benefits as ends in themselves and as means to other ends.

This process is currently threatened by the state of research on the values of sport, exercise, and play. We do not yet know some of the benefits of kinesiology's activities, so we need to proceed on the basis of partial information and what we currently know.

Fortunately, our four values—health, knowledge, skill, and fun—are so fundamental and so well researched that we believe we can produce them to one degree or another. To be sure, we do not understand all there is to know about how to create them or to what degree we bring them into being. While it might be good to get into the scientific details on these issues, ours is a philosophic journey. We must be content with the realization that health, knowledge, skill, and fun are realistic values for us to prioritize. We can proceed with confidence that we are spending our time wisely by reviewing values that we can produce.

Weighing the Reasons

In the second step, weighing the reasons, I propose three criteria for determining what Baier (1958) calls the rules of superiority. These criteria allow us to evaluate the evidence gathered from surveying the facts. For example, suppose we now have a list of all the known benefits of skill and knowledge in front of us. The problem is that both lists appear impressive. Under skill we see "freedom to move," "ability to express oneself creatively," and many other benefits. Under knowledge we notice "capacity to understand and play by game rules," "ability to avoid mistakes in dieting and exercising," and other good things.

Our tendency here may be to fall back on our personal biases. And it is conceivable that our biases would serve us well. But because we are doing philosophy, we need to look for a set of defensible rules for determining which of these good things should count more. We have to be able to give objective reasons for our choices.

This is a critical and difficult step to take. When we apply these rules to the factual evidence, they commit us to certain conclusions. If we do not like the conclusions, our primary recourse is to dispute the original rules of superiority. However, if we want to change the rules, we must have good reasons for doing so. The following sections detail the principles that will serve as our rules of superiority.

Rule 1: Criterion of Intrinsic Value

Values that are good in themselves are superior to values that lead to good things (Frankena 1973). The traditional way of saying this is that intrinsic values are superior to extrinsic values. Intrinsic values, or end values, are regarded as good in themselves. Excellence, happiness, and knowledge are common end values. If we were asked what the realization of excellence, happiness, or knowledge in dance is good for, we could respond, "Each one is good in itself. Experiencing such things as excellence, happiness, or knowledge needs no further justification. Such encounters themselves are the things for which we aim."

Extrinsic values, or means values, are regarded as good because they lead to values that are good in themselves. Sport practice sessions and therapeutic exercise interventions, for example, are often thought to have means value. If we were asked what routine drills and uncomfortable fitness activity are good for, we could respond, "They are not much good in themselves, but they are still valuable because they lead to things that we really want, like improvement, excellent play, and health."

Most activities in life have both intrinsic and extrinsic value. Fitness training and even repetitive drills can sometimes be

© Photodisc

It is possible to assess virtually any experience in both intrinsic and extrinsic terms.

enjoyable in their own right, even though they also lead to even more intrinsically valuable experiences. On the other hand, playing well has strong intrinsic value, but it also has extrinsic merit; for example, pleasure can serve as motivation for further practice or the acceptance of new challenges. While activities may have greater or lesser components of intrinsic and extrinsic goodness, it is possible to assess virtually any experience in both intrinsic and extrinsic terms.

It is unlikely, therefore, that any objectives of kinesiology are wholly intrinsic or wholly extrinsic. The four values of health, knowledge, skill, and fun have both intrinsic and extrinsic merit. But they may not have equal amounts of each kind of value. This first rule of superiority, therefore, will allow us to examine these values on their relative strength as intrinsic and extrinsic values. All else being equal, we will judge those that have greater intrinsic strength as superior.

Are there any good reasons for preferring end values to means values? The rationale goes like this: End values have independent worth. They carry their cash value, as it were, on their own persons. They lack nothing; they wait for nothing. Their merits are self-contained. Means values have dependent worth. Their value is derived from the end values to which they lead. Their glory is not self-contained. They need end values for their own worth to show.

This one-way dependency presents end values as superior to means values. It acknowledges that we want to experience the good life, not just spend our energy getting there. It also acknowledges that, from time to time, we are willing to endure experiences that are not part of the good life, so long as they eventually lead us to this destination. It does not, however, depict extrinsic values as unimportant. Experiences that lead to intrinsically satisfying states of affairs may be tremendously valuable—but again, primarily as means to those more important things that we experience as valuable in themselves.

In chapter 12, when we review the extrinsic power of each of the four values, we will discriminate between greater and lesser extrinsic value on the basis of its usefulness. How useful are health, knowledge, skill, and fun as a means to producing other good experiences? We will employ four criteria to answer this question:

◆ Whether the means is necessary or optional
◆ Whether the means is narrowly or broadly useful
◆ Whether the means leads to important intrinsic values or trivial ones
◆ Whether the means are efficient (without significant cost) and durable (likely to be of continuing value)

Rule 2: Criterion of Satisfaction

All else being equal, experiences that include satisfaction carry more intrinsic power than those that do not. Happiness, or what Frankena calls satisfactoriness (1973, 89), is a broader concept than pleasure or fun. It is not limited to excited emotional states, nor is it confined to the so-called animal pleasures. It can even include experiences that have a measure of discomfort, such as long-distance races, that we nevertheless live with an overall feeling of contentment. Satisfaction often comes from doing what we want to do, even if such projects introduce difficulties or hard work.

Corollary of Purity   *Satisfaction that brings little or no harm into the world is preferred to satisfaction that brings greater harm.* We may experience some satisfaction in soundly defeating a weak opponent. The experience of succeeding dramatically and scoring effortlessly may be pleasurable and intrinsically valuable for that reason. Yet the behavior itself may not be defensible because it causes another person pain and possibly harms one's own integrity. This sort of behavior is less valuable than behavior that includes the same experience of succeeding without hurting the opponent—for instance, in a close, well-played game against a worthy competitor.

Corollary of Durability   *Satisfaction that is durable or dependably recurring is preferred to satisfaction that is temporary or erratic* (Fraleigh 1986; Parker 1957). When we experience success by winning the big game, for example, the satisfaction is temporary. The good feeling lasts a while and sometimes can even be recalled years later. But there is another game to be played; there is another challenge to be met. The memories of fans are short, and the heroes of today are often forgotten tomorrow. This experience of success is less valuable than one that lasts or is recurring. The steady and repetitive satisfactions that come with good skills and a good reputation, for instance, are preferred over pleasures that come with the short-lived flush of victory.

When we win a big game, the euphoria is often temporary.

Are there good reasons for adopting this second rule of superiority and its two corollaries? Will it help us objectively choose values that more effectively produce the good life? The rationale is as follows: Rule 2 places a fair amount of importance on what some have called the "pleasure principle." This principle is based on the recognition that pleasant experiences are intrinsically good because they need no further justification. We seek pleasure because we want to experience it, not because we want it to lead to something else.

However, I have tempered this pleasure principle in two ways. First, I have broadened the notion of pleasure from narrow, short-term experiences to broader, more durable satisfaction. Satisfaction encompasses more of life than pleasure does and gets closer to the heart of what it means for an experience to be good for its own sake. We would not normally want to claim, for example, that the experience of playing baseball is enjoyable only when we are having a particularly fine sensuous experience, like hitting a fastball on the meat of the bat. Baseball can also be enjoyable when we conjure up a strategy, review game statistics, or watch a pitcher from the on-deck circle—that is, when little or nothing sensuous is going on.

Second, I am not claiming that satisfaction is the only thing that makes an experience worth having. That is why I included the phrase *all else being equal* in rule 2. This keeps us from having to judge experiences simply on the amount of pleasure or the balance of pleasure over pain that they produce (Frankena 1973). It seems reasonable to claim that experiences that include enjoyment *and* excellence (using fine technique in hitting a golf ball out of the deep rough onto a distant green) are superior to those that are only enjoyable (feeling a delightfully warm breeze blow through your hair as you prepare to hit a shot from the rough). Similarly, experiences that are characterized by satisfaction *and* creativity (doing a compulsory dive well and with personal flair) are superior to those characterized simply by satisfaction (doing the dive well but unimaginatively).

The two corollaries also require justification. The first corollary is based on the recognition that pleasure is not absolutely good. Satisfactory experiences are not self-justifying to the extent that any manner of producing pleasure is acceptable. Say there is a certain professional hockey player who derives a great deal of pleasure from viciously checking opponents into the boards when they do not see him coming. He defends his behavior by claiming that this is part of the game and that such physicality provides a great deal of satisfaction. However, everyone knows that this behavior is unethical. No matter how pure the enjoyment is, and thus no matter how intrinsically valuable the experience is, this behavior is insupportable. It makes sense then to allow factors like harming another human being to detract from satisfying experiences.

The corollary related to durability also seems to be sensible. Given our limited time, energy, and ability to find and experience satisfaction, we want to invest our resources wisely. We do not want to waste our talents chasing something that gives a temporary high but then leaves us hurting, tired, or empty.

Seeking intrinsic pleasure does not justify harming others.

Rule 3: Criterion of Coherence

Satisfactory experiences that build a coherent and meaningful life take precedence over those that are isolated moments of pleasure (MacIntyre 1984; Bellah et al. 1985, 1991; Singer 1995). A coherent, meaningful life brings with it durable satisfactions. This criterion is about making sense of our lives, of seeing and living a pattern in daily activities that is interesting and worthy. When we say that life has meaning, we are indicating that it is reasonably consistent, has poignancy, has a goal, and is recognizably ours.

Perhaps the most fundamental experience of a coherent life comes with developing and living a story. A story has a beginning, middle, and end, and all three are related to one another. A story goes someplace. Its characters have roles to fulfill, work to do, celebrations to hold, and love to experience. A story does not develop on its own. History and culture are two primary sources of plots, goals, and aspirations, so rule 3 implies that positive cultural traditions take precedence over mathematical solutions, and an intelligent community consensus trumps logically pure philosophic ideals.

There are countless stories, and we are not entirely free to choose the ongoing plot that we wish to take up. Parents, ancestors, and genes have much to say about which stories suit us. As we mature, move through school, prepare for the work and play of our lives, make commitments to mates or choose to remain single, and start careers, we continue to define our stories and achieve increasing degrees of meaning and satisfaction.

On the other hand, if we have no narrative, if our activities are somewhat arbitrary and disconnected, it is more likely that we will see the world as somewhat meaningless. Our actions are controlled by appetites and other forces that operate apart from rooted meaning. Disconnected from our past, meandering through our present, and uncertain about any future direction, we experience ourselves as living in a strange land.

The rationale goes like this: We need rule 3 for breaking ties. This is so because rule 2 presents us with several problems (Frankena 1973, 90-91). Different kinds of satisfaction are difficult, if not impossible, to compare with one another. How would we evaluate the pleasure of watching ballet in contrast to the satisfaction of understanding, for the first time, how the Krebs cycle works and why people feel pain in conditions of oxygen debt? It is possible that they are incomparable and simply may have to be appreciated for what they are. We need a way to choose between incomparable satisfactions, and rule 3 helps us to do this.

Similar satisfactions, on the other hand, seem to be comparable. But here a different problem shows up. It is difficult to measure pleasure. How would we ever determine the exact quantity of pleasure in a given experience or, worse yet, in some future event? How could we ever be certain that we had effectively measured the pleasure in each of 10 lacrosse goals we had scored during the season or be certain that a goal in the play-offs would offer more enjoyment than all of these goals combined? It is highly impractical to discriminate greater from lesser intrinsic values based on quantity of pleasure. Once again, rule 3 acts as a tiebreaker.

But why should the standard be coherence and meaningfulness? Why not excellence, for example? First, meaning seems to be a doorway through which virtually all human behavior must pass. If I score a winning goal and thereby achieve a bit of excellence, its value is uncertain until I know its importance for me—what it means in my life. If I gain some excellence as part of a lifelong, passionate journey, that is one thing. But if I gain it as a result of pushy parents or a selfish, demanding coach, if it is an angry or reluctant reaction to negative circumstances, that is quite another thing. Excellence on its own may be cold, even if it is impressive. However, when it is woven into a story, its powerful intrinsic value can strike home.

Second, a meaningful life includes and fosters excellence. People care about things that are meaningful, and they are likely to become good at whatever those things are. If parenthood is deeply meaningful, parents will spend the time and energy necessary to achieve excellence in that role. If kicking soccer goals is meaningful, players will practice until they get it right.

On the other hand, there are many forces that promote excellence: economic necessity, guilt, fear, and duty, to name only four. While some people will eventually develop a love for an activity they do even if it was forced upon them, many will not. They will continue to perform excellently even though it means little to them. Or they will eventually change jobs, burn out, or drop out. Meaning seems more often to bring excellence than the other way around. Consequently, if forced to choose which value to start with, I would pick a coherent, meaningful life.

Finally, meaning is a democratic value in contrast to excellence. Not all of us can achieve something that is truly excellent. Most of us cannot even approach the achievements of the best athletes, the best actors, the best writers, or the best of anything. To reach the highest excellence, we might have to neglect much else that embellishes life, like friendships, family, even an ability to relax. But as regular human beings, we can fight for and find meaning, molding an interesting narrative out of our lives. We do not have to be extremely gifted or put our lives out of balance to experience meaning, but we do have to be dedicated to those things that make up our narrative.

While these arguments may be persuasive, they certainly are not conclusive. We cannot prove that coherence and meaningfulness are the most powerful measure for intrinsic value. Nevertheless, they provide a useful measuring stick. As you will see, this criterion will effect how we prioritize health, knowledge, skill, and fun. It also carries some exciting implications for kinesiology.

Philosophic Exercise

Rule 3 may have the most far-reaching consequences of any judgment made so far. The fact that it may be controversial makes it all the more important for you to pause at this junction in your philosophic travels.

You may want to do some experimental hiking down another path by substituting another criterion for the third rule of superiority or by adding one or two more rules to the list. Two criteria for the good life that have received a great deal of attention are

◆ experiences of freedom, authenticity, choice, and responsibility (Meier 1988; Slusher 1967), and

◆ experiences of excellence (Novak 1976; Simon 2004; Weiss 1969).

As we attempt to prioritize fitness, knowledge, skill, and pleasure in the next chapter, you may want to apply these two criteria to determine the strength of these four values.

REVIEW

Your work in this profession should be aimed at making a contribution to the good life. Four traditional values of kinesiology—fitness, knowledge, skill, and fun—are prime candidates for such contributions. There are at least three reasons for prioritizing these values:

◆ Focusing on one value more than the other three can make a tremendous difference in the scope and nature of your work.

◆ You have already made value judgments on these and many other matters of worth. Because value judgments are unavoidable, you might as well make them on the basis of reason and reflection.

◆ A profession that has not committed itself to a direction by prioritizing values may accomplish much, but none of it very well. It may also appear to lack focus, placing it in jeopardy.

We can rank values in two steps: surveying the facts and weighing the reasons. Surveying the facts involves cataloging the good things that come with fitness, knowledge, skill, and pleasure. Weighing the reasons requires an identification of criteria for good living. We can use three such criteria:

◆ Intrinsic values count more than extrinsic ones.

◆ Intrinsically valuable experiences that include durable satisfaction count more than those that lack it.

◆ Intrinsically valuable experiences that promote a coherent, meaningful existence count more than those that are pleasurable but less connected with a person's life.

LOOKING AHEAD

In the next chapter you will use the method we developed here to rank the four traditional values. You will also attempt to answer the question about whether or not movement is essential to the good life. In the process, you will review four movement-based lifestyles to see how they might be desirable.

CHECKING YOUR UNDERSTANDING

1. *What is the difference between moral and nonmoral values? Give some examples of each. Which moral and nonmoral values are most important to you? That is, how would you define the good life for yourself?*

2. *What are four traditional values of kinesiology? Describe examples of their presence in the profession today. Which of the four philosophies do you find most attractive and why?*

3. *Why is it important to prioritize values? Give at least three reasons.*

4. *How can we prioritize values? What does it mean to survey the facts and weigh the reasons? Identify three criteria that we can use to weigh the reasons.*

The Active Lifestyle

© Photodisc

We cannot make movement any more important than it is. We cannot force movement experiences to have high intrinsic value if, in fact, they do not. Nevertheless, the criteria identified in chapter 11 provide a framework for distinguishing the higher from the lower, a more powerful mission for kinesiology from a less significant role—in short, a vision for what we could be.

In this final chapter, we will attempt an analysis that will help us see what direction our profession needs to take if we believe skillful movement to be a cultural diamond in the rough—something that is often overlooked but has tremendous potential to add value to human living. This journey requires that we ask a number of questions.

◆ Under this more ambitious mission, how would we conceptualize our four main values and how might we rank them?

◆ If we emphasize activity as something that improves quality of life, where exactly does that improvement show up?

◆ What can we say to those individuals who do not move and still claim that their life is entirely satisfactory?

◆ Is movement central to the good life?

HEALTH AND FUN: POWERFUL EXTRINSIC VALUES

All four traditional values have strength as tools or means, but two of them, health and fun, are particularly strong in this regard. Kinesiology literature usually describes health and fun as useful check points that help us arrive at final destinations. They are also often lined up in a three-part sequence of causation:

CHAPTER OBJECTIVES

In this chapter, you will

◆ *examine the extrinsic and intrinsic value of health, knowledge, skill, and fun;*

◆ *look at four arguments for claiming that the good life is a physically active life;*

◆ *reflect on four descriptions of the good life that emphasize movement and physicality; and*

◆ *draw conclusions about activity and the good life.*

◆ If an activity is not fun, people will not persist.

◆ If people do not persist, they will not receive the health benefits that come from activity.

◆ If people are not healthy, they cannot get what they want out of life.

By promoting persistence, fun is a means to health. By promoting vitality and longevity, health is a means to the good life. And the good life is what we really want. To see if fun and health are up for the job, we need to survey the facts, a step we discussed in chapter 11.

Surveying the Facts: Health

Health would appear to have great extrinsic value. We can see its power in the many roles it plays in helping us meet our objectives. By surveying the following facts, we should see the potential of activity-related health as an extrinsic value.

◆ *Aerobic fitness* is the ability to move at a moderate to low intensity, where energy is produced with oxygen. Aerobic fitness allows you to work on a physically demanding yard project, take a 2-hour bike ride, and play 30 minutes of basketball with your child. Aerobic fitness has the capacity to promote productivity, long periods of play, even a longer life.

© Empics

Health is a powerful tool.

◆ *Anaerobic fitness* is the ability to move at a high intensity, where energy is produced without oxygen. Anaerobic fitness lets you move a piano or sprint for the winning score in touch football. One example of the extrinsic power of anaerobic fitness is its capacity to allow individuals to save a life in a physically taxing emergency.

◆ *Agility* is the ability to move your whole body quickly and gracefully. The benefits of agility include taking part in virtually any sport, working in physically oriented vocations, and reacting to an immediate danger, like jumping out of the way of an oncoming cyclist. We can see the extrinsic power of agility in the way it promotes success and fame in sports like basketball.

◆ *Body composition* refers to the combination of elements that constitute the body, particularly the amount of fat, bone, and muscle. Good body composition allows you to move quickly and gracefully, play a demanding game such as basketball, and increase your chances for a long life. Part of the extrinsic power of good body composition is its ability to promote vitality and to improve appearance and self-esteem.

◆ *Body size* and *shape* refer to weight, height, body composition, and body design. Having a good body size and shape promotes a positive self-image, allows you to fit into narrow places, and relieves back pain. An example of the extrinsic power of body size and shape is its promotion of self-acceptance.

◆ *Flexibility* is the capacity to move your appendages through a full range of motion. Good flexibility helps you do simple household chores that involve bending, reaching, and stooping; take off tight boots; and stretching for a wide throw at first base in a picnic softball game. We can observe the extrinsic power of flexibility in the way it promotes self-reliance, particularly among the elderly.

◆ *Strength* refers to the muscular capacity to apply force to our limbs and to objects in the environment. Strength gives you the ability to change car tires, carry heavy luggage, or hold a physically demanding job. Like flexibility, an example of the extrinsic power of strength is its capacity to foster independence, particularly among the elderly.

Weighing the Reasons: Health

Activity-related health is a condition of biological well-being that permits physical functioning, enhances chances for a long life, and improves vitality and appearance. Accordingly, health is an outstanding extrinsic value. To the extent that health promotes the continuation of biological existence, health probably does not have a serious rival. Without our health, as we say, we have nothing.

As we discussed in chapter 11, there are four criteria for judging extrinsic value on the basis of utility. A highly useful extrinsic value is necessary, is broadly useful, leads to important intrinsic values, and is efficient (without significant cost) and durable (likely to be of continuing value).

Activity-related health scores very well on the first three criteria for evaluating tools. It is necessary, it is broadly useful, and it leads to important intrinsic values—namely, everything we live for. However, when it comes to the fourth criterion, health has two weaknesses. Activity often comes with costs such as discomfort, inconvenience, financial expense, and sometimes boredom. In addition, activity-related health is not particularly durable. One can work for months to lose weight or improve cardiovascular endurance and then forfeit all in a matter of weeks. Activity-related health requires maintenance.

Intrinsic scores for health, on the other hand, are not nearly as good. We do not live *for* health; we live *from* it. It is health that allows us to do everything else in life. Health is normally in the background of our daily life, and whenever it takes center stage, such as when we become seriously ill, we treat it as the means that will allow us to continue with our life interests and relationships, not as an end in itself. Health is not typically what lends significance to daily living. We never read epitaphs on gravestones that say, "John Jones, loving father of three, was a healthy person," or "Susan Smith, an individual of integrity and courage, had good cardiovascular endurance."

Some might argue that experiencing life without pain is an intrinsic value. To an extent this is true. If we are not well, if we have a disfigured body, or if we are severely injured, we are quickly reminded of how important vitality, appearance, and pain-free functioning are to daily living. To be sure, the intrinsically satisfying life is filled with basic activities and an absence of pain. Nevertheless, this on its own does not produce a good life.

On our third criterion, coherence, health does not fare very well. We do not typically build our personal stories around health and fitness. When we experience good health day in and day out, we are not inclined to conclude, "We've achieved everything there is to achieve in life." Rather, we find meaning on the foundation of whatever level of health we possess and whatever type of body we have. While it feels good to be free of pain and physically normal, it feels better to experience love, adventure, and excellence.

We do not live for health; we live from it.

Philosophic Exercise

Do the intrinsic and extrinsic power of health change with different circumstances? What about for individuals in developing countries? Those who have crippling arthritis? The very old?

For some individuals health and discomfort are more central. Would this change the ranking of health from high extrinsic to high intrinsic value? Or would it only further emphasize the extrinsic value of health?

Surveying the Facts: Fun

Many kinds of fun can serve as means for continued participation. By surveying the following facts, we should gain a more complete picture of fun as an extrinsic value.

◆ *Testing fun* refers to the satisfaction of solving problems. The benefits of testing fun include playing a challenging but not impossible game like golf, finding new answers, and anticipating whether or not you can achieve a good score. An example of the extrinsic power of testing fun is its ability to keep athletes on task for long periods of arduous participation.

◆ *Contesting fun* refers to the satisfaction of trying to perform better than someone else. The benefits of contesting fun include enjoying the closeness of a hard-fought game, appreciating victories, and finding satisfaction in the achievements and future challenges that come with defeats. We can see the extrinsic power of contesting fun in its ability to promote improved performance, success, and fame.

Aesthetic fun is satisfaction related to experiences of beauty.

◆ *Sensuous fun (sedate)* refers to the satisfaction that comes from comfortable body states or experiences. Sedate sensuous fun is enjoying the way the body feels after a long run, hitting a golf ball on the sweet spot, or taking a long shower after a strenuous workout. Part of its extrinsic power lies in its ability to bring us back to these settings again and again.

◆ *Sensuous fun (dramatic)* refers to the satisfaction that comes from ecstatic body states or experiences. Dramatic sensuous fun is the thrill of careening down a ski slope, rappelling down a

200-foot cliff, or driving a shoulder into an oncoming football running back. We can see the extrinsic power of dramatic sensuous fun in its ability to refresh and to make the rest of life seem more worthwhile.

◆ *Aesthetic fun* refers to the satisfaction that comes from beauty. Aesthetic fun allows us to encounter harmony, grace, balance, and flow in physical activities. Aesthetic fun has extrinsic power in that it promotes a sense of peace and well-being.

◆ *Ludic fun* refers to the satisfaction that comes from experiences that we appreciate for their own sake. Ludic fun means appreciating doing something because we choose to rather than because it must be done, and relishing the absence of real-world pressures. The power of ludic fun lies in its capacity to bring us back to activities and thereby promote better health, lower stress levels, and develop traditions.

Weighing the Reasons: Fun

Fun and the anticipation of more fun are useful in two senses. First, they are central motivators in human experience. Second, they help develop culture (Huizinga 1950).

The motivational power of fun is obvious. We look forward to parties, vacations, and evenings in the presence of friends because they promise to be fun. We seek out physical activities that we expect to be fun and then return again and again to those that meet our expectations. We abandon anything that is not fun, usually sooner rather than later.

Culture develops through experiences that have intrinsic meaning, or activities that we choose to do because they are fun. Music, literature, art, games, dance, and sport are potential playgrounds—places where we choose to spend our time, not places where we are forced to reside. While we are having fun, symbol systems develop, traditions emerge, and messages about value are sent and received.

We can better appreciate the centrality of fun as motivation when we observe two of its alternatives, boredom and anxiety. If movement lacks challenge, if it has no interesting problems to solve, it becomes boring and people look for things to do that are more fun. On the other hand, if movement is too unpredictable, if it is too challenging and movements in front of others start to become embarrassing, it produces anxiety. Once again, people look for other things to do that are more fun. Fun lives in the space between boredom and anxiety (Csikszentmihalyi 1990). It is fun that brings people back to places where this space can be found. It is a universally effective tool for motivation.

As noted in chapter 7, studies on adherence suggest that logic, reason, and understanding are not sufficiently powerful motivators. Even individuals who have experienced serious cardiac health problems and who fully understand the importance of exercise for their continued existence quit exercising. We need something more, something on the affective side of life. People do not live by reason, prudence, and duty alone. Any kinesiologist who ignores fun or removes it from of an activity environment is courting disaster.

Fun is a universally effective tool for motivation.

Like activity-related health, fun scores well on our three criteria for extrinsic value. It is a necessary means for positive motivation. It is broadly useful, not narrow in its application. And by promoting continued activity, it leads to the good life. In the extent to which fun produces well-being, its tool value is anything but trivial. It is efficient and can cost little. The durability of fun, however, is less certain. People often tire of activities. An activity that was fun yesterday may lose its luster today. But this is not fatal in the presence of a clever kinesiologist who can make modifications to revitalize a tired activity and bring fun back onto the scene.

It seems that fun would also score well on the intrinsic side. Fun experiences are ends in themselves. We want to fill our hours with fun, period. Thus fun has good intrinsic value and satisfies the first criterion. But it does not do as well on criteria 2 and 3. Fun is not the same as satisfaction. It is narrower and less durable. Its narrowness comes from the fact that it must be pleasant. Satisfaction meets these qualities, but it is broader. It can be gratifying even if it is not particularly pleasant. It can be meaningful, even if it is not wholly enjoyable.

Fun's lack of durability is related to criterion 3—coherence. We can chase fun as isolated moments of pleasure. And if we string enough fun events together, we might have a reasonably good day. But the criterion of coherence requires that we do more than chase isolated moments of fun. We have to build something that is meaningful, something that connects our past to our present and our present to our future. To meet criterion 3, fun would need to become meaningful.

Philosophic Exercise

Have I been too hard on fun? Does it have more intrinsic power than I have suggested? Can we live a good life by going from one fun time to another?

If you were to distinguish between two levels of experiences, one called fun and the other called delight, how would you do so? What characteristics would you attribute to each one? While this is a difficult task, we have all had some experiences that were fun and others that were truly delightful. What is the difference?

KNOWLEDGE AND SKILL: POWERFUL INTRINSIC VALUES

The two remaining values of kinesiology have powerful intrinsic value. Both knowledge and skill are related to liberation from narrow thinking, fears, and superstitions that prevent us from achieving our potential. Knowledge and academic skills are associated with the liberal arts, with those subjects that make us better people, improve our tastes in the arts, and give us an understanding of how things have come to be and how we might make them better. Physical knowledge and skill could also meet these criteria and provide the kind of education that is designed to improve the quality of our lives.

Surveying the Facts: Knowledge

Knowledge takes the form of theories, propositions, and statements. Knowledge can be mulled over, symbolized in words, stated, and restated. It is abstract in that it has an existence apart from the particular situations that it describes or explains. If we have knowledge of how to swing a baseball bat, for example, we can talk about it away from the field and without actually moving a bat. This is knowledge as understanding.

The intrinsic value of movement-related understanding is not particularly great unless we are theoreticians of health or movement. People want to be healthy and experience the joys of movement, not merely understand these things. Knowing the theory behind our inability to hit a golf ball straight gives little solace if we cannot improve our game.

But there is a second kind of knowledge that has even greater intrinsic value. This is encounter- or recognition-knowing. It is the experience of living through insight firsthand. It involves what could be called personal embodied wisdom.

All movement domains—exercise, dance, sport, work—are full of wisdom. The only problem is actually living it rather than reading or talking about it. Here is an example from golf.

Many books discuss a certain paradox related to power and driving the ball. If the golfer relaxes, takes a more rhythmic swing, and stays more fluid before exploding at the bottom of the arc when contacting the ball, the drive is likely to go farther. Trying harder often results in shorter drives, while trying less hard often results in longer drives. The relaxed swing is an adventure for the improving golfer. Each step reveals some new wisdom about this movement paradox—firsthand, lived experience. This embodied wisdom becomes an intrinsically valuable gem worth remembering and returning to again and again.

Let's look at four gems of movement wisdom. I have phrased them as paradoxes to reflect the fact that their truth-value is difficult to uncover. This is an attempt to survey the facts of lived movement wisdom in terms of its intrinsic value.

◆ "The best game plan is no plan." Many athletes start an event with an idea of how they plan to attack the environment (e.g., pacing themselves in a distance run) or an opponent (e.g., going after an opponent's weak backhand in a tennis match). However, little by little, as performers become more comfortable, they leave the script and respond intuitively to what is happening under the precise conditions of the event. This can be called the experience of no plan. Rigid scripts are a product of worry and a lack of trust. When calm confidence descends on the athlete, scripts disappear and a wonderful responsiveness to the movement world replaces it. This is the power of no plans.

◆ "Instead of shooting the arrow, let the arrow shoot itself." This phrase comes from Kenzo Awa, the Zen master introduced in chapter 7 (Herrigel 1971). While this statement refers specifically to a single art, it applies to all sporting activities where we have to shoot, hit, swing, pirouette, or otherwise intentionally perform a skillful task. The Zen master's suggestion indicates that fine performers are not conscious of what they are doing when they release an arrow, hit a golf ball, or sprint for the finish line. These things should happen automatically, when the time is right, without thinking about them. This special kind of automatic movement has been called a peak experience (Maslow 1962), deep play (Ackerman 1999), playing in the zone (Murphy and White 1995), and flow (Csikszentmihalyi 1990). Whatever its name, it has always been described as effortless and wonderful. This is the intrinsic power of not thinking.

◆ "Getting close to the ball means getting away from it." This bit of wisdom is gradually encountered by beginners in team games like soccer. When young children first play the game, the ball is the attractor and acts like a magnet. Little girls and boys follow the ball around in a pack. Eventually these children begin to feel a new truth. One day they get away from the ball and find an open space

© Photodisc

When we row against the current, we row with it.

where they can receive a pass, effectively placing them closer to the ball. When athletes begin to feel space appropriately, they have an ever-growing sense of being at home. Fine athletes may reach a point where they are continuously at home in the pool, on the field, or in the gymnasium. Feeling at home is a peaceful, centered, balanced experience. This is the intrinsic power of being in the right place.

◆ "When we row against the current, we row with it." This comes from Craig Lambert's experience as recounted in *Mind Over Water* (see pages 151-152). Lambert knows intellectually that forward progress in the shell can occur only because the water resists the oars. He also knows that the water impedes the hull of the boat and that the craft will eventually stop if rowing ceases. Nevertheless, he reports that at some point the friction disappears. It is as if a stream of water beneath the hull is flowing with the boat, not against it. You will recall that he called this frictionless state *swing*. Sometimes in life, hard becomes easy, and a restraint becomes a boost. Lambert may have described this wonderful experience best when he wrote, "The appetite for swing is limitless." This is the intrinsic power of harmony.

Weighing the Reasons: Knowledge

When people encounter these unfolding truths as they get into better shape, increase their strength, and develop their skill, they most assuredly are aware of it. The activity becomes unmistakably different. Reflection and verbalization might have to come later, particularly if the game or activity is still in progress. But this matters little, for it is not the truth in verbal form that matters. Fancy language about swing, Lambert might say, is but an insignificant surrogate for the magnificent experience itself.

Lived wisdom scores well on the three rules of superiority. As we saw, it has outstanding intrinsic value. Lived experiences of insight are nothing short of wonderful. If some coach or trainer could bottle and sell the prerequisites to such ecstatic living, all of us who are inclined toward the active lifestyle would grab our credit cards immediately. Lived wisdom also scores well on the criterion of satisfaction. These experiences cut deeper than fun does. They tend to be more memorable, more durable, and more personal. Sometimes they show up at moments of physical discomfort and frustration. Perhaps that is why they are more than just fun. "Fun" does not capture how gratifying these achievements are.

On the third criterion, coherence, lived wisdom also passes muster. We solve the previous paradoxes by living our unique bodies through the world's challenges. When hard becomes easy, when heavy becomes light, when the best script becomes no script, these revelations become important pages in our personal movement story. Last year, we struggled to get the timing right. Six months ago, we had momentary glimpses of peaceful, rhythmic flow. Then today, for the first time, it all came together. Without thinking, it just happened and it was unforgettable. Throughout this activity journey we move through a series of related events, encountering bits of kinesthetic wisdom and building on them.

Surveying the Facts: Skill

Skills allow us to do things, from baking cakes and fixing cars to solving math problems and hitting tennis balls. Usually skills are grounded in a variety of habits. If the habits are sound, we are free to attend to other things that the activity demands. A piano player does not need to attend to proper fingering, and a basketball player does not need to watch hand and ball while dribbling up court. These correctly-habituated performers can see a larger picture, anticipate future moves, and exercise the fine perception and touch that are needed for highly successful performances (Sudnow 1978).

Wisdom and skill are two sides of the coin of human freedom. As we gain skills, we enjoy greater access to wisdom. The unusual experience of less effort resulting in more power normally does not come until after gaining considerable skill through training and practice. Conversely, when performers brush up against wisdom, it reinforces the skills that produced such experiences. In effect, wisdom says, "Do it precisely that way again," or "Keep working in the same direction." And as importantly, repeated encounters with wisdom provide tremendous motivation to keep honing our skills. The encountered wisdom of, say, moving away from the ball to get closer to it, provides freedom from narrow thinking. In turn, the activity skills that allow a player to feel the right place on a soccer field provide a freedom to move in ways that were not there before.

Let's review five basic human freedoms that come with skill development. Once again, this review allows us to survey the facts related to the intrinsic value of the skills.

◆ Freedom to discover. Discovery involves skills of noticing and recognizing. As we learn to jump more effectively, we develop the senses that allow us to make jumping discoveries. As our cardiovascular endurance increases, we can make discoveries about distances and places that were previously inaccessible. This is the intrinsic power of discovery: Discoveries are not always earth-shattering, but even when they are less notable, they are typically good. Thus we readily engage in the process of discovery and rely on a battery of sensory skills to do so. Discovery quiets our curiosity—at least for a time.

◆ Freedom to explore. Exploration is a primary avenue for discovery. It includes our investigative skills. These skills determine where we can go to make our discoveries. If we have strong exploration skills, our discoveries are likely to be richer. If we have weak exploration skills, discoveries will be correspondingly impoverished. The process of exploring can be exciting, involving the adventure of heading into uncharted territory. From childhood on, most of us love to explore. This is the intrinsic power of exploration.

◆ Freedom to express. Eleanor Metheny (1972) was fond of describing sport as being, "a flow of meanings without speech" and "of as many meanings as of men" (226). In physical activity, human beings need to have a way of telling their story. They need to get it out, whether in play or work, by pen or football. The intrinsic power of expression is clear: When we express our individuality, it feels good. Sport is not much fun when our movement is awkward and wooden. On the other hand, sport gains life when we become expressive and add personal style to our movements.

◆ Freedom to invent. Polanyi and Prosch (1975) argue that inventiveness is a hallmark of human intelligence. According to these authors, inventiveness requires the reconciliation of at least two things that appear to have little to do with one another. Reconciliation unveils a previously hidden relationship.

For instance, no one in baseball saw a relationship between metal and running until someone put metal and shoes together in the form of baseball spikes. There was a time when people thought that throwing a football, retaining possession, and improving field position were contrary ideas, until Sammy Baugh invented the forward pass. And experts in track and field thought that a back-to-the-ground position and gaining optimal height in high jumping were contradictions, until someone named Fosbury showed them to be very compatible indeed. This is the intrinsic power of inventiveness: Inventors are clever and insightful. People who are inventive in solving problems experience a freedom that is not available to others.

Reconciliation of supposed incompatibles unveils previously hidden relationships.

◆ Freedom to create. The difference between inventiveness and creativity, according to Polanyi and Prosch (1975), is this: Whereas contradictions melt away once an invention takes place, disconnected elements re-emerge once creative behavior ends. For example, once Fosbury pointed out the connection between a certain positioning and jumping, their compatibility was easy to see. Once the invention is made, the apparent contradiction dissolves forever.

This is not so with creativity. Here there are contradictions too, but they are so opaque, durable, and complex that their resolution can be only temporary. Art inspires us, but when the spell is broken we are left only with sounds, colors, shapes, and patterns. The intrinsic power of creativity is this: When we are stirred either as a creative performer or as a spectator who appreciates the artistic, we are grateful. Deep, special meaning always moves us.

Weighing the Reasons: Skill

When people possess activity skills, they experience themselves as competent. They enjoy a freedom to go places, do things, and solve problems that others will never know. They operate in the physical world with ease and confidence. They enjoy five of the most basic acts known to humankind—discovery, exploration, expression, invention, and creativity. As embodied creatures, this is no mean accomplishment.

Activity-related skill scores well on the three criteria. First, its intrinsic merit is undeniable. Skill literally liberates. It opens the world, bringing competence and confidence. Living life in this way is most agreeable. As we saw in chapter 9, successfully meeting skill-demanding challenges is one of the best ways to fill our days.

As for criterion 2, skill moves beyond fun to satisfaction. We need little or no skill simply to have fun, but skill *is* required for most accomplishments, and it is in accomplishments that we find satisfaction. When we patiently win our freedom through training and practice, we would do the experience an injustice if we referred to it merely as fun. Such achievements are always successes. Thus, skill-grounded freedom does well on the third criterion of coherence. As skill develops we grow slowly toward freedom. It is all part of a single path of competence that is grounded in where we came from, where we are now, and where we would like to be tomorrow.

Activity-related skill has considerable extrinsic value, particularly for the aging. Their independence and thus their quality of life depend a great deal on their motor skills, such as their ability to drive cars, dress themselves, bathe, and so on. But these are basic skills whose deployment depends on overall health, not patient practice. Skillful movements by the elderly may point to the extrinsic value of health and not to motor skill specifically.

Skill is an important tool for promoting fun. In physical education, for example, activities are not particularly enjoyable in the absence of skill.

Students must develop at least a degree of skill if they are to appreciate the activity. To the extent that skill promotes a positive affect, and to the extent that the positive affect keeps people moving, skill is important for promoting persistence.

Requirements for activity skills have lessened over the past two centuries across most of the globe. Unless one wields a hammer for a living, is a professional athlete, or is in some other physically demanding profession, the utility of activity-related skill is not great. High-level skills are not even required for health or fitness. Walking on a treadmill and lifting free weights do not impose significant demands for skill development.

Conclusions: Auxiliary Profession or Part of the Liberal Arts?

How we rank the four traditional values depends very much on our vision of ourselves. If we see ourselves as an auxiliary profession, one that performs a subsidiary role in promoting good living, then we would rank health and fun at the top. After all, they carry the strongest extrinsic values our profession can offer. Fun promotes persistence in the active lifestyle. The active lifestyle promotes health and vitality, life itself. And of course, we need to have life before worrying about promoting a good life.

If, on the other hand, we hope to be more than an auxiliary profession, we need to look toward the two values that have stronger intrinsic value, encounter-knowing and skill. These different facets of insight free us to know and to do. They decrease our ignorance and increase our confidence and our ability to act. In short, they involve experiences of freedom—of knowing, seeing, discovering, and creating. Moments of such unfettered delight *are* the good life.

If we are smart about all of this ranking business, we may be able to have our cake and eat it too. Remember, this is not an either–or exercise. I confessed in this text's introduction to one of my own biases, that dichotomies are often more harmful than helpful in the real world. Ranking does not necessarily mean excluding; it means prioritizing. I want health *and* I want freedom. I want organic vitality *and* I want a meaningful life.

In order to get both, it might be best to aim high and think of kinesiology as part of the liberal arts. Perhaps, we should conceptualize movement as part of the good life. If we aim at the quality of life that movement provides, health is a likely by-product. Those who love running, who can hardly let a day pass without hiking or fishing, who have made activity part of who they are—all these people are also likely to receive the health benefits of active living.

None of these individuals gets up from their chairs specifically to be healthy, but it happens anyhow. They move because they receive daily invitations to move that are simply irresistible. When they are in their movement domains, they encounter personal meaning and delight.

Delight trumps fun on most every occasion. If we can help our students and clients discover the delight of a personally significant activity, we have won. We have not simply made them healthier and thinner so they can seek out the good life. We have given them a piece of the good life itself. Because this piece of good living involves activity, they may get healthier and thinner as a bonus. But even if they do not, they will still fill their hours with delightful experiences that matter.

Those who are more attracted to sedentary freedoms may argue that we are not seeing things clearly. What matters, they might say, are experiences of enlightenment and liberty, whether they involve movement or not.

We could respond that, in fact, it does matter. We are embodied creatures. Our intelligence, our ability to solve problems, our cherished freedoms to understand and to do—all of this and more—developed as we moved (Sheets-Johnstone 1999). To suggest that human beings are neutral to movement is to ignore our biological history. To suggest that the good life is neutral to movement is to ignore the fact that we are bodies. It is folly to think that evolution, logic, or mind will take us beyond our earthly roots.

Nevertheless, we all know happy and well-adjusted people who do not move very much. Because their lives present a challenge to the kinds of bold claims I just made, we need to examine the patterns of good living available to those who embody the active lifestyle.

FOUR VERSIONS OF THE ACTIVE LIFESTYLE

Undoubtedly, many styles of active living are comparably good. Thus the four profiles are not meant to be comprehensive. Similarly, the individual emphases identified here are not mutually exclusive. They overlap and tend to develop together. In all probability activity-oriented people live all four profiles in various intensities and combinations. Regardless, it is useful to describe the different directions that active living can take.

The Strenuous Life

For American philosopher William James (1842-1910), the good life came from engaging the world, from struggling for improvement in an open existence whose future is uncertain. As McDermott (1967-1977) notes, "For James, it is precisely the ability of man to enter into the relational fabric of the world, in a participative and liberating way, which enables him to become human" (xxxi-xxxii).

Participation carries high demands. It requires both vision and action, both a sense of possible improvements and a will to pursue them. It is not an easy life of either pessimistic resignation or self-indulgent comfort.

James once visited Chautauqua Lake in New York and spent a week at its well-known assembly grounds. It was a place where people were "spell-bound by the charm and ease of everything, by the middle-class paradise, without a sin, without a victim, without a blot, without a tear." But James felt stifled in this utopian environment. "This order is too tame, this culture too second-rate, this goodness too uninspiring. This human drama without a villain or a pang; this community so refined that ice-cream soda water is the utmost offering it can make to the brute animal in man; this city simmering in the tepid lakeside sun; this atrocious harmlessness of all things—I cannot abide with them. Let me take my chances again in the big outside worldly wilderness with all its sins and sufferings" (McDermott 1967-1977, 647).

For James the good life lay at a great distance from the easy life. The good life is built on doing and suffering and creating. If there are insufficient natural problems, if no wars need to be fought, then we must find other challenges. Human beings create meaning in a quest that requires "order and discipline, the tradition of service and devotion, of physical fitness, unstinted exertion, and universal responsibility" (McDermott 1967-1977, 670).

James also understands that we live a connected life. As biological creatures our intelligence is tethered to our physicality, and our physicality is tethered to our emotions, our will, and our reflections. Motor activity is not inherently inferior any more than ideas are inherently superior. Human beings are capable of narrow, hateful ideas and of moving in fearful, untruthful ways. This has the effect of leveling intentional human behavior. In fact, James was incensed by the cultural distinctions on which people often pin so much of their identity. To be an intellectual as opposed to a common laborer, a person of means as opposed to one who is not well-off, or to be a physical educator as opposed to a professor in some more respected discipline—for James, these differences are pretensions. There is no substance to them.

James argued that all human beings, nobles and commoners alike, are built to meet challenges, find creative solutions, and solve problems. This requires a "little more humility on [our] own part, and tolerance,

© Photodisc

All human beings are built to meet challenges.

reverence, and love for others; and [we] gain a certain inner joyfulness at the increased importance of our common life" (McDermott 1967-1977, 658).

Sport and exercise are particularly conducive to James' view of the good life. Both provide clear goals or objectives. Both present significant challenges. Both require the virtues needed for good living, such as strong will, courage, a willingness to suffer, and a commitment to progress. We might speculate that James would be particularly supportive of extreme sports, those activities that place unusual demands on their participants. While he might be quick to point out that people could abuse such settings and engage in these sports in unhealthy ways, he would also be impressed by the fact that these settings are a good fit for human beings. They offer opportunities for snow-capped heroic challenges, and we are built to climb just these kinds of mountains.

James might well be suspicious, on the other hand, of efforts to soft-sell exercise rather than challenge people to higher levels of health and fitness. While research supports certain claims about health benefits from moderate exercise, it also allows us to dodge arduous practice in favor of comfort and ease. James would likely recommend that kinesiologists go in another direction. Human beings respond better to inspiring challenges, he would say, not comforting guarantees.

Finally, James might be very supportive of physical-education classes (Anderson 2002). He doubted the preeminent utility typically attributed to theory. At the same time, he honored the knowing that occurs when we rub shoulders with the world, develop good habits, and begin to feel things with greater sensitivity. He called this "knowledge of acquaintance." This practical knowing can go toe to toe with any abstraction. Consequently, it would be a mistake to substitute the theory of movement for actual movement. And James provides a foundation for arguing that judges in game 1 of the dualistic tournament in chapter 5 made a terrible mistake in awarding victory to theory over practice. James would likely argue for shared honor.

James provides a holistic vision of the good life that is friendly to kinesiology. He believed that human beings should fight for meaning as they face challenges and live a strenuous existence toward progress. This is not an optimistic, idyllic life. Nor is it a life of resignation to the ultimate meaninglessness of everything. It sits in the middle, requiring vigor, hope, and meaning, without any guarantees.

The Sensuous Life

In many ways the aesthetic is the source of our satisfactions. Every place we go has its potentially beguiling fragrances, feels, forms, colors, and sounds. Every project we undertake has its rhythms, tensions, climaxes, and resolutions. We are naturally attracted to what we call in a generic sense, "the beautiful." But we never fall in love with beauty in the abstract. We meet it in particular moments from our own particular embodiment. We meet it on the soccer field in a smooth and effortless movement, in the mountains when we see lacy Canadian hemlocks moving with the wind against a dark blue sky, and in the delicious exhaustion of accomplishment when we finish a marathon.

Such rich experiences, however, are not a birthright. Many human beings do not have the eyes to see, the fingers to touch, or the muscle memory to feel these experiences. They have not been, in the deepest sense of the words, physically educated.

It is not difficult to see why. In the Western world, at least, we have been making a number of trade-offs. We have traded the outdoors for the indoors, walking for riding in a car, physical recreation for television, and speaking to a friend in person for corresponding via e-mail. The point here is not that technology is evil. Nor is this a romantic call for a return to nature. Rather, it is an observation about a discrepancy between our sensory potential and our failure to develop that potential and reap the deep satisfactions that lie within our grasp.

From an anatomical perspective, we are built to live sensory-rich lives. Because we developed not only as embodied but as moving creatures, our brains have developed to allow us to sense our position, determine direction, interact with physical objects, distinguish odors, and appreciate texture and color. Four of Gardner's (1985) original six intelligences are based on sensory discrimination. The other two, numerical and linguistic intelligence, arguably have deep roots in human experiences related to time and space.

From a human perspective, we are also built to live sensory-rich lives. The following testimony from a computer programmer suggests that life in front of a screen is somehow deadening (Ullman 1995). "Real time was no longer compelling. Days, weeks, months, and years came and went without much physical change in my surroundings. Surely I was aging. My hair must have grown, I must have cut it, grown

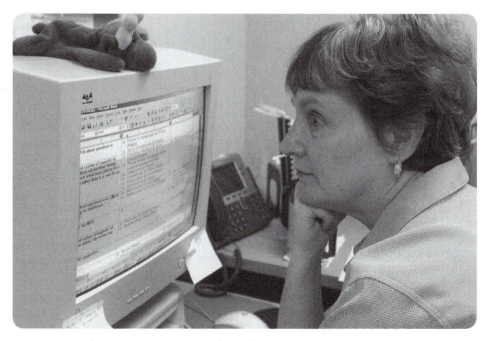

We waste our human powers sitting in front of a computer screen.

more gray hairs. Gravity must have been working on my late-thirties body, but I didn't notice. I only paid attention to my back and shoulders because they seized up on me from long sitting. Later, after I left the company, there was a masseuse on staff. That way, even the back and shoulders could be ignored" (133-134).

By way of contrast, many others have testified to the great satisfactions of discriminating sensation. Emerson once wrote that encounters with nature "are medicinal, they sober and heal us. These are plain pleasures, kindly and native to us. The mind loves its old home: as water to our thirst, so is the rock, the ground, to our eyes, and hands, and feet. Cities give not the human senses room enough. . . . He who knows the most, he who knows what sweets and virtues are in the ground, the waters, the plants, the heavens, and how to come to these enchantments, is the rich and royal man" (1937, 224-225).

The great English poet Wordsworth (in Eliot 1910/1938, 678) once wrote, "The world is too much with us; late and soon,/Getting and spending we lay waste our powers." We might revise his words to address the aesthetic version of the good life as follows: "The sensory world is now too little with us; sitting in front of a computer screen—with a diminished sense of real time and space, and with little chance to encounter actual textures, colors, sounds, and fragrances—we lay waste our human powers."

From this perspective, the good life includes significant experiences of aesthetic delight in movement, nature, art, music, and other parts of the sensory world. It includes the aesthetic drama of sensory-based tests and vigorous games. To access these delights, we must be physically educated in art, music, sport, and active forms of recreation.

The Spiritual Life

Some versions of the good life aim high—toward religious conversion, revelation, bliss, transcendence, or some other sort of ecstasy. Spirituality, broadly defined here to include both theistic and nontheistic commitments, would change our lives significantly. This might occur as we experience radical love, intimate belonging, or profound tranquility. Movement has played a major role in promoting spiritual experiences.

For example, *The Rule of St. Benedict* (Fry 1981) provides a series of ascetic guidelines—laws of austerity related to food, drink, sexuality, comfort, and other physical accommodations. Monks were on a strict regimen of work, prayer, reading, and reflection. The purpose of these extreme experiences was to allow these spiritual athletes to achieve "a purity of heart, a state in which his own inner turmoil is quieted so that he can listen to the Spirit within him" (95). Spiritual leaders of this stripe well understood the connection between physicality and spirituality, austerity and tranquility. Profane space, given the right practice, the right attitude, and considerable patience, could become sacred space.

Many athletes report experiences of spiritual clarity on the heels of an ascetic withdrawal from the world. Ackerman (1999) quotes writer Thaddeus Kostrubala, who likens running "to one of the major techniques of meditation, and sometimes prayer, employed by virtually all disciplines East and West: the constant repetition of a particular word or series of words . . . the same process occurs in the repetitive rhythm of slow long-distance running. Eventually, at somewhere between 30 and 40 minutes, the conscious mind gets exhausted and other areas of consciousness are activated" (195).

Many Eastern approaches to spirituality aim to help us change ourselves. Herrigel (1971) did not take up archery to gain a vision of a transcendent deity or to see what scores he could achieve. He entered a kind of spiritual contest with himself to see what kind of harmony he could establish with the bow, what kind of tranquility he could experience when releasing the arrow. After years of arduous practice, when he finally experienced the arrow shooting itself, he had been transformed. His old ego was dead. His desires for more of everything had been quieted. His inability to live in the now had been replaced by a consciousness that automatically saw more, felt more, and enabled him to do more.

Passionate involvement in sport may provide occasions for spiritual revelations. Novak reported such an experience when he suggested that viewing the courageous determination of great athletes in the face of defeat provided "a momentary glimpse into the fiery heart of the Creator" (1976). This revelation taught him something about how we are meant to live.

From this perspective, the good life is the transformed life—one that has been moved in a significantly positive direction by revelation, ecstatic experience, or some other dramatic change in one's quality of life. The good life is lived in love, service, insight, or tranquility. Austerity, discipline, sensation, and passion have long been partners to those who seek this ambitious plane of good living.

The Excellent Life

The final profile of the good life focuses on excellence. Many commentators have identified excellence as a primary redeeming feature of competitive activity (see Simon 2004; Novak 1976; Weiss 1969). Nobody champions mediocrity. Nobody recommends that we fall short of our potential. Nevertheless, commentators do disagree on the form that excellence is to take.

My own preference is a balanced excellence that is a trademark of many versions of the liberated person. Earlier in this chapter, we looked at two traditions of liberal education. Each is powerful, but neither can stand on its own. The first tradition is understanding, or wisdom. This wisdom can be

Balanced excellence may be the ideal.

explicit: We can write it down, dissect it, and rebuild it. It can also be implicit: We can know, use, and trust it, even if we cannot fully explain it.

The other tradition of liberation is skill, or knowing how. Skills allow us to be successful parents, balance our checkbooks, understand world politics, play the piano, change flat tires, and so on. As kinesiologists, we are responsible for sensory skills, work skills, game skills, play skills, and athletic skills. Such skills free us by allowing us to go more places and do more things. When our skills are significantly developed we can discover, explore, express, and create.

From this account, the excellent life is a balance of knowledge and skill that provides increasing degrees of freedom—more choices, less fear, more creativity, less ignorance. The quality of life is improved because we can appreciate more and experience more. All this is done with confidence, with a sense of being at home in different environments.

This leads toward an ideal that used to be called the Renaissance person—an individual who knows about many subjects and who is skilled in a variety of areas. We do not need to play five instruments, speak seven foreign languages, compete in two varsity-level sports, quote Shakespeare, and be able to discuss the merits of quantum physics. But this vision of the good life suggests that we need to press ourselves in many of these directions. Because the world is a storehouse of diverse treasures, we need to develop the knowledge and skill to interact creatively with some of these different places—music, art, language, and skillful movement places. Such is the life of balanced excellence.

Philosophic Exercise

Can you come up with any additional profiles? What would you call them? What would the lives of individuals who live these profiles be like? Do you believe that any of these lifestyles rival the previous four in terms of potential for human gratification? In terms of popularity?

If you think you've uncovered a particularly good one, please mail it to me. Who knows, it may make the next edition of *Practical Philosophy*, and I will be sure to acknowledge your contribution with a footnote.

SUMMARY: THE GOOD LIFE, HEALTH, AND MOVEMENT

We are now in a position to address one of our most significant questions: Can a person live a good life with only average health and without moving any more than is absolutely necessary? Can a person be overweight, in poor cardiovascular shape, inclined to stay indoors, and still experience a high-quality existence?

I think that the answer would have to be yes. It *is* conceivable. In fact, many of us know people who eat too much and live sedentary lives, but who are also intelligent, loving, playful, productive, and content. If they have good luck, good genes, and good health care, they may also live to a ripe old age. We also know people who have a disability that prevents them from living the kinds of vigorous lives that able-bodied people can live. Yet they too are capable of crafting meaningful lives.

Fitness and movement, in short, are not indispensable. Nevertheless, to diminish embodiment and movement is to go against the human grain. We are built to play, test ourselves, and compete, in the world of time and space, color and form, texture and sound. Everything we are, from our smallest cellular building blocks to our largest aspirations, points us in that direction (Booth et al. 2002).

Why, then, would we fight it? Why would we work so hard to find the good life only in chairs, when all of our elements and the entire human history invite us to spend at least some of our time elsewhere? Why would we confine our intelligence and creativity to chairs when our potential spills out of such limiting places?

Our critics might say that we could expedite evolution by refusing to move. Maybe we could elevate humanity to some higher state of pure mind by staying put and denying our embodiment. Quite possibly we should try harder to rid ourselves of those bodies that so dramatically limit us.

I don't know about you, but such utopian speculations are not appealing to me. Thus, I am going to give in to my human impulses, get away from this computer, and have a run. I hope you too will now put down the book, leave your chair, and celebrate your own humanity in one of your favorite movement playgrounds.

REVIEW

When we set high goals for ourselves in kinesiology, when we strive to improve quality of life, we find that fitness and fun serve important roles as extrinsic or tool values, and that skill and knowledge go a long way toward defining our intrinsic objectives. We can pursue knowledge as explicit understanding as well as tacit, lived wisdom. Skill is a kind of knowledge that promotes the freedom to discover, explore, express, invent, and create. We have seen the quality of the active lifestyle in the four prototypes—the strenuous, sensuous, spiritual, and excellent lifestyles. While we can achieve good living without activity, such patterns go against the grain of our capabilities as human beings. We are built to move and we are ready to find meaning in movement.

CHECKING YOUR UNDERSTANDING

1. *Identify the two values that have superior extrinsic value. Try to find one argument that shows their strength as an extrinsic value, or a tool, and one argument that shows their weakness as an intrinsic value, or something that we value for its own sake.*

2. *Identify the two values that have superior intrinsic value. Give examples of their intrinsic attraction. See if you can give one concrete example of understanding, wisdom (implicit understanding), and skillful knowing.*

3. *What are the five human projects that skill promotes?*

4. *Which of the four profiles of the active lifestyle is most appealing to you? See if you can give one or two reasons for your choice.*

5. *Does a person have to embody an active lifestyle in order to lead a good life? Why or why not?*

APPENDIX: CASE STUDIES

On Sportsmanship and "Running Up the Score"[1]

Nicholas Dixon, Alma College

Reprinted, by permission, from N. Dixon, 1992, "On sportsmanship and 'running up the score'," *Journal of the Philosophy of Sport* XIX: 1-13.

Dixon Formulates a Thesis

I wish to argue against a widely-held view concerning sportsmanship. I call this view the *Anti-Blowout* thesis (AB):

> AB: It is intrinsically unsporting for players or teams to maximize the margin of victory after they have secured victory in a one-sided contest[2]

Having elaborated on the thesis in Section I, I present my main arguments against it in Section II. Section III is devoted to showing that none of several currently favored theories of sportsmanship supports the AB thesis. Section IV is a qualified conclusion.

I

The sporting community (players, coaches, and journalists) seems almost unanimous in condemning the pursuit of lopsided victories, which is described in such derogatory terms as "running up the score" and "showing up" the losing team. For instance, the University of Michigan's 61-7 defeat of Houston's football team in 1992 was greeted with howls of delight that Houston had been given a taste of its own medicine. The "grossly classless behavior" which, according to a Detroit sports journalist, earned Houston such heavy retribution, was its own habit of running up the score against outmatched opponents. Similarly, in the early 1980s, a Big-Ten football coach was outraged when the opposing team, already ahead by several touchdowns, scored another touchdown on a long passing play in the game's closing moments. After the play, the coach led his entire team onto the field and drew its attention to the scoreboard, which indicated the few seconds remaining to play. They stood there for several seconds contemplating the scoreboard, presumably vowing bloody revenge for this humiliation when the teams met the following season.

Apparently the sporting thing for victorious teams to do on such occasions would be to "go easy" on their opponents. They should insert second- and third-string players, and mercifully run out the clock with time-consuming running plays, gracefully coasting to victory without compounding the losers' suffering.

The AB thesis is widely held in both college and professional sport, especially football. It is also applied to some extent in basketball, and even in baseball. For instance, eyebrows would be raised if the visiting team, already ahead 12-0 in the top of the ninth inning, attempted to pad the lead by bunting and stealing bases.

The few passing references to this issue that I have been able to find by philosophers indicate that they share the AB view, albeit in a less extreme form. For instance, Randolph M. Feezell (2: p. 2) states that "running up the score on an opponent . . . is bad form, somehow inappropriate because it violates the nature of what sport is about." He considers the fictitious coach Smith, who intimidates both players and referees, ruthlessly pursues victory by all means short of cheating, believes that the only thing wrong with cheating itself is being caught, *and would willingly run up the score if it improved his team's rating and tournament seeding:* "Smith has an impoverished view of sport, an impoverished experience of sport, and it is just such views and attitudes that tend to generate unsportsmanlike behavior in sport" (2: pp. 4-5).

Warren P. Fraleigh (3: pp. 180-190) discusses what he calls "the problem of right action in the uneven contest" at considerable length, showing the complexity of the moral considerations that are relevant to this matter. However, he does not attempt to defend a position on this issue, since his goal is rather to use this example to illustrate a *method* of dealing with value conflicts in general. A virtue of his analysis is that he shows that many options are open to the team leading by a wide margin, ranging from actually allowing the losing team to score a few "consolation" points, to aggressively pursuing an even greater margin of victory. Intermediate tactics include substituting less competent players, or trying out new tactics and strategies (3: p. 181). What is of most interest for my discussion is that Fraleigh (3: p. 184) includes as a reason against tactics that increase the chance of a lopsided victory the fact that "such action would be viewed by other sports agents and spectators as 'running up the score,' intentionally, which is a negatively sanctioned act and contrary to courtesy."

Finally, in a discussion of Fraleigh's views, R. Scott Kretchmar (8: p. 28) suggests in passing that Fraleigh may have to defend the view that, even when a team has an invincible lead, its players are obligated to play their hardest until the end of the game. This is because Fraleigh believes that the central nonmoral value involved in all sporting contests is "knowledge of relative abilities to move mass in space and time in the ways prescribed by the rules" (8: p. 28). Such knowledge is possible only if both teams play to the maximum of their abilities for the duration of the contest. Kretchmar suggests that other nonmoral values may deserve consideration alongside, even in opposition to, the acquisition of knowledge. In the context of uneven contests, one such value would be avoiding the "psychically painful embarrassment" experienced by those who suffer heavy defeats (8: p. 28).[3] Though Kretchmar does not directly raise the issue, this value could be used in support of the AB view.

II

Dixon Clarifies the Problem

I agree that it would be churlish to refuse to relent in a friendly, recreational racquetball game against a completely outmatched opponent. What was meant to be fun would be turned into an exhausting, frustrating ordeal for the other player. In contrast, holding off would help her to improve her game and would lead to longer rallies, making the game more enjoyable for both players. In the same way, an experienced adult chess player should not repeatedly overwhelm a young child whom she is teaching how to play. This might fuel the adult's ego, but would also very likely discourage the child to the point of destroying her interest in chess. Deliberately making weak moves, and even allowing the child to win occasionally, would be a far more appropriate way to help the child to enjoy and improve her game. In both cases, "going for the jugular" would destroy the purpose of the game: recreation and nurturing, respectively.

In contrast, my main thesis in this paper is that there is absolutely nothing intrinsically wrong with pressing for a lopsided victory in a *competitive* game, whether it be football, basketball, soccer, or any other sport. While values such as mercy and mutual enjoyment are also relevant to competitive sport, the introduction of the element of competition makes complaints voiced by proponents of the AB view inappropriate. The distinction I draw between recreational and competitive sports parallels that made by James W. Keating (7) between sport and athletics,[4] though in section IIIB I will consider an objection to his distinction.

It might be *unwise* for a coach to risk injuries to key players and waste a golden opportunity to give second-string players some playing time and perhaps try out novel plays and strategies in a low-risk setting. However, I reject the received wisdom among AB advocates that winning a game by a wide margin is not just unwise, but positively *unsporting.*

One line of argument for this mistaken belief is a rather distasteful attitude toward sport: Winning is the only thing that matters. If this were so, it would indeed be gratuitous to continue to score points long after victory, the game's only goal, has been secured. However, the premise is false: Winning is *not* the only thing that matters. Players who win blowouts can be justly proud of their display of athletic excellence, the personal and team records they have set, and the excitement provided for fans.

Even if it is granted that there is more to sport than winning, the feeling persists that there is still something cruel in inflicting one-sided defeats. Underlying this feeling is an attitude toward sport that can be used to mount a second, more plausible argument for the AB thesis: Players who suffer lopsided defeats have been humiliated and diminished as human beings. The fact that the AB thesis is most often cited in football and basketball, both of which involve considerable contact, suggests that the macho notion of sport as a test of manhood is also involved.[5]

This attitude has lost sight of the element of play in all sports, at whatever level, and regardless of their business aspect.[6] Moreover, even on a view such as Fraleigh's (3), which regards the determination of athletic superiority as the essential value of sport,[7] there is absolutely no disgrace in suffering a heavy defeat by a far stronger team. While they do indicate athletic ability, neither victory nor defeat affects one's worth as a human being. What *does* reflect players' character is how hard and fairly they play, and how they conduct themselves in defeat and victory.

It might be countered that a lopsided defeat does humiliate the loser, not as a human being, but *as an athlete,* and that this is why it is unsporting to inflict such defeats. Athletes take pride in their ability and effort, and blowouts are an affront to this pride.

My response involves distinguishing between weak and strong humiliations. In the weak sense of "reducing to a lower position,"[8] any defeat, not just a blowout, is by definition a humiliation of the loser qua athlete. Inflicting humiliation in this harmless sense is the inevitable outcome of most competitive activities. Only in the strong sense of causing shame or disgrace does humiliating someone become a moral issue. And it isn't clear that an athlete is humiliated qua athlete in this stronger sense by the fact that her opponent is far stronger. The only cause for shame after a heavy defeat would be knowing, for example, that I did not play to the best of my ability, or that I gave up trying. A heavy defeat is in and of itself no cause for shame.

More appropriate occasions for feelings of strong humiliation would be the revelation of a moral fault (e.g., cheating), a nonmoral character fault (such as the lack of persistence I show if I give up too easily in my defeat), or an act of gross stupidity or incompetence. Suffering a heavy defeat to a far stronger athlete or team reveals no such failing. In general, the fact that someone else is far better than me at *x*-ing strongly humiliates me neither qua *x*-er nor as a human being. Why should sport be regarded differently than other activities? Even if one confines attention to the person *qua athlete,* then, the claim that she is strongly humiliated by a heavy defeat indicates an inflated estimate of the importance of the outcome of sporting contests.

The AB thesis seems to require that a team which is far stronger should *conceal* the extent of its superiority by easing up. An analogy from the academic world may be helpful. When a student makes a comment in class that indicates a misunderstanding of an elementary point, the sensitive instructor will give the comment the most favorable reading possible and gently lead the student to a better understanding. At a professional meeting, in contrast, an academic will not hesitate to point out an error made by a peer. This can be done in a respectful, nonconfrontational way, just as a team can win a contest by a wide margin while still showing respect for its opponents. The suggestion that an academic should diplomatically try to conceal the error made by her peer is condescending. A vastly superior team should treat its opponents just as an academic would treat a colleague, not as she would treat a student.

None of this is to deny that malevolent coaches and players may maximize the margin of victory precisely in order to humiliate their opponents. The wrongness of such actions consists in the *intention* to harm, since, if my analysis is correct, such defeats do not actually humiliate the losers in the strong, harmful sense. Such behavior is just as reprehensible as any deliberate attempt to humiliate others, and may justly be called "running up the score." My point is that one can also pursue a lopsided victory *without* any intention to humiliate one's opponent, and that there is nothing wrong with such victories. Heavy defeats are not intrinsically humiliating in the strong sense that is prima facie morally wrong.

However, partly because some teams arguably do intend to humiliate the opponents they beat by a wide margin, a connection has been forged in American sporting consciousness between lopsided victories and humiliation. Even if the winning team has no such malevolent intentions, the losers are likely to *infer* them, and to *feel* humiliated, anyway. Consequently, an objection to my view is that respect for the feelings of opponents should prevent teams from pursuing victory by a wide margin, however innocent the motives behind the victory would have been.

Certainly the way an action will be perceived is one of the factors that should be considered in evaluating that action. However, if people's negative perception of the action is based on a misconception—as I claim is the case with the view that lopsided victories strongly humiliate the opponent—it carries little weight as an objection to the action. For instance, the fact that interracial relationships would have shocked and even offended people in southern states in the 1950s sheds more light on the prejudice of the offended people than it does on the morality of interracial relationships. Those who lose sporting contests by a wide margin may *feel* humiliated, but, if my argument in the last few paragraphs is sound, they have not *in fact* been strongly humiliated, either as human beings or as athletes. Consequently, the existence of such feelings does not justify moral condemnation of teams pursuing victory by a wide margin. We might hope that, as a less inflated estimate of the importance of the outcome of sporting contests prevails, such groundless feelings of humiliation will become less and less common. Consequently, malicious athletes and teams will be less and less tempted to inflict heavy defeats in a misguided attempt to harm their opponents.

When one strips away these two mistaken attitudes toward sport—winning is the only thing that matters, and heavy defeat is a serious affront to one's humanity or to one's status as an athlete—there remains no good reason to criticize teams for pursuing high scores in one-sided victories. As long as the winning team shows respect for the losers (which is perfectly compatible with winning a soccer game by 10 goals, or a football game by 50 points), no apology is needed for an exciting display of skill and athleticism. What *does* show a lack of respect for outmatched opponents is mocking and taunting them, and this will often be a distinguishing feature of the deliberate attempts to humiliate opponents that I do condemn.

An unlikely source of support for my view was provided by the opponents of the U.S. "Dream Team" in the 1992 Olympic basketball tournament. Despite being thoroughly outmatched, they played with great enthusiasm and spirit, clearly enjoying every minute they shared the court with the NBA legends. They understood, far better than proponents of the AB thesis, that a lopsided defeat in sport need mean no more than a lopsided difference in ability.

What *was* distasteful was the jingoistic buildup to the Olympics, fueled by NBC's promotional "spots" for the Dream Team's imminent display of American superiority. This chauvinism has nothing to do with sportsmanship, and everything to do with the mistaken view that sport is a test of the worth of a human being or a nation.

III

My concern in this section is not to propose a new analysis of sportsmanship. Instead, my purpose is to show that my view comports far better than the AB thesis with the most plausible models of sportsmanship that have been proposed.

A

Dixon Searches for Arguments

I will consider first an influential account of sportsmanship developed by Keating (7). His view is best understood in contrast to a model of sportsmanship that *would* condemn lopsided victories: the "Eton" view of sport prevalent in English public (i.e., exclusive and private!) schools in past centuries.[9] Sport was played by gentlemen for the intrinsic pleasure of playing, rather than for the purpose of winning. Amateurism was encouraged, excessive preparation for a sporting event was considered bad form,[10] and players and coaches were expected to value a "good game," an equal contest, as more important than achieving superiority. Since even strenuous efforts to win a game were frowned upon, this model would clearly not tolerate the pursuit of victory by a wide margin.

Keating's account of sportsmanship is based on the distinction between recreational ("sport") and competitive ("athletics") contests. The different purpose of each of these two activities gives rise to a different conception of sportsmanship. Since the purpose of recreational sport is "pleasant diversion—the immediate joy to be derived in the activity itself—the pivotal or essential virtue in sportsmanship is generosity" (7: p. 34). While generosity does not require the adoption of the Eton model, it calls for moderation on the part of the person or team with an insurmountable lead in a friendly game. Such moderation will help "to avoid all unpleasantness and conflict and to cultivate, in their stead, an unselfish and cooperative effort" (7: p. 34). This insight underlies my own support for the AB thesis in purely recreational sport. What little plausibility the Eton model has is confined to recreational sport. It is wholly inadequate, however, when applied to competitive sport, and hence cannot be used to undercut my arguments against the AB thesis in the context of this type of sport.

Competitive sport (athletics), according to Keating (7: p. 33), has the different purpose of "the objective and accurate determination of superior performance and, ultimately, of excellence." The corresponding concept of sportsmanship is hard but fair play. A similar view of the purpose of competitive sport is expressed by Warren P. Fraleigh: "to provide equitable opportunity for mutual contesting of the relative abilities of the participants to move mass in space and time within the confines prescribed by an agreed-upon set of rules" (3: p. 41).

While this paradigm clearly excludes cheating, in no way does it deem lopsided victories as unsporting. If anything, if the runaway winner eases up in the later stages of the game, the purpose of determining athletic excellence is *undermined*. It is true that the contestants' "relative abilities" have already been determined by this stage in the sense of a *rank ordering*. However, an eight-goal margin of victory may more accurately reflect, for instance, the relative abilities of two soccer teams than a still-comfortable three-goal difference. The margin of victory gives a tangible *quantitative measure* of the relative abilities of the teams. Those who complain that continuing to score goals long after victory has been achieved is gratuitous and unsporting are guilty of a simplistic reduction of the comparative purpose of competitive sport to the categories of "winners" and "losers." Moreover, the interest of competitive sport goes beyond a comparison between the contestants. We are also interested in assessing their abilities in comparison with other athletes and teams, both past and present, as is evidenced by the assiduous attention given to sporting records. The attempt to make quantitative comparisons between contestants, and to maintain the integrity of sporting records, would be sabotaged if easing up in a sporting event once victory is secured were to become common practice.[11]

In defense of the AB thesis, it might be objected that the actual context of many blowouts is far removed from the accurate measure of athletic ability Keating and Fraleigh believe is central to sport. In college athletics, lopsided victories often result from a team's desire to "pad" its record, and thus improve its national ranking, by deliberately scheduling weak opponents. Such blowouts are meaningless as a measure of the ability of the winning team, since the outmatched losers present no serious challenge. Since the goal of measuring athletic ability is not met, the charge remains that lopsided victories involve the gratuitous infliction of suffering.[12]

I have three responses. First, this objection is confined to the Fraleigh/Keating view of the purpose of competitive sport discussed in this subsection. Lopsided victories may serve *other* goals of sport, such as providing excitement for fans, and hence may avoid being gratuitous.

Second, I reject the assumption that a lopsided victory over an outmatched opponent gives no measure of athletic excellence. While the superior team's victory may never be in doubt, its manner of victory can be most revealing. Even when the opponent is weak, an exciting display of offensive firepower, full of skill and imagination, can be a testament to a team's strength. By the same token, a narrow, lackluster victory over a clearly inferior team will often justifiably result in a lower national ranking for the winning team. Throughout the world of soccer, including the World Cup, "goal difference" is used as a tie-breaker. Of all the methods of tie-breaking, this is the least controversial, since people recognize that the ability to score and prevent goals over a series of games, especially over a whole season, is a reliable measure of excellence in soccer. More generally, as pointed out previously, the practice of record keeping in sports reflects the belief that scores in a game, season, or career are a meaningful basis for comparison between athletes and teams.

Third, and most important, the objection is addressed primarily to the *scheduling* of contests that are known in advance to be uneven, not to lopsided victories themselves. This type of scheduling may result in an unrealistically inflated win–loss record for the stronger team, and hence undermine the reliability of national standings (although those responsible for the standings may be able to take into account the quality of a team's opponents when they decide on its ranking). However, the arguments I have presented so far indicate that once a contest has been scheduled, there is nothing unsporting about pursuing victory by a wide margin, as long as respect is shown for the losing team.

In sum, if the primary purpose of competitive sport is to determine relative athletic ability, then the pursuit of emphatic victories may be not only compatible with sportsmanship, but even required by it. However, we now need to consider rival models of sportsmanship based on different views of the purpose of sport.

B

Dixon Provides a Second Argument

Randolph Feezell (2) rejects the sharp distinction between recreational and competitive sport (sport and athletics) that underlies Keating's two-level theory of sportsmanship. Whereas Keating excludes keen competition from his account of recreational sport, and playfulness from his account of competitive sport, Feezell argues that both the serious desire to win and a sense of playfulness are involved, in varying degrees, in all sport. The person who engages in sport

> is simultaneously player and athlete. His purpose is to win the contest *and* to experience the playful and aesthetic delights of the experience. His attitudes are at once both playful and competitive, and these color his relationship with his fellow participants. He sees his opponent as both competitor and friend, competing and cooperating at the same time. (2: p. 6)

Keating's account of sportsmanship in *competitive* sport, which is my main concern in this paper, is inadequate, Feezell argues, because it would sanction brutal, no-holds-barred competition, as long as one stays within the letter of the rules of the game. Such an attitude is actually more like an instance of bad sportsmanship, since it "ignores the unwritten rules of playing . . .and tends to destroy the spirit of play" (2: p. 7).

Once we recognize that "sport is a formal, competitive variety of human play" (2: p. 7), a more appropriate model of sportsmanship would accommodate the playfulness that Keating confines to purely recreational sport. At the same time, the person whose attitude is so playful that she makes no serious effort to win the game is being unsporting in a completely different way: failing to respect the importance of trying one's hardest in competitive sport. Feezell's model of sportsmanship is an Aristotelian mean

> between excessive seriousness, which misunderstands the importance of the play-spirit, and an excessive sense of playfulness, which might be called frivolity and which misunderstands the importance of victory and achievement when play is competitive. (2: p. 10)

A certain degree of seriousness is needed in order to experience the pleasure of competition, but at the same time this very seriousness creates the danger of alienating, unsporting behavior.[13]

In defense of Keating, Feezell's accusation that Keating's account of sportsmanship in competitive sport would permit an unsporting obsession with winning within the letter of the rules may be unfair. After all, Keating (7: p. 35) bases his account of sportsmanship on his belief that *honorable* victory is the goal of participants in competitive sport. The player who constantly badgers the referee, and who rudely but legally tries to "psych out" her opponent, may not violate the purpose of an "objective and accurate determination of superior performance," but her victory is certainly not honorable. However, Keating's account of sportsmanship may be circular, in that exactly what kind of behavior is honorable is the very point in question in explaining sportsmanship.

At first blush, Feezell's account of sportsmanship, which includes playfulness as well as competitiveness, would be less tolerant of one-sided victories than would the Keating/Fraleigh model, which puts primary emphasis on sport as a fair and accurate assessment of the relative ability of the contestants. Shouldn't the competitive urge to achieve a high score be tempered by a generous desire to ease up and soften the impact of defeat on the losers? As we saw in section I, Feezell himself believes so. However, I have two arguments that show why Feezell's account of sportsmanship does not support the AB thesis.

First, the value of generosity that calls for easing up in one-sided games is a moral value more germane to the model of sportsmanship, to be discussed in the next subsection, based on altruism. Playfulness is a more aesthetic, even hedonistic concept, which does not clearly require generosity. This is not to suggest that the spirit of playfulness places no moral demands on competitors. Not only cheating, but any form of disrespect for opponents, is directly contrary to the spirit of playfulness. The trash talking and taunting of opponents practiced by some basketball players and admired by some sports journalists and fans are clearly ruled out by Feezell's account of sportsmanship. However, as I argued in section II, beating an outmatched team by a wide margin is in itself not in the least disrespectful. The belief that it is disrespectful is based on the mistaken notion, criticized previously, that a heavy defeat diminishes losers as human beings, or disgraces them as athletes.

Second, continuing to play strenuously even after victory has been secured is actually more congruent with the spirit of playfulness than is easing up. There is nothing in the least bit playful when the football team that is ahead by five touchdowns devotes the entire fourth quarter to grinding out time-consuming, conservative running plays, motivated by the desire to avoid "showing up" the outmatched opponents. Such time-wasting would be openly booed by soccer fans. It reinforces the distinctly *un*playful attitude that the game is effectively over once the sole goal of winning has been guaranteed. Genuine playfulness would consist of continuing to entertain the fans with exciting, innovative plays, taking advantage of the freedom that is provided by having already secured victory. Not only would this enable the winning team to celebrate its excellence, it would also give the opponents the opportunity to demonstrate their pride and character by continuing to compete hard and fairly against superior opponents, and to score "consolation" points. The opponents of the U.S. basketball team in the 1992 Olympics were especially gracious in this regard.

None of this is to deny the value of substituting backup players for starters in uneven contests. Aside from the prudence of not risking injury to key players, team morale will be improved by sharing the fun, and these values may well outweigh the importance of creating scoring records and giving an objectively accurate measure of the winning team's superiority. In any event, inserting second-string players does not guarantee that the margin of victory will be minimized. They are perfectly justified in taking advantage of their rare minutes of playing time by playing hard. It would be unfair to demand that they refrain from inflicting heavy defeats, and thus deny themselves the opportunity to showcase their abilities.[14]

My point in this subsection has been that neither starters nor backups are required to ease up in uneven contests by Feezell's model of sportsmanship as a mean between competitiveness and playfulness.

C

Dixon Provides a Final Argument

The strongest support for the AB thesis comes from models of sportsmanship that put more explicit emphasis on moral values.[15] Peter J. Arnold (1: p. 66) has developed a model of sportsmanship "as a form of altruistically motivated conduct that is concerned with the good or welfare of another." He argues that there is more to sportsmanship than the mere observance of the rules of the game or the unwritten rules of fair play. The paradigm case of sportsmanship is the athlete who acts altruistically, even if this action diminishes her chance of victory, for instance, the runner who stops to help a badly injured competitor (1: pp. 67-69).

Arnold does not characterize such sportsmanlike acts as supererogatory, since this is the language of duties, albeit "imperfect" ones, based on universal principles.[16] Instead, he puts altruism and sportsmanship in the context of an ethic of care, based on the sympathetic responses we have to particular individuals.[17]

Arnold's view makes more stringent demands on the athlete than any of the other models of sportsmanship we have considered. The sporting athlete not only facilitates a fair contest that accurately reflects the participants' abilities, and behaves in the spirit of playfulness; she also responds altruistically to her rival should the need arise, even if this impairs her chance of victory. The question before us is whether the altruistic athlete will take pity and refrain from lopsided victories over outmatched opponents. In other words, does Arnold's model of sportsmanship support the AB thesis?

In considering this question, we should first note that Arnold's account of sportsmanship differs from the others we have examined in one crucial respect. These other models present sportsmanship in the form of mandatory moral prescriptions. For instance, the person who cheats, or who violates the playful spirit of sport, exhibits the vice of bad sportsmanship. Arnold, in contrast, regards sportsmanlike acts as those that go beyond the call of duty (though, for reasons already explained, he prefers to characterize them as altruistic, rather than as supererogatory, a term which belongs to the ethics of duty). His examples of sportsmanship are heroic acts of altruism, where an athlete jeopardizes her own chances of victory out of sympathy for the plight of a rival. While few would deny Arnold's claim that such actions "exemplify the best traditions of sportsmanship," the competitor who does *not* perform them is guilty of no moral failing.[18] Viewed in this light, the practice of easing up on outmatched opponents is at best an optional act of mercy, and players who do not do so are innocent of bad sportsmanship.

Moreover, the account of victories by a wide margin that I have developed throughout this paper indicates that suffering a heavy defeat is hardly the kind of disaster that calls for spontaneous acts of altruism by the victor. To paraphrase a point made earlier, a lopsided defeat need reflect only a lopsided difference in performance, and in no way disgrace the loser. Heroic acts of altruism are better reserved for athletes who are genuinely in need of help, such as Arnold's (1: p. 67) example of the marathon runner who, "at the cost of victory, stops to help a fellow runner in a state of distress." Though he uses it to illustrate a different model of sportsmanship, another of Arnold's (1: p. 63) examples also indicates a more appropriate occasion for the altruism which he endorses: Tennis player Mats Wilander corrected a call made by the umpire in the French Open in 1982, even though the call had been in his favor and had given him match point.

The exercise of altruism in the case of the bad tennis call would also be endorsed by the Keating/Fraleigh view of sportsmanship as facilitating a fair and accurate measurement of the rivals' abilities. Wilander's sportsmanlike intervention ensured that the game's outcome depended on a fair application of the game's rules, and not on an error by the umpire. In contrast, when the reason for a one-sided victory is nothing other than a vast difference in ability, there is no need to "go easy" on the losers in the name of the Keating/Fraleigh view of sportsmanship.

Arnold's model of sportsmanship fails to support the AB thesis. First, it relegates sportsmanship to the status of optional acts of altruism, making it inappropriate to condemn the failure to perform such acts as easing up on outmatched opponents. Second, even within the realm of optional acts of altruism they are better reserved for fellow competitors who are genuinely in need of help than extended to people whose only misfortune is to be losing a competitive sporting contest by a wide margin.

IV

This paper should not be construed as endorsing the obsessive pursuit of massive victories in competitive sport. The value of resting key players, giving second-string players valuable and enjoyable game experience, and trying out untested strategies may often outweigh the value of pursuing victories that accurately reflect the full extent of the winning team's superiority. Even less should it be construed as endorsing the cruel, contemptuous attitude toward the losers exhibited by the team that runs up the score in a deliberate (but misguided) attempt to humiliate its opponents. Any plausible model of sportsmanship, including those examined here, requires that all competitors show mutual respect at times. Mocking, taunting, and gloating at outmatched opponents is despicable. The sportsmanlike victors should thank the losers for the game, and console them for their obvious disappointment.

My only goal has been to show that no sound arguments, including those based on the models of sportsmanship currently in favor, give any good reason for condemning the pursuit of victory by a wide margin as intrinsically unsporting. It might be objected that this only shows the inadequacy of current models of sportsmanship, and that we should develop a new model that *does* condemn pursuit of runaway victories. However, the models considered here are all supported by careful theoretical arguments and produce plausible analyses of sporting behavior in a wide variety of situations. To reject them, and to build an ad hoc theory, all in the name of the unshakable intuition that lopsided victories are unsporting, creates the suspicion that the intuition is no more than a prejudice.

Interesting though it is in its own right, discussion of the AB thesis is most valuable for the light it sheds on prevailing American attitudes toward sport. While the thesis is ostensibly offered as a merciful corrective to ruthless competition, further analysis has revealed, ironically, that it presupposes views that are ill suited to the spirit of sportsmanship.

First, the AB thesis may be based on the view, condemned by all plausible accounts of sportsmanship, that winning is the only thing that matters in sport. Second, it assumes that suffering a heavy defeat is an affront to one's status as an athlete, if not as a human being. While this mistaken attitude is in itself inoffensive, it reflects a gross overestimation of the importance of the outcomes of sporting contests, and this overestimation may well be associated with unquestionably unsporting behavior. Huge financial incentives already exist for cheating, illicit drug use, and other violations of sportsmanship in both college and professional athletics. To add to these financial incentives the view that defeat brings disgrace on the loser only increases the temptation to resort to unsporting means to achieve victory.[19]

NOTES

[1]To conform to standard usage, and to avoid unwieldy expressions, I have reluctantly used the term *sportsmanship*. I trust that my routine use of *she* as a generic personal pronoun will allay any concerns that my use of *sportsmanship* has a masculinist intent.

[2]I add the qualifier *intrinsically* because, as I explain in section II, I do condemn those who pursue lopsided victories *in order to* humiliate their opponents. If my main argument is sound, however, even these deliberate attempts do not actually humiliate the losers in a morally objectionable way.

[3]One wonders why Kretchmar classifies this as a nonmoral value. Minimizing suffering is very much a moral value, at least on a utilitarian approach.

[4]See section IIIA for more detail on Keating's view.

[5]It may be no coincidence that both football and basketball are time-based sports, in which the contest continues for a specified time, regardless of the score. A point may be reached, well before time expires, when one team has no realistic chance of winning. The AB thesis is most plausible in precisely such situations in time-based sports. In score-based sports such as tennis, on the other hand, play continues until a certain score has been reached, regardless of the time elapsed. In such sports, dramatic comebacks are feasible until the final point has been played, and we are unlikely to criticize as unsporting the behavior of a player who pads her lead in order to reduce the likelihood of such a comeback.

What this shows is that there is a reason for trying to maximize the margin of victory in score-based sports that does not exist in time-based sports. I maintain, however, that in neither case is it unsporting to pursue one-sided victories. I am grateful to Michael Meyer for the distinction between these two kinds of sport.

[6]See section IIIB for a more detailed discussion of the role of play in sport.

[7]See section IIIA.

[8]*Webster's Ninth New Collegiate Dictionary* (Springfield, MA: Merriam-Webster, Inc., 1990), p. 587.

[9]See Arnold (1: p. 62), and Keating (7: pp. 32-34).

[10]British disdain for what was considered as excessive American zeal for training is given a remarkably favorable portrayal in the 1981 film *Chariots of Fire*.

[11]I do not mean to suggest that sporting scores are "transitive," in the sense that if A beats B by x points, and B beats C by y points, it follows that A will beat C by $x + y$ points. The value of keeping records, rather, is that figures such as the total points or goals scored by a player or team over a season can provide a meaningful measure of excellence and basis for comparison with other players and teams, both past and present.

[12]I am grateful to a reviewer of the *Journal of the Philosophy of Sport* for this objection.

[13]See Hyland (5: pp. 68-69).

[14]I am grateful to a reviewer of the *Journal of the Philosophy of Sport* for this point.

[15]*All* theories of sportsmanship are evaluative, in that sportsmanship is an inherently normative concept. Sportsmanship is by definition a virtue, and being a bad sport is by definition a moral failing. I distinguish Arnold's view because he defines sportsmanship in terms of the moral virtue of altruism, whereas the other views define it in terms of facilitating the nonmoral goals of sport.

[16]For the distinction between perfect duties ("duties of justice") and imperfect duties ("duties of benevolence"), see Kant (6: pp. 191-195).

[17]For two formulations of an ethic of care, see Gilligan (4) and Manning (9).

[18]A more comprehensive account of sportsmanship would combine mandatory requirements of the kind explained by Keating, Fraleigh, and Feezell, along with Arnold's insight that the highest level of sportsmanship is exemplified by optional acts of altruism that exceed these minimal requirements. Developing such an account is beyond the scope of this paper.

[19]I am grateful to the reviewers of the *Journal of the Philosophy of Sport* for helpful suggestions, to Sterling Harwood for encouraging me to write this paper and for extensive written feedback, and to Mike Meyer for his incisive and generous criticisms.

BIBLIOGRAPHY

1. Arnold, Peter J. "Three Approaches Toward an Understanding of Sportsmanship." *Journal of the Philosophy of Sport,* X (1984), 61-70.

2. Feezell, Randolph M. "Sportsmanship." *Journal of the Philosophy of Sport,* XII (1986), 1-13.

3. Fraleigh, Warren B. *Right Actions in Sport: Ethics for Contestants*. Champaign, IL: Human Kinetics, 1984.

4. Gilligan, Carol. *In a Different Voice: Psychological Theory and Women's Development*. Cambridge, MA: Harvard University Press, 1982.

5. Hyland, Drew A. "Opponents, Contestants, and Competitors: The Dialectic of Sport." *Journal of the Philosophy of Sport,* XI (1985), 63-70.

6. Kant, Immanuel. *Lectures on Ethics*. Translated by Louis Infield. New York: The Century Company, 1930.

7. Keating, James W. "Sportsmanship as a Moral Category." *Ethics,* LXXV (October 1964), 25-35.

8. Kretchmar, R. Scott. "Ethics and Sport: An Overview." *Journal of the Philosophy of Sport,* X (1984), 21-32.

9. Manning, Rita C. *Speaking From the Heart: A Feminist Perspective on Ethics*. Lanham, MD: Rowman and Littlefield, 1992.

ON PERFORMANCE-ENHANCING SUBSTANCES AND THE UNFAIR ADVANTAGE ARGUMENT

Roger Gardner,
Kentucky Wesleyan University

Reprinted, by permission, from R. Gardner, 1989, "On performance-enhancing substances and the unfair advantage argument," *Journal of the Philosophy of Sport* XVI: 59-73.

Gardner Formulates a Thesis

Following the Ben Johnson track disqualification episode at the 1988 Olympics, one of the more common rationales used to argue against Johnson's use of the steroid Stanozolol was that it provided him with an unfair advantage. This notion of unfair advantage is frequently used to support the banning of performance-enhancing substances in sport (1, 4, 5, 10, 13, 16). But whereas this argument is routinely employed and may represent one of our more intuitive objections toward such substances, it has not been subjected to the type of philosophical scrutiny it deserves. Even among those who have addressed the general ethical issues surrounding athletic use of performance-enhancing substances (e.g., 2, 6, 7, 11, 14, 16, 18), and, in so doing, may have commented on the question of unfair advantage (in most cases then maintaining that the argument is problematic), the argument has escaped careful study.

In this paper I explore the ethical status of competitive advantages that might be gained through performance-enhancing substances. I attempt to answer the question of whether such a line of reasoning can offer a compelling justification for prohibiting their use in sport.

Before beginning, several qualifications are in order. First, this essay deals only with issues surrounding those substances used in athletics to improve performance. Two of the more identifiable substances are amphetamines and anabolic steroids. I will not be addressing the use by athletes of substances taken for purposes of altering mood or behavior—so-called recreational drugs (e.g., alcohol or cocaine). It needs to be understood, however, that many substances commonly associated with "recreational" usage have been used and can be used as performance enhancers; for example, alcohol has been used to reduce anxiety, cocaine to offset fatigue. The distinguishing feature would seem to be intent. Any and all such substances, when intentionally used to improve athletic performance, are then acceptable examples of performance-enhancing substances.

Second, the jury is still out on whether many of the substances to be discussed do in fact enhance performance. The question of efficacy as well as degree of efficacy would seem pivotal to any opposition to performance enhancers that is grounded in concern for the possible competitive advantages to be gained through use; if there is no advantage to be gained—unfair or otherwise—then there is no reason for concern and no justification for proscription.[1] The importance of efficacy notwithstanding, it is a matter to be left to scientific debate and a matter to be sidestepped here. For purposes of philosophical discussion, this paper will be argued from the standpoint that *if* a particular substance were to provide its suspected (or hoped for) qualities of enhancement, would it then also provide the athlete with competitive advantages that could be considered unacceptable in sport?

A third stipulation is that my comments are devoted to ethical issues related to unfair advantage only. In other words, as indicated by Fost (6), Brown (2), and Lavin (11), there are at least four ethical arguments around which opposition to performance-enhancing substances is usually centered: harm, coercion, unnaturalness, and unfair advantage. The principal focus in this paper is the unfair-advantage argument. And even though it can prove difficult to isolate these four rationales and address each one individually, an attempt to do so would seem an important step toward a better understanding of the overall problem.

Finally, nothing I say should be taken as advocating the use of performance-enhancing substances. The aim of this paper is to subject a common objection to performance enhancers to rational and ethical examination to see if it can offer a compelling justification for prohibiting use.

WHAT IS AN UNFAIR ADVANTAGE?

Gardner Clarifies the Problem

Ben Johnson's steroid-enhanced performance is often viewed as having created a condition of inequality among competitors. Any subsequent advantage Johnson may have gained is thereby characterized as unfair and, in turn, as unacceptable in sport. In what sense though is such an advantage unfair, and does unfair necessarily mean unacceptable or for that matter immoral? Before any determination can be made as to the ethical nature of advantages gained through the use of performance-enhancing substances, it is first necessary to understand what we mean by unfair advantage.

To claim unfair advantage would seem to imply that an athlete's or team's chances for success have been improved in an unacceptable manner. This would suggest, in turn, that if the manner of improving one's chances for success is acceptable, it is a fair advantage. Such being the case, two issues arise. First, it would appear that it is not the advantage per se that we object to, because gaining a competitive edge in skill or strategy is an essential feature of sport. Instead, what we object to is the way in which the athlete acquires the advantage. For instance, one possible way to gain an advantage during competition is to improve one's own capabilities. Yet, depending on the circumstances, we could either accept or reject an athletic advantage so gained. A major league baseball player might want to gain an advantage by improving his ability to hit home runs. If such ability is acquired by increasing upper-body strength through weight training, we would tend to classify any advantage gained as fair and acceptable. On the other hand, if the increased ability to hit home runs is secured by using a corked bat (an illegal process of altering the bat's structure in order to increase bat speed), any subsequent advantage is viewed as unfair and unacceptable. So, when we say an athlete has an unfair advantage, it would seem that we are objecting to the actions or circumstances that have created the gained advantage.

The second point is that in order to distinguish between acceptable and unacceptable advantages in sport, it appears that we need simply to determine whether the advantage is fair or unfair. However, unlike the preceding example, unfair may not always be the equivalent of unacceptable. For instance, in international competition athletes from some countries gain an advantage in certain sports due to more favorable climates or sporting traditions. It is often commented in just such a context that countries such as Austria and Switzerland have an unfair advantage over America when it comes to winter sports. Or consider that American athletes, in a similar manner, would seem to have an unfair competitive advantage over third-world athletes because of better facilities and sophisticated training techniques. And it could perhaps be argued that some athletes gain a decided and unfair advantage over others due to superior skill or physique. Does it not seem unfair when, say, Steffi Graf, the world's number one-ranked tennis player, is matched against the 128th-ranked player; or when a basketball team that averages 6'10" in height plays one that averages 6'2"? Such conditions of inequality and any ensuing advantages gained, although intuitively unfair, would appear to fall into a class of unfair but accepted (or at least tolerated) advantages in sport.[2]

Whether the prima facie advantage is considered unfair does not then seem to provide a clear distinction between acceptable and unacceptable advantage. More is required. And, what is needed may have to do with the first point discussed; that is, the way in which the advantage is gained. I would contend that in many instances what determines acceptability is not whether an athlete has an advantage or whether the advantage itself seems unfair but our ethical evaluation of the way in which the advantage is acquired. In other words, depending on the circumstances, although a condition of inequality may indeed be unfair, we might not consider the athlete morally blameworthy for exploiting the resulting advantages.

For instance, returning to the aforementioned examples, the Swiss skier is able to benefit from resources and climatic conditions that are more conducive for training than are those available to the skiers of many other nations. Exposure to such training in turn could provide a significant and seemingly unfair advantage during competition with those other nations. But because the advantage results from geographic location (something we perhaps cannot control), it does not seem unethical for the Swiss skier to benefit from that advantage. Likewise, though it may indeed seem that Steffi Graf has an unfair advantage over the lower ranked players, if the advantage is acquired through, say, genetic endowment, then we might not hold her morally culpable for benefiting from that advantage on the tennis court. The means used to secure an advantage would seem to have quite a bit to say about the eventual acceptability of that advantage. And in that sense, the issue of fairness is perhaps more properly placed with the means and not the resulting advantage. A further example will help to clarify this matter.

In the late 1970s, Bruce Sutter, then with the Chicago Cubs, was perhaps the first pitcher to develop an effective split-finger fastball. This pitch, due to the way the ball is held and to the imparted spin, makes a drastic and sudden downward movement just as it approaches home plate. Sutter acquired the pitch through the guidance of a pitching coach and countless hours of practice. The split-finger fastball gave Sutter a decided advantage over the hitter; in fact, some commented that it seemed unfair to have to face such a pitch. During this same time period, a pitcher for the San Diego Padres, Gaylord Perry, had a pitch with the same sharp downward movement as Sutter's. This pitch gave Perry a similar advantage over the hitter and, likewise, opposing hitters may have felt it unfair to have to face such a pitch. In Perry's case, however, it is suspected that he secured his advantage (the drastic and sudden ball movement) by applying a foreign substance to the ball. Though some say Perry used the pretense of throwing spitballs simply as a ploy to break the concentration of the hitter (he was caught throwing a "loaded" pitch only once in his more than 20-year career), let us say for purposes of argument that he did indeed achieve his advantage through the use of a foreign substance. Most would view Sutter's advantage as acceptable, Perry's as unacceptable. What distinguishes the two?

Both pitchers had the same advantage per se: a pitch that was difficult to hit due to its sudden drop. And it would seem we do not object to either pitcher having an advantage over the hitter; trying to gain such an edge is part of pitching. We also do not object if in each case the advantage (or the difficulty of hitting the pitch) seems unfair. But we do object (in Perry's case, not Sutter's) to the way in which the advantage was gained. What determines acceptability is our evaluation of how each pitcher created ball movement. So it is here and not with respect to the advantage itself that "fair" or "unfair" may more clearly indicate both acceptability and morality. That is, Sutter's use of a split-finger fastball is evaluated as a fair and ethical way to gain an (unfair) advantage over the hitter. Perry's use of a spitball is evaluated as an unfair and unethical way to gain the same advantage.[3] This raises of course the more significant question of what determines our ethical evaluations (in this case, for instance, it might be the rules of baseball—a spitball violates those rules), and still leaves unanswered the critical issue of why, ultimately, some methods of gaining an advantage are permitted in sport and others are not. What is the initial justification for the rule?

In sum, to object to a specific advantage by claiming that the athlete has an unfair advantage may not provide a clear indication as to whether it is unacceptable. Instead, because it is the way the advantage is gained that concerns us, a better indication might be provided by claiming that the athlete has an unfairly gained advantage. And even though this approach may ultimately encounter similar problems, at this time it would seem to resolve the intuitive difficulties posed by cases such as those previously discussed. In any event, regardless of where one posits the term unfair (whether it is associated with the advantage itself or the method of securing the advantage), the point of agreement and the central issue is that, in each instance, we usually mean to declare the situation unacceptable for reason of fairness. And, in each instance, we are still left with the more significant task of justifying why it should be unacceptable. Understanding this, my attention now turns to whether using performance-enhancing substances to gain an advantage can be justified as unacceptable in sport.

Let me begin by dispensing with an obvious objection to gaining an advantage through currently banned performance enhancers: Such advantages are illegally gained. One area of sport in which we desire equality is with respect to following the rules, and illegally gaining an advantage is considered (in most cases) unacceptable and unethical. But although there may be little denying this position, it fails to justify substance prohibitions. If one's only objection to a substance-acquired advantage is that use of the substance is currently against the rules, the problem could be avoided by legalizing the substance. What is ethically required is to establish initial justification for the rule. The question to be addressed is therefore as follows: If all performance-enhancing substances were allowed, what justification could then be offered for prohibiting this attempt to gain an advantage in sport? The unrestricted use of performance enhancers would raise concern in regard to two areas of athletic advantage: (a) an advantage over other athletes, and (b) an advantage over the sport.

AN ADVANTAGE OVER OTHER ATHLETES

Gardner Searches for Arguments

Under a condition of unrestricted use the possibility would exist, due to perhaps unequal access or choice, that both users and nonusers of performance enhancers would be competing on the same playing field. The argument could thereby be made that due to this inequality, performance advantages would be available to some and not to others. Some athletes, for instance, would benefit more than others by having greater access to effective substances and to information and advice about their use. In addition, an individual's financial ability or a nation's technological advancement would lead to inequalities in regard to the availability of the "best" substances. One response to this is that any advantages that might accrue from limited availability could be avoided through equal access (2, 6, 19). But although equal access might indeed suggest a greater sense of fairness, it is not clear that it would be a required condition for permitting performance enhancers.

Athletic performance can be enhanced by the availability of many things, things which would not seem to implicate greater access as an unacceptable means to gaining an advantage. It is advantageous to be exposed to good coaches and trainers, to have access to modern training facilities and equipment, and to benefit from the advice of knowledgeable physiologists and biomechanists. Yet having unequal access to these or similar means for improving performance due to such things as economic standing, technological advancement, or available knowledge does not seem to evoke cries for universal or equal access. As a consequence, many athletes routinely gain a performance advantage over other athletes without raising ethical concerns. So, although we might wish to see such advantages eliminated and may feel that equal access would be the ideal condition of sport (i.e., athletes would then be given an equal opportunity to improve and develop to their true performance capabilities, and outcomes would reflect only the differences in the competitors themselves [5]), equal access to means for enhancing performance does not appear to be a necessary condition of sport. It would follow then that unequal access to performance enhancers and knowledge and advice about their use would not be a sufficient reason for disallowing them in sport.[4]

Irrespective of the degree of accessibility, and even if equal access were achieved, users and nonusers might still be competing against one another due simply to choice. An athlete might have access to performance enhancers but opt (for whatever reason) not to use them to try to gain an edge. Would this in turn result in an unacceptable advantage for those who chose to be users? There are many avenues to improved performance that the athlete may or may not choose to pursue. But merely because some athletes may choose not to utilize a certain (legal) method of improvement, we do not then claim that other athletes, who have so chosen, have somehow unjustly gained an advantage.[5] Any advantages users might gain over nonusers due solely to choice would appear permissible on similar grounds.

Another argument that might be made against unrestricted use of performance enhancers is that inequalities would exist not just between users and nonusers but among users. In other words, even if universal access were achieved and even if all athletes chose to use the same substance, it could still be argued that athletes might not react to substances equally. If all competitors in the 1988 Olympic 100-meter race used Stanozolol, perhaps Johnson would still have gained a performance advantage due to the better physiological ability of his body to utilize the substance. Simon (18: p. 11), indirectly framing this objection, has stated that this probable difference in reaction to substances suggests that competitive success and failure would be determined by the innate capacity of the body to react to a substance, and that this reaction might vary unequally among competitors.[6] It is not clear however that such inequalities would result in unacceptable or unethical advantages over other athletes.

There are many innate differences or inequalities in athletes that might enable some to benefit more than others. In men, for instance, differences in the innate amount of testosterone in the blood can vary over threefold. This considerable variance in testosterone levels predisposes men with high levels to excel and gain an advantage in sports in which muscular strength and size are important. Along similar lines, every athlete has a unique response to the variety of available training stimuli. There are inequalities in the predispositions of athletes to benefit from weight training and endurance training and diet. There are discrepancies in the capacity to physiologically benefit from currently permitted substances, such as caffeine (permitted in limited quantities), bicarbonate (offsets the buildup of lactic acid), and amino acids. Gaining an advantage through inequalities in innate capabilities is unavoidable and it hardly seems unethical; nor from a practical standpoint do such discrepancies seem to be distinguishable.

There would therefore seem no necessity to restrict substance use based on the position that inequalities would exist in the innate capacities of athletes to benefit from a performance enhancer. In fact, when we begin discussing advantages gained over others as a result of differences in the athletes themselves—innate or acquired—we encounter a formidable problem: This is one area of sport where we may not want equality.

To this point, we have been discussing conditions that could lead either to users competing against nonusers or to disparity among users. However, in both cases, the ultimate concern is that through substance use inequalities will be created in the eventual performance capabilities of the athletes themselves. Put another way, the two principal qualities of athleticism that would be most affected by substance use are ability (strength, endurance, speed, power, etc.) and physique (height and weight). Yet, some might consider it illogical to oppose gaining an advantage through differences in these qualities.

It does not seem unreasonable to desire equality in the structure of the game, in respect to following the rules, and even in regard to access during the preparatory phase of a game; but, it might seem unreasonable to desire equality in the ultimate abilities (skills and strategies) of individual athletes.[7] Now we may, in order to see a close contest, prefer competition between participants who are relatively even in ability but, in the end, the idea is not for all to come out equally or to have equal ability. Sport in fact would seem dependent upon differences in performance capabilities. After all, if we wanted to avoid the accumulation of advantages and disadvantages due to inequalities in ability, then we would try to equalize individual skill levels by allowing those lacking in ability to compensate for their disadvantage through the structure of the game (e.g., a 5-yard head start), or we would build and program robot athletes as equals. And although there are some attempts to equalize skill levels through such things as handicapped golf tournaments, this is not the case in true athletic competition. Any disparities that substance use might create in abilities such as strength or speed would not seem to suggest sufficient cause for proscription.

Substance-gained advantages in either height or weight would also seem permissible. There are no attempts in elite sport—that is, the highest levels of competition—to equalize or limit the heights of competitors. If, then, certain substances (e.g., human growth hormone) could influence an athlete's height, any advantages gained over other athletes would seem allowable. With respect to weight, though there are branches of sport in which possible advantages gained through weight discrepancies are eliminated (e.g., boxing, crew, judo, amateur and Olympic wrestling, and weight lifting), there are also those activities in which weight is not legislated and any advantages so gained are accepted (e.g., lacrosse, football, gymnastics, etc.). In either case, regardless of one's weight and regardless of whether one acquires that weight (loss or gain) through a substance, differences could be accommodated for (equalized) through weight classes, or, as they are in sports with no weight limitations, simply permitted.

As before, objecting to performance enhancers on grounds that inequalities would be created among athletes does not provide strong justification for banning their use. Advantages gained due to differences in the performance capabilities of athletes are not only accepted in sport, they are usually desired. This point would seem crucial, and it serves to reestablish the contention made at the beginning of this essay: It is not the advantage per se that we object to but the action or circumstances that have created the gained advantage. What has made justification of prohibition problematic up to this point is that whatever possible (objected to) advantages can be gained through substance use, can be and are gained through currently accepted means. Therefore, in order to determine the permissibility of certain substances, perhaps the focus should not be on the potential advantages; instead, the focus should be on the use of performance enhancers as a means for gaining an advantage.

Perhaps securing an advantage through the use of proscribed substances can somehow be distinguished from gaining the similar advantage through accepted modes of enhancement. Consider the following two cases: (a) One way to gain an advantage over other competitors in endurance events is to increase the oxygen-transporting capacity of the blood. Two theoretical ways this can be achieved are high-altitude training and blood boosting. Blood boosting is a process by which athletes increase their blood volume and hemoglobin count through injecting supplemental blood—either their own or a donor's (usually a blood relative)—prior to an event. Receiving a transfusion from a donor was the method used by U.S. cyclists during the 1984 Olympics. (Seven riders have either admitted to this or were named by witnesses; 15: pp. 32-35). (b) Another way to gain an advantage in some activities is to increase body weight through adding muscle. Muscle mass can result from such things as genetic endowment, arduous training and diet, or human growth hormone (hGH). HGH is a hormone produced by the pituitary gland and shown to affect the growth of skeletal muscle and bone as well as visceral organs and tissues. Previously extracted from the pituitary glands of human corpses, it can now be produced synthetically. HGH is used to treat children with stunted growth; it is also used (since at least 1983) to promote muscle growth in athletes (4: p. 113).

In the first case, we do not object to differences in the endurance capabilities of athletes resulting from increased hemoglobin count, provided that increase is the result of high-altitude training. In the second case, we do not object to discrepancies in the size of skeletal muscles, provided that size results from genetic endowment or training (e.g., weight lifting). In each case, we are not objecting to the advantage, but to the way in which the advantage is gained. So what is there about blood boosting and human growth hormone that somehow distinguishes these methods of securing an advantage and seems to render their effects unacceptable? The most obvious difference is that the advantages gained by blood boosting and hGH are achieved through the use of a (supplemented) substance. However, if the basis of our objection is to be that using a substance is an unacceptable means to gaining an advantage, then the inconsistencies are more than apparent.

There are many legal substances used by athletes in their attempt to gain an advantage over competitors—for example, amino acids, protein powders, vitamin and mineral supplements (sometimes injected), caffeine (legally limited to 12 micrograms per milliliter of urine, about seven cups of coffee), glucose polymer drinks, and injections of ATP (a naturally produced chemical involved in muscle contraction). The list could go on and on. Clearly we do not object to gaining an advantage through the use of a substance; it is only particular substances to which we are opposed. This being the case, it seems that some form of definitive criteria would have to be established in order to differentiate between permissible and prohibited substances. Yet, such criteria do not seem to exist.

Others (6, 11, 12) have indicated the difficulty (and perhaps interminability) of attempting to establish a working distinction between "good" and "bad" substances that relies solely on characteristics or properties of the substances themselves. For example, trying to distinguish food from nonfood, restoratives from additives, or drugs from nondrugs is fraught with ambiguity. Likewise, the notions of naturalness and/or harm have thus far proven incapable of providing principled distinctions between acceptable and unacceptable performance enhancers. The problem is that regardless of the criteria or morally objectionable properties we try to use to define proscribed substances, permitted substances either fit the same criteria or possess similar properties.[8]

Gardner Provides a Further Argument

Given this difficulty, instead of focusing on the substance itself, perhaps there is something about the way a substance allows one to acquire an advantage that will provide a compelling acceptable/unacceptable distinction. For instance (as is often suggested), maybe substance use represents a shortcut to improved performance; that is, the advantages gained (enhanced capabilities) are not actually earned by the athlete.

Returning to the above cases, it seems through blood boosting and hGH that the athlete is indeed provided a shortcut to endurance and muscle mass, respectively. For instance, whereas in high-altitude training the athlete is perhaps putting in long hours of hard work in order to gain a competitive edge, in receiving a blood transfusion from a donor no such training effort is required; therefore, any subsequent advantage would seem unearned. Would discrepancies created in the amount and intensity of required training render substance use an unacceptable or unethical means for seeking a competitive advantage?[9]

To the contrary, in sport the notion of effort would not seem to carry sufficient moral weight for justifying prohibition. The amount and intensity of effort required to become an elite athlete greatly varies among competitors. But because it may be "easier" for some, we do not then claim that they have unethically gained any ensuing competitive advantage. Due to genetic predisposition and endowment, Nancy Lopez may have developed her golfing abilities in a rather accelerated and effortless fashion; Jose Canseco of the Oakland A's baseball club may have developed his large physique in the same manner. Although not actually earned through effort, any resulting advantage they gain over their competitors is permitted. We do not accuse Lopez and Canseco of immorally gaining an advantage simply because others may have to work twice as hard and long to acquire ability or size.[10]

In a related fashion then, though some may work long and hard to gain an advantage in endurance or muscle size, the fact that others might gain such advantages through the effortlessness of blood boosting or hGH (or genetic endowment) would not seem to render the method of acquiring those advantages unacceptable.[11] Much the same could be said for using other performance enhancers as well.

Another distinction that might be offered is that the acquired capabilities are somehow separate or external to the athlete. Perhaps the body weight and endurance promoted through the respective uses of hGH and blood boosting is analogous to using lead-filled water bottles in cycling (to increase the weight, and thus the speed, of the rider and bike during mountainous descents) and using the subway during New York City marathons. The objection now being that the extrinsically gained capabilities (advantages) are not directly related to the ability or physique of the athlete per se (or related to the athlete's legal equipment). And it would appear some proscriptions could be justified along these lines (e.g., spit or scuffed balls and corked bats in baseball, stickum in football, and weighted gloves in boxing). But in order for this rationale to be applied to substance-enhanced advantages, the acquired capabilities must somehow be shown to be independent of the athlete (like lead-filled water bottles) in ways that similar capabilities acquired through permitted modes of extrinsic enhancement are not. How do the capabilities and accompanying advantages that result from training techniques, running shoes, or legal substances differ? Before addressing this issue, it needs to be pointed out that the focus of the overall argument may now have shifted.

To this point the discussion has centered on those circumstances that might result in one athlete having a competitive edge over another. It has been shown that any inequalities that might surface among athletes due to unrestricted use of performance enhancers would not provide justificatory grounds for proscription. Whether an athlete could gain an advantage through greater access, choice, better physiological response, or improved ability or physique would not in turn seem to create unacceptable or unethical situations in sport. Further, it has been suggested that there is perhaps no defensible distinction between using proscribed substances as a means to gain an advantage and using other currently accepted methods to gain the similar advantage (e.g., high-altitude training, weight lifting, permitted substances, or genetic endowment). However, in all instances the overriding moral consideration has been that one athlete might unjustly gain an advantage over another. With the justification proposed above (i.e., enhancement extrinsic to the athlete), this may no longer be the concern.

In each preceding example of extrinsically enhanced capabilities the method for gaining the advantage could have been permitted, thereby avoiding any subsequent (prima facie) inequality among athletes. We could allow all wide receivers stickum, or all cyclists lead-filled water bottles, or, following from this, all athletes hGH and additional blood. So it would seem that more is involved here than just a concern for possible advantages one athlete might gain over another.

And as before, justifying prohibition along these lines would prove problematic. Instead, perhaps what renders a substance-gained advantage unacceptable, and what we may be ultimately objecting to, is not that an advantage is gained over other athletes but that one is gained over the sport itself—either its intended purpose or its conceived obstacles.

AN ADVANTAGE OVER THE SPORT

Gardner Provides a Final Argument

Consider again the Ben Johnson incident. One might object that the capabilities Johnson acquired through Stanozolol infringed upon the purpose of the 100-meter race or somehow made the activity less demanding than it should have been. In this case, what makes gaining advantage through substance use unacceptable is not that Johnson had an edge over other competitors, but that he had one over the activity. The purpose of the 100-meter race is to determine who can cover that distance fastest on foot. In the process, the competitors encounter and attempt to overcome certain obstacles, such as depletion of leg strength. If the competitors decided to use, say, motorcycles, then both of these intended conditions would be compromised. Would allowing unrestricted use of steroids in the 100 meters be somewhat like providing the participants with motorcycles? More generally, does the use of performance-enhancing substances somehow alter the intended purpose or difficulty of an activity (i.e., does it change what the sport was originally designed to test) and, if so, would this provide sufficient justification for prohibiting use?

It would seem that some rules have been enacted to prevent the athlete from gaining an advantage over the activity or, in other words, from in some way threatening the integrity of the sport. Such rules revolve primarily around performance-enhancing equipment (innovations, modifications) and, to a lesser extent, changes in athletic technique (e.g., using a midair somersault in the long jump). The most recent example comes from the sport of golf. Square- or U-grooved irons were banned from the PGA tour as of January 1, 1990. Tour players can now use only those clubs with traditional V-shaped grooves. The reason behind the ruling is that tests and anecdotal accounts of players suggest that U grooves give the golfer an advantage, especially out of the rough (9). They create a higher spin rate, which translates into better ball control (3: p. 54). The fact is, since U grooves first came on the scene in 1985 many touring professionals have been opposed to their use because of a concern that they devalue true golf skill and consolidate the talent (3).

We have here two related objections. First, square grooves make shots out of the rough easier (or less a matter of true golfing ability) than they should be, for all players. Gaining an advantage in such a manner is unacceptable not because it provides one golfer an advantage over another (although it might do so),[12] it is unacceptable because an advantage is gained over the sport itself—the intended "test" of the rough, for example, is avoided. Second, and as a consequence, the quality of golf (or the difference between various skill levels) is being equalized. This second objection represents the reverse of an earlier argument. That is, what is being objected to here is not that performance enhancement will create inequality among athletes, but that it will lead to parity. In the end, U grooves are more responsible for the performance than is the golfer.

Now it could be argued that a similar line of reasoning could be used to justify the banning of previously mentioned and parallel cases of extrinsic enhancement (e.g., corked bats, stickum, etc.). Employing this as a general rationale, however, is problematic.

It is not always the case that creating and altering equipment or technique (consider the Fosbury Flop) in order to gain an advantage is prohibited. Golf itself offers a clear example of this. In 1932 Gene Sarazen invented the sand wedge. Like U grooves, the sand wedge made it easier for the golfer to contend with a designed obstacle, in this case sand. In point of fact, there have been many changes and innovations in equipment that have resulted in the enhancement of athletic performance (e.g., tennis rackets, baseball gloves, vaulting poles, archery bows, bicycles, etc.). Such extrinsic enhancement, while assuming greater responsibility for the athlete's performance, and perhaps making the task in question less difficult,[13] has nevertheless been permitted. At the same time, it would seem an argument could be offered that athletic skill remains at a premium, diverse levels of talent are still displayed (i.e., equality has not been created), and the purpose or test of the sport, although perhaps altered somewhat from its historical beginnings, appears to maintain its (perhaps evolving) integrity.[14]

Returning to the context of performance-enhancing substances; it is not always the case then that extrinsic advantages gained over a sport are prohibited. But for purposes of argument let us contend, along the lines of U-grooved golf clubs, that this is our justification for banning certain performance-enhancing substances. That is to say, gaining enhancement (speed, endurance, strength, power, physique, etc.) through certain substances is unacceptable because it threatens a sport's integrity. The substance, in the end, is more responsible for any gained advantage than is the athlete, and hence we are no longer testing the athlete but the substance. Even if this is to be the main objection to performance enhancers, there are several ways in which the argument proves problematic, ways that relate to the by now familiar dilemma of trying to establish principled distinctions.

How does attempting to gain an advantage over the physical and mental obstacles of a sport through the use of prohibited substances differ from trying to do so through training, coaching, diet, technology, use of physiologists, biomechanists, and psychologists; or, for that matter, how does it differ from using permitted substances such as amino acids or (loading) carbohydrates? Whereas many athletes reach their level of performance due directly to the use of a coach, sport psychologist (biofeedback, hypnosis), or special diet, others may reach theirs through the use of substances such as steroids. It could thereby be argued that the extrinsic assistance of the psychologist or diet, like the steroid, is responsible for the resulting performance of the athlete. And, in turn, the purpose of the sport becomes not just a test of the athlete but of the athlete's scientists or diet and how efficiently the athlete can utilize what each has to offer. Is this not comparable to the claim that with the use of substances such as steroids we are no longer appraising the athlete but the substance and the efficiency with which the athlete's body can utilize that substance?

It seems that the responding argument would rely upon the notion of sport as a measure of human performance and attempt to claim that the capabilities provided athletes through substance use are nonhuman, or unnatural. So, one might want to argue that the psychologist, biomechanist, diet, and so on are simply bringing out the best in the athlete, and the athlete (qua human) is still ultimately responsible for the performance and any gained advantage. The resulting capability is not external to the athlete, like U-grooved irons, but inherent within the athlete. The enhancement allowed for through the scientist or diet simply permits the athlete to overcome some "undesired inhibitor" (16: p. 42) to better performance (e.g., anxiety, poor technique, or glycogen depletion in the muscles), and thereby reach his or her full potential. Yet, it would seem the similar argument could be made with respect to the use of substances such as amphetamines or steroids. That is, the substance brings out the inherent ability of the athlete by assisting him or her to overcome certain performance inhibitors, in this case perhaps passiveness and muscle exhaustion. If the limiting condition is to be humanness, then the objectionable enhancement must be shown to be nonhuman.

We thus return to the basis for the original objection: capabilities separate from the athlete. Because, clearly, the burden confronting the U-groove argument is the need to establish that the substance-influenced advantage gained over a particular sport is independent of the athlete's human capabilities (like using a motorcycle in the 100 meters). Moreover, and even if this could be shown, it would still have to be made clear how this form of extrinsic (unnatural) capability or advantage differs from those which, although they seem independent of the athletes, we accept (e.g., those resulting from running shoes or carbohydrate loading).[15] And it is at this point that we must look to an entirely different line of philosophical and ethical reasoning; that associated with trying to define and understand the natural/unnatural distinction.

In summary then, I have suggested that our primary concern regarding performance-enhancing substances may be that athletes would unjustly gain an advantage over the intended purpose or test of a sport. Such an argument, however, is problematic and would seem contingent upon the need to show that the capabilities acquired through a (proscribed) substance are extrinsic to the athlete and in some way unnatural (i.e., did Ben Johnson have "corked" legs?).

To conclude, the purpose of this essay has been to demonstrate that arguments opposing the use of performance-enhancing substances that are grounded primarily in a concern for the athletic advantages that might be gained through such use are, at the least, problematic and, at the most, unable to provide a compelling justificatory defense for proscription. Given a condition of unrestricted use, any moral concern that users may unjustly gain advantages over other athletes appears to be unwarranted. Such being the case, it has been suggested that the critical area of concern in this matter may not be opposition to one athlete gaining an advantage over another but that, through substance use, an athlete may gain an advantage over the sport itself. Yet, this line of argumentation also proved problematic and, at this stage, does not seem to offer sufficient justification for banning performance-enhancing substances.[16]

NOTES

[1]At least no justification on grounds of unfair advantage. One might still search for justification on other grounds, say, for instance, harm.

[2]Some may have a philosophical objection with this and want to argue that such things as geography, ability, and technology, though certainly advantages, are not necessarily unfair. This claim, however, would at least seem to suggest more analysis; because, at this point in time, such advantages do not seem to be *clearly* fair either.

[3]As to the morality of Perry's suspected actions, consider that in February of 1989 the Baseball Writers Association of America succeeded in keeping Perry out of the Hall of Fame on moral grounds. Several writers have admitted to ignoring Perry because they evaluated his accomplishments as morally questionable (8).

[4]The fundamental mode of argumentation throughout this essay will be to indicate contradictions and inconsistencies in current policies and rationales. To point out these inconsistencies is not to advocate tolerance for any of them or to suggest that because we allow *a* we should then allow *b*. Further, as one anonymous referee put it, "it does not follow from the fact that people would not regard *X* as unfair that *X* is indeed not unfair." Because these are philosophically important matters, addressing them would seem to be the next step. The first step is to point out inconsistencies and to thereby suggest that concern over performance enhancers may involve other issues, in this case, issues other than fairness. (My thanks to W. Fraleigh, S. Kretchmar, and the anonymous referee for bringing this to my attention.)

[5]Fraleigh (7) and Murray (14) argue that when it comes to harmful performance enhancers, athletes confront not just choice but coercion. Such an objection is dependent upon the issue of harm and is more properly couched in the harm and coercion arguments. If, for instance, relevant substances were harmless, then clearly the simple act of choice would not represent an unacceptable means to gaining an advantage over others.

[6]The basis for Simon's objection is not so much that athletes will react to substances unequally, but that such differences are athletically irrelevant. This ultimately is more a concern for changes in the nature of sport than it is for inequality and advantages some athletes might gain over others.

[7]Brown (2: p. 17) and Földesi and Földesi (5) make the similar point.

[8]Fost (6), in general, and Lavin (11: p. 39), more specifically, also identify this dilemma. In Lavin's case, he then wants to offer "consensus disapproval" as the distinguishing criterion. Although this is not the place to address Lavin's position, it might be said that accepting an argument that seems practically (democratically) strong but is nonetheless logically weak seems more like resignation than justification; it merely satisfies the status quo.

[9]Some maintain that the ability of anabolics to aid in muscle recovery allow one to increase the intensity and frequency of workouts; in effect, permitting the athlete to work harder.

[10]In fact, genetic endowments would seem to suggest moral neutrality. Rawls (17) argues that an individual does not deserve the products of genetic endowments, as such endowments are bestowed by a blind genetic lottery.

[11]Of course one might argue that although it may be true that genetically determined advantages are unmerited, they are at least the result of natural occurrences; substance-enhanced advantages are not. This is a

significant objection but one that seems little concerned with effort and more properly placed within the unnaturalness argument.

[12]That is, square grooves might provide the lesser player with an advantage over the better player. It could be argued that the lesser player does not need golfing skill to equal the performance of the better player. This points out that there may not be an absolute line of distinction between an advantage over the sport and an advantage over other athletes. It would seem, however, that the two can be sufficiently separated.

[13]In some cases an equipment change may not make an activity necessarily less difficult, but it may still improve performance; that is, the same effort may be required but a better performance results (e.g., solid disk wheels in cycling, fiberglass vaulting poles, artificial track surfaces).

[14]There may be a sense that there is a baseline beyond which, but only beyond which, the intended purpose of a sport is sufficiently challenged. So, in the sport of cycling we may allow titanium components, solid disk wheels, and aerodynamic helmets and handle bars—which Greg LeMond credits for having significantly contributed to his winning of the 1989 Tour de France—but we will not allow a motor to be attached to the bicycle. It is not clear where exactly this baseline may be, but it might be found in the distinction that surfaces later in the essay, the notion of testing *human* ability.

[15]Perry (16) argues for such a distinction. The critical elements of his argument, however, are unnaturalness and harm.

[16]My thanks to Bill Harper, Larry May, and three anonymous *JPS* referees for their input into this project.

BIBLIOGRAPHY

1. Beckett, A. "Philosophy, Chemistry and the Athlete." *New Scientist* 103 (1984): 18.
2. Brown, W.M. "Drugs, Ethics, and Sport." *Journal of the Philosophy of Sport* VII (1980): 15-23.
3. Diaz, J. "Has Golf Gotten Too Groovy?" *Sports Illustrated* 67, No. 5 (August 3, 1987): 52-59.
4. Donohoe, T., and Johnson, N. *Foul Play: Drug Abuse in Sports.* New York: Basil Blackwell, 1986.
5. Földesi, T., and Földesi, G. "Dilemmas of Justness in Top Sport." *Dialectics and Humanism* 1 (1984): 21-32.
6. Fost, N. "Banning Drugs in Sports: A Skeptical View." *Hastings Center Report* 16 (1986), 5-10.
7. Fraleigh, W. "Performance-Enhancing Drugs in Sport: The Ethical Issue." *Journal of the Philosophy of Sport* XI (1985): 23-29.
8. Gammons, P. "Morals and Immortals: Ferguson Jenkins and Gaylord Perry Should Be in the Hall." *Sports Illustrated* 70, No. 10 (March 1989): 78.
9. Hershey, S. "A Groovy Decision: PGA Told to Rough It Without U-Grooved Irons." *USA Today* (March 1, 1989): 2C.
10. Hyland, D. "Playing to Win: How Much Should It Hurt?" *Hastings Center Report* 9 (1979): 5-8.
11. Lavin, M. "Sports and Drugs: Are the Current Bans Justified?" *Journal of the Philosophy of Sport* XIV (1987): 35-43.
12. Michels, R. "Doctors, Drugs Used for Pleasure and Performance, and the Medical Model." In *Feeling Good and Doing Better.* Edited by T. Murray, W. Gaylin, and R. Macklin. Clifton, NJ: Humana Press, 1984: 175-184.
13. Moorcroft, D. "Doping: The Athlete's View." *Olympic Review* (October 1985): 634-635.

14. Murray, T. "Drugs, Sports, and Ethics." In *Feeling Good and Doing Better*. Edited by T. Murray, W. Gaylin, and R. Macklin. Clifton, NJ: Humana Press, 1984: 107-126.

15. Pavelka, E. "Olympic Blood Boosting." *Bicycling* XXVI, No. 3 (April 1985): 32-35.

16. Perry, C. "Blood Doping and Athletic Competition." *International Journal of Applied Philosophy* I (1983): 39-45.

17. Rawls, J. *A Theory of Justice*. Cambridge, MA: Harvard University Press: 1970.

18. Simon, R. "Good Competition and Drug-Enhanced Performance." *Journal of the Philosophy of Sport* XI (1985): 6-13.

19. Torrey, L. *Stretching the Limits*. New York: Doss, Mead and Company: 1985.

BIBLIOGRAPHY

AAHPERD (American Alliance for Health, Physical Education, Recreation and Dance). 2003. American Association for Leisure and Recreation. www.aahperd.org (accessed January 19, 2004).

Ackerman, D. 1999. *Deep play.* New York: Vintage.

American Psychological Association. 1995. Mind–body connection: Rallying the troops inside our bodies. http://helping.apa.org/mind_body/pnia.html (accessed December 13, 2003).

Anderson, D. 2002. The humanity of movement, or, it's not just a gym class. *Quest* 54: 87-96.

Arendt, H. 1958. *The human condition.* Chicago: Univ. of Chicago Press.

Baier, K. 1958. *The moral point of view: A rational basis of ethics.* Ithaca, NY: Cornell Univ. Press.

Bellah, R., R. Madsen, W. Sullivan, A. Swidler, and S. Tipton. 1985. *Habits of the heart: Individualism and commitment in American life.* Berkeley: Univ. of California Press.

Bellah, R., R. Madsen, W. Sullivan, A. Swidler, and S. Tipton. 1991. *The good society.* New York: Knopf.

Blair, S., J. Kampert, H. Kohl III, C. Barlow, C. Macera, R. Paffenbarger Jr., and L. Gibbons. 1996. Influences of cardiorespiratory fitness and other precursors of cardiovascular disease and all-cause mortality in men and women. *JAMA* 276 (July 17): 205-210.

Blakemore, C. 2003. Movement is essential to learning. *Journal of Health, Physical Education, Recreation and Dance* 74 (November-December): 9, 22-25, and 41.

Blakemore, C. 2004. Brain research strategies for physical educators. *Journal of Health, Physical Education, Recreation and Dance* 75 (January): 1, 31-36, and 41.

Booth, F., M. Chakravarthy, S. Gordon, and E. Spanngenburg. 2002. Waging war on physical activity: Using modern molecular ammunition against an ancient enemy. *Journal of Applied Physiology* 93 (July): 3-30.

Bouchard, C. 2001. Physical activity and health: Introduction to the dose-response symposium. *Medical Science in Sports and Exercise* 33:S347-350.

Brown, M. 1980. Drugs, ethics, and sport. *Journal of the Philosophy of Sport* 7:15-23.

Burke, M., and T. Roberts. 1997. Drugs in sport: An issue of morality or sentimentality? *Journal of the Philosophy of Sport* 24:99-113.

California Department of Education (CDE). 2002. Physical fitness testing and SAT9. www.cde.ca.gov/statests/pe/pe.html (accessed May 20, 2003).

Cassirer, E. 1944. *An essay on man: An introduction to a philosophy of human culture.* New Haven, CT: Yale Univ. Press.

Centers for Disease Control and Prevention (CDC). 1997. Guidelines for school and community programs to promote lifelong physical activity among young people. *Morbidity and Mortality Weekly Report* 46:1-36.

Charles, J. 2002. *Contemporary Kinesiology.* 2nd ed. Champaign, IL: Stipes.

Clark, A. 2003. "Natural-Born Cyborgs," in *The New Humanists: Science at the Edge* (New York: Barnes & Noble), 67-77.

Clifford, C., and R. Feezell. 1997. *Coaching for character: Reclaiming the principles of sportsmanship*. Champaign, IL: Human Kinetics.

Coles, R. 1989. *The call of stories: Teaching and the moral imagination*. Boston: Houghton Mifflin.

Cooper, M. 1998. *Playing in the zone: Exploring spiritual dimensions of sport*. Boston: Shambhala.

Corbin, C. 2002. Physical activity for everyone: What every physical educator should know about promoting lifelong physical activity. *Journal of Teaching in Physical Education* 21:128-144.

Corbin, C., R. Pangrazi, and B.D. Franks, eds. 2002. *Research digest: President's council on physical fitness and sports*. Vol. 3.

Cox, H. 1969. *Feast of fools: A theological essay on festivity and fantasy*. New York: Harper and Row.

Csikszentmihalyi, M. 1975. *Beyond boredom and anxiety*. San Francisco: Jossey-Bass.

Csikszentmihalyi, M. 1990. *Flow: The psychology of optimal experience*. New York: Harper Perrennial.

Daily Business Journal Online. 2002. Workers rethinking priorities: Jobs more stressful, survey finds. www.business-survival.com/reportsJobStress.html (accessed January 24, 2004).

Dawkins, R. 1989. *The selfish gene*. New York: Oxford Univ. Press.

Dennett, D. 1991. *Consciousness explained*. Boston: Little, Brown.

Descartes, R. 1641/1960. Meditations on first philosophy. Trans. L.J. Lafleur. New York: Bobbs-Merrill.

Dishman, R., ed. 1988. *Exercise adherence: Its impact on public health*. Champaign, IL: Human Kinetics.

Dishman, R., ed. 1994. *Advances in exercise adherence*. Champaign, IL: Human Kinetics.

Dixon, N. 1992. On sportsmanship and 'running up the score.' *Journal of the Philosophy of Sport* 19:1-13.

Dixon, N. 1998. Why losing by a wide margin is not in itself a disgrace: Response to Hardman, Fox, McLaughlin, and Zimmerman. *Journal of the Philosophy of Sport* 25: 61-70.

Dixon, N. 2000. The inevitability of disappointment: Reply to Feezell. *Journal of the Philosophy of Sport* 27:93-99.

Ellis, M. 1973. *Why people play*. Englewood Cliffs, NJ: Prentice Hall.

Emerson, R.W. 1937. Nature. In vol.5 of *The Harvard classics: Essays and English traits by Ralph Waldo Emerson*, ed. C. Elliot, 223-237. New York: P. F. Collier and Son.

Feezell, R. 1999. Sportsmanship and blowouts: Baseball and beyond. *Journal of the Philosophy of Sport* 26:68-78.

Ferguson, J. 1979. *The Satires: Commentary, notes and introduction*. New York: St. Martin's Press.

Fink, E. Summer 1960. The ontology of play. *Philosophy Today* 4:95-110.

Fraleigh, W. 1984. *Right actions in sport: Ethics for contestants*. Champaign, IL: Human Kinetics.

Fraleigh, W. 1986. The sports contest and value priorities. *Journal of the Philosophy of Sport* 8:65-77.

Frankena, W. 1973. *Ethics.* 2nd ed. Englewood Cliffs, NJ: Prentice Hall.

Fry, T., ed. 1981. *The rule of St. Benedict.* Collegeville, MN: The Liturgical Press.

Gardner, H. 1985. *Frames of mind: The theory of multiple intelligences.* New York: Basic Books.

Gardner, H. 1999. *Intelligence reframed.* New York: Basic Books.

Gardner, R. 1989. On performance-enhancing substances and the unfair advantage argument. *Journal of the Philosophy of Sport* 16:59-73.

Gilligan, C. 1982. *In a different voice: Psychological theory and women's development.* Cambridge, MA: Harvard Univ. Press.

Gleick, J. 1987. *Chaos: Making a new science.* New York: Penguin Books.

Glover, J. 2000. *Humanity: A moral history of the twentieth century.* New Haven, CT: Yale Univ. Press.

Gough, R. 1995. On reaching first base with a "science" of moral development in sport: Problems with scientific objectivity and reductionism. *Journal of the Philosophy of Sport* 22:11-25.

Greene, B. 2004. *The Fabric of the Cosmos: Space, Time, and the Texture of Reality.* New York: Alfred A. Knopf.

Griffin, L., T. Chandler, and M. Sariscsany. 1993. What does "fun" mean in physical education? *Journal of Physical Education, Recreation, and Dance* 64(7): 63-66.

Griffin, L., and Butler, J., eds. 2004. *Examining teaching games for understanding model.* Champaign, IL: Human Kinetics.

Griffith, R. 1970. Anthropodology: Man afoot. In *The philosophy of the body: Rejections of Cartesian dualism,* ed. S. Spicker, 273-292. Chicago: Quadrangle Books.

Gruneau, R. 1983. *Class, sports, and social development.* Amherst, MA: Univ. of Massachusetts.

Hall, E. 1990. *The hidden dimension.* New York: Anchor Books.

Hardman, A., L. Fox, D. McLaughlin, and K. Zimmerman. 1996. On sportsmanship and running up the score: Issues of incompetence and humiliation. *Journal of the Philosophy of Sport* 23:58-69.

Hardman, A. 1999. Change in sport: A critical evaluation of normative constraints in sport. PhD diss., Pennsylvania State Univ.

Harper, W. 1973-76. *Play factory advocate.* 4 vols. Emporia, KS: William A. Harper.

Herrigel, E. 1971. *Zen in the art of archery.* New York: Vintage Books.

Hetherington, C. 1910. Fundamental education. *Journal of Proceedings and Addresses of the National Education Association* 48:350-357.

Hill, J., and J. Peters. 1998. Environmental contributions to the obesity epidemic. *Science* 280:1371-1374.

Holowchak, A. 2002. Ergogenic aids and the limits of human performance in sport: Ethical issues and aesthetic considerations. *Journal of the Philosophy of Sport* 29:75-86.

Huizinga, J. 1950. *Homo ludens: A study of the play element in culture.* Boston: Beacon Press.

Jackson, S., and M. Csikszentmihalyi. 1999. *Flow in sports: The keys to optimal experiences and performances.* Champaign, IL: Human Kinetics.

Josephson Institute. 2002. The ethics of American youth: 2002 report card. www.josephsoninstitute.org (accessed January 2004).

Keen, S. 1990. *To a dancing god: Notes of a spiritual traveler.* New York: Harper Collins.

Keen, S., and A. Valley-Fox. 1989. *Your mythic journey: Finding meaning in your life through writing and storytelling.* Los Angeles: Jeremy P. Tarcher.

Kidder, R. 1994. *Shared values for a troubled world: Conversations with men and women of conscience.* San Francisco: Jossey-Bass.

Kimiecik, J., and A. Harris. 1996. What is enjoyment? A conceptual–definitional analysis with implications for sport and exercise psychology. *Journal of Sport and Exercise Psychology* 18:247-263.

Kleinman, S. 2000 Summing up: A chronological retrospective or dancing the body Electra. *Quest* 52 (February): 89-101.

Kretchmar, S. 1975. From test to contest: An analysis of two kinds of counterpoint in sport. *Journal of the Philosophy of Sport* 2:23-30.

Kretchmar, S. 1990. Moral callouses in sport. *Strategies* 4 (September-October):5, 27.

Kretchmar, S. 1994. *Practical Philosophy of Sport.* 1st ed. Champaign, IL: Human Kintics.

Kretchmar, S. 1995. T.D. Wood: On chairs and education. *Journal of Health, Physical Education, Recreation and Dance* 66 (January): 12-15.

Kretchmar, S. 1996. Movement and play on higher education's contested terrain. *Quest* 48 (November): 433-441.

Kretchmar, S. 1999. The ethics of performance-enhancing substances in sport. *Bulletin: International Council of Sport Science and Physical Education* 27 (Fall): 19-21.

Kretchmar, S. 2000a. Movement subcultures: Sites for meaning. *Journal of Physical Education, Recreation and Dance* 71 (May-June):19-25.

Kretchmar, S. 2000b. Moving and being moved: Implications for practice. *Quest* 52 (August): 260-272.

Kretchmar, S. 2001. Duty, habit and meaning: Different faces of adherence. *Quest* 53:3, 318-325.

Kretchmar, S. 2004. Understanding the delights of human activity. In *Examining a teaching games for understanding model,* eds. L. Griffin and J. Butler. Champaign, IL: Human Kinetics.

Lambert, C. 1998. *Mind over water: Lessons of life from the art of rowing.* Boston: Houghton Mifflin.

Lasch, C. 1979. *The culture of narcissism: American life in an age of diminishing expectations.* New York: Warner Books.

Lewis, C.S. 1947. *The abolition of man.* New York: Macmillan.

MacIntyre, A. 1984. *After virtue.* 2nd ed. Notre Dame, IN: Univ. of Notre Dame Press.

Marcel, G. 1950. *The mystery of being.* Vol. 1. Trans. G. S. Fraser. Chicago: Henry Regnery.

Maslow, A. 1962. *Toward a psychology of being.* Princeton, NJ: Van Nostrand.

McCloy, C. 1940. *Philosophical bases for physical education.* New York: Appleton-Century-Crofts.

McCloy, C. 1966. How about some muscle? In *Anthology of contemporary readings: An introduction to physical education,* eds. H. Slusher and A. Lockhart, 13-17. Dubuque, IA: Brown.

McDermott, J., ed. 1967-1977. *The writings of William James: A comprehensive edition.* Chicago: Univ. of Chicago.

Meier, K. 1988. "Embodiment, Sport, and Meaning," in *Philosophic Inquiry in Sport.* eds. W. Morgan and K. Meier. (Champaign, IL: Human Kinetics), 93-101.

Meilaender, G.C. 1984. *The theory and practice of virtue*. Notre Dame, IN: Univ. of Notre Dame.

Merleau-Ponty, M. 1962. *Phenomenology of perception*. Trans. C. Smith. New York: Routledge and Kegan Paul.

Metheny, E. 1972. "The Symbolic Power of Sport," in *Sport and the Body: A Philosophical Symposium* (Philadelphia: Lea & Febiger), 221-226.

Midgley, M. 1994. *The ethical primate: Humans, freedom, and morality*. New York: Routledge.

Mokdad, A., B. Bowman, E. Ford, F. Vinicor, J. Marks, and J.P. Koplan. 2001. The continuing epidemics of obesity and diabetes in the United States. *JAMA* 286(10):1195-1200.

Morgan, W. 1982. Play, utopia, and dystopia: Prologue to a ludic theory of the state. *Journal of the Philosophy of Sport* 11:30-42.

Morgan, W., and K. Meier, eds. 1994. *Philosophic inquiry and sport*. 2nd ed. Champaign, IL: Human Kinetics.

Morgan, W. 1994. *Leftist theories of sport: A critique and reconstruction*. Urbana, IL: Univ. of Illinois.

Murphy, M. 1972. *Golf in kingdom*. New York: Viking.

Murphy, M., and R. White. 1995. *In the zone: Transcendent experience in sports*. New York: Penguin.

National Association for Sport and Physical Education (NASPE). 1992. *Outcomes of quality physical education programs*. Reston, VA: American Alliance for Health, Physical Education, Recreation and Dance (AAHPERD).

National Association for Sport and Physical Education (NASPE). 2004. *Moving Into the Future: National Standards for Physical Education, Second Edition*. Reston, VA: McGraw-Hill.

Neale, R. 1969. *In praise of play: Toward a psychology of recreation*. New York: Harper and Row.

Newell, K. 1990a. Physical education in higher education: Chaos out of order. *Quest* 42 (December): 3, 227-242.

Newell, K. 1990b. Physical activity, knowledge types, and degree programs. *Quest* 42 (December): 3, 243-268.

Niaura, R., J. Todaro, L. Stroud, A. Spiro, K. Ward, and S. Weiss. 2002. Hostility, the metabolic syndrome, and incident coronary heart disease. *Health Psychology* 21:6, 588-593.

Novak, M. 1976. *The joy of sports: End zones, bases, baskets, balls, and the consecration of the American spirit*. New York: Basic Books.

Ogden, C., et al. 2002. Prevalence and trends in overweight among U.S. children and adolescents, 1999-2000. *JAMA* 288:1728-1732.

Parker, D. 1957. *The philosophy of value*. Ann Arbor: Univ. of Michigan Press.

Pennington, T., and J. Krouscas. 1999. Connecting secondary physical education with the lives of students. *Journal of Physical Education, Recreation, and Dance* 70 (January): 34-39.

Pieper, J. 1952. *Leisure: The basis of culture*. New York: Pantheon Books.

Pinker, S. 2002. *The blank slate: The modern denial of human nature*. New York: Viking Penguin Books.

Plato. 1951. *Phaedo*. Trans. F. J. Church. New York: Liberal Arts Press.

Plato. 1975. *The republic of Plato*. Trans. F.M. Cornford. New York: Oxford Univ.

Polanyi, M. 1958. *Personal knowledge: Towards a post-critical philosophy*. Chicago: Univ. of Chicago Press.

Polanyi, M. 1966. *The tacit dimension.* Garden City, NY: Doubleday.

Polanyi, M., and H. Prosch. 1975. *Meaning.* Chicago: Univ. of Chicago Press.

President's Council on Physical Fitness and Sports. 2001. Tracking of physical activity across the lifespan. *Research Digest* 3 (September): 14, 1-6.

President's Council on Physical Fitness and Sports. 2002. Dose-response issues concerning the relations between regular physical activity and health. *Research Digest* 3 (September): 18, 1-6.

President's Council on Physical Fitness and Sports. 2003. Increasing physical activity in communities: What really works? *Research Digest* 4 (December): 4, 1-6.

Raju, P. 1985. *Structural depths of Indian thought.* Albany: State Univ. of New York Press.

Ridley, M. 2003. *Nature via nurture: Genes, experience, and what makes us human.* New York: Harper Collins.

Robinson, J.P., and G. Godbey. 1997. *Time for life: The surprising ways Americans use their time.* University Park, PA: Penn State Univ.

Ryle, G. 1949. *The concept of mind.* New York: Barnes and Noble.

Sage, G. 1990. *Power and ideology in American sport: A critical perspective.* Champaign, IL: Human Kinetics.

Scanlan, T., and J. Simmons. 1992. The construct of sport enjoyment. In *Motivation in Sport and Exercise,* ed. G.C. Roberts, 199-215. Champaign, IL: Human Kinetics.

Scheffler, I. 1965. *The conditions of knowledge.* Glenview, IL: Scott, Foresman.

Schmitz, K. 1972. Sport and play: Suspension of the ordinary. In *Sport and the Body: A Philosophical Symposium,* ed. E. Gerber, 25-32. Philadelphia: Lea and Febiger.

Schneider, A. 1994. Why Olympic athletes should avoid the use and seek the elimination of performance-enhancing substances and practices from the Olympic Games. *Journal of the Philosophy of Sport* 20-21:64-81.

Searle, J. 1999. *Mind, language and society: Doing philosophy in the real world.* London: Weidenfeld and Nicholson.

Seefeldt, V., ed. 1986. *Physical activity and well-being.* Reston, VA: American Alliance for Health, Physical Education, Recreation and Dance.

Sheets-Johnstone, M. 1999. *The primacy of movement.* Philadelphia: John Benjamins.

Shellenbarger, S. 2004. Work-life trends: some signs of hope. Career Journal.com (accessed July 7, 2004).

Siedentop, D., ed. 1994. *Sport education: Quality physical education through positive sport experiences.* Champaign, IL: Human Kinetics.

Siegel, B. 1986. *Love, medicine and miracles: Lessons learned about self-healing from a surgeon's experience with exceptional patients.* New York: Harper and Row.

Simon, R. 1985. Good competition and drug-enhanced performance. *Journal of the Philosophy of Sport* 11:6-13.

Simon, R. 2004. *Fair play: Sports, values, and society.* 2nd ed. San Francisco: Westview Press.

Singer, P. 1981. *The expanding circle: Ethics and sociobiology.* New York: Farrar, Straus, and Giroux.

Singer, P. 1995. *How are we to live? Ethics in an age of self-interest.* Amherst, NY: Prometheus Books.

Slusher, H. 1967. *Man, sport and existence: A critical analysis.* Philadelphia: Lea and Febiger.

Smith, A. 1985. Sport is a western yoga. In *Sport inside out: Readings in literature and philosophy,* eds. D. Vanderwerken and S. Wertz. Fort Worth: Texas Christian Univ.

Sudnow, D. 1978. *Ways of the hand: The organization of improvised conduct.* Cambridge, MA: Harvard Univ. Press.

Suits, B. 1972. What is a game? In *Sport and the body: A philosophical symposium,* ed. E. Gerber, 16-22. Philadelphia: Lea and Febiger.

Suits, B. 1977. Words on play. *Journal of the Philosophy of Sport* 4 (Fall): 117-131.

Suits, B. 1978. *The grasshopper: Games, life and utopia.* Toronto: Univ. of Toronto Press.

Suppaporn, S., and L. Griffin. 1998. Undergraduate students report their meaning and experiences of having fun in physical education. *Physical Educator* 55(2): 57-67.

Suzuki, D. 1956. *Zen Buddhism.* New York: Doubleday Anchor.

Torres, C. 2002. Play as expression: An analysis based on the philosophy of Maurice Merleau-Ponty. PhD diss., Penn State University.

Ullman, E. 1995. Out of time: Reflections on the programming life. In *Resisting the virtual life: The culture and politics of information,* eds. J. Brook and A. Boal, 131-144. San Francisco: City Lights.

U.S. Department of Health and Human Services (USDHHS). 1996. *Surgeon General's report on physical activity and health.* Washington, DC: U.S. Government Printing Office.

U.S. Department of Health and Human Services (USDHHS). 2001. *Healthy People 2010.* Conference edition. Washington, DC: U.S. Government Printing Office.

U.S. Congress. Senate. 2003. *Improved nutrition and physical activity act* (IMPACT). Washington, DC: U.S. Government Printing Office.

Vogel, P. 1986. Effects of physical education programs on children. In *Physical activity and well-being,* ed. V. Seefeldt, 455-509. Reston, VA: American Alliance for Health, Physical Education, Recreation and Dance (AAHPERD).

Vanderwerken, D., and S. Wertz, eds. 1985. *Sport inside out: Readings in literature and philosophy.* Fort Worth: Texas Christian.

Wallace, B.A. 2000. *The taboo of subjectivity: Toward a new science of consciousness.* New York: Oxford Univ. Press.

Wankel, L. 1993. The importance of enjoyment to adherence and psychological benefits from physical activity. *International Journal of Sport Psychology* 24:151-169.

Weil, A., ed. 1997. *The roots of healing: The new medicine.* Carlsbad, CA: Hay House.

Weiss, P. 1969. *Sport: A philosophic inquiry.* Carbondale, IL: Southern Illinois Univ. Press.

Whitehead, J., and C. Corbin. 1997. Self-esteem in children and youth: The role of sports and physical education. In *The Physical Self: From Motivation to Well-Being,* ed. K.R. Fox, 175-204. Champaign, IL: Human Kinetics.

Williams, J. 1964. *The principles of physical education.* 8th ed. Philadelphia: Saunders.

Williams, J. 1965. Education through the physical. In *Background readings for physical education,* eds. A. Paterson and E. Hallberg, 191-196. New York: Holt, Rinehart, and Winston.

Wilson, J. 1993. *The moral sense.* New York: Free Press.

Wiren, G., and R. Coop. 1978. *The new golf mind.* Norwalk, CT: Golf Digest/NY Times.

Wordsworth, W. 1910/1938. "The world is too much with us." In ed. C.W. Eliot. *The Harvard Classiscs: English Poetry,* vol. 41, New York: P.F. Collier and Son.

Zernike, K. 2003. Fight against fat shifts to the workplace. *New York Times,* October 12, sec. 1.

INDEX

Note: The italicized *f* and *t* following page numbers refer to figures and tables, respectively.

ABOUT THE AUTHOR

R. Scott Kretchmar, PhD, is a professor of exercise and sport science at Penn State University in University Park, Pennsylvania. Having previously served as chair of the Department of Kinesiology for seven years at Penn State, Kretchmar brings to light in this book his experiences from administration, skill teaching, theory instruction, coaching, and playing as an athlete. Kretchmar, a Fellow in the American Academy of Kinesiology and Physical Education, is former president of the International Association for the Philosophy of Sport, and served as editor of the *Journal of the Philosophy of Sport*. He has been named an Alliance Scholar by the American Alliance for Health, Physical Education, Recreation and Dance (AAHPERD) and a Distinguished Scholar by the National Association for Kinesiology and Physical Education in Higher Education (NAKPEHE).

In his leisure time, Kretchmar practices what he preaches, remaining active as a marathon runner and as a competitive table tennis player.